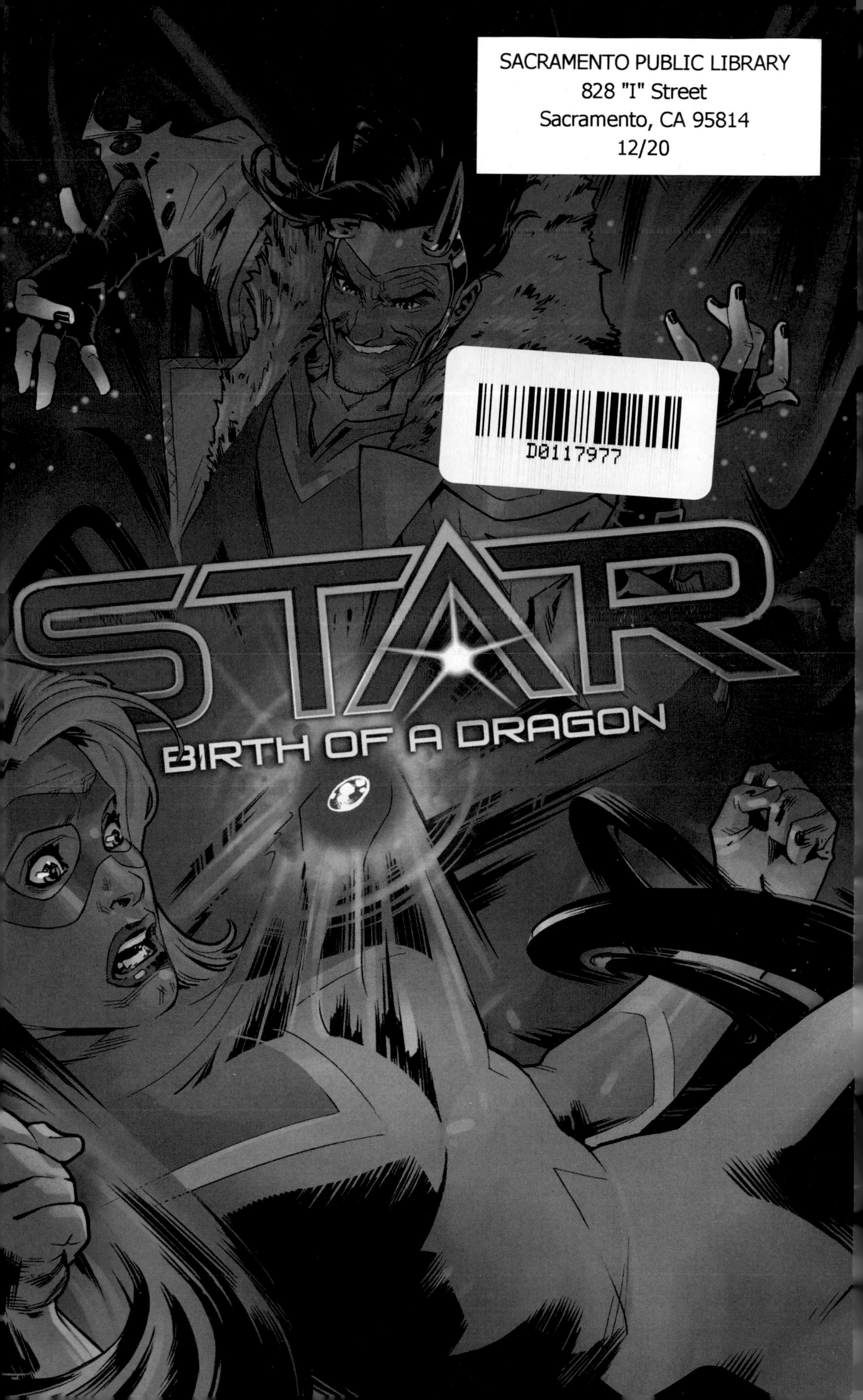
STAR
BIRTH OF A DRAGON

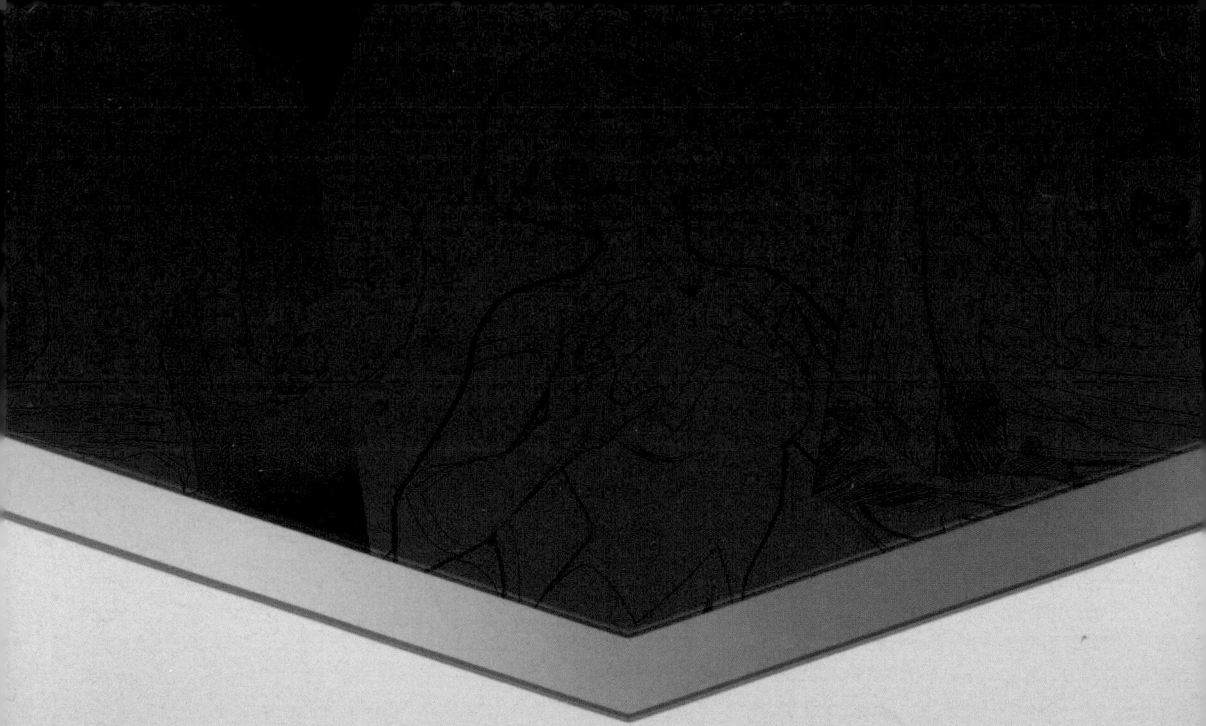

RIpley Ryan was a successful reporter for *Ms. Magazine*. The day she was assigned to interview super hero Captain Marvel . . . everything changed.

Traumatized by a months-long kidnapping at the hands of Nuclear Man, Ripley made a devil's bargain with a Kree scientist to gain super-powers — but that scheme failed after she nearly killed the entire population of New York City.

Barely alive after Captain Marvel punched a hole in her chest, Ripley lost her powers and wound up in the Raft prison facility. But she quickly escaped after discovering a new power, one that she barely understands . . .

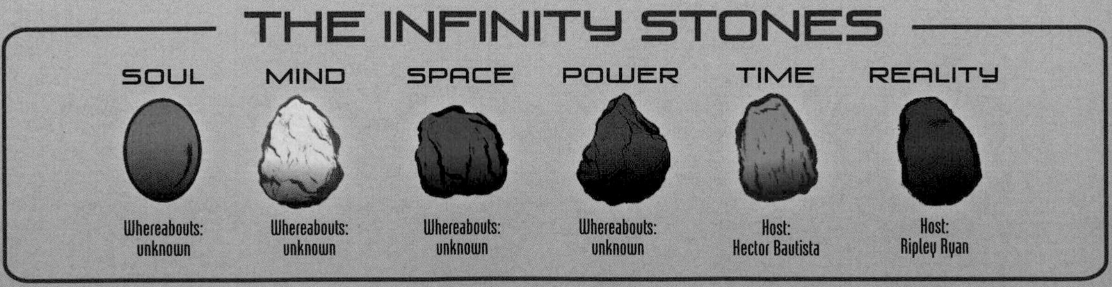
THE INFINITY STONES
SOUL
MIND
SPACE
POWER
TIME
REALITY
Whereabouts: unknown
Whereabouts: unknown
Whereabouts: unknown
Whereabouts: unknown
Host: Hector Bautista
Host: Ripley Ryan

STAR: BIRTH OF A DRAGON. Contains material originally published in magazine form as STAR (2020) #1-5. First printing 2020. ISBN 978-1-302-92458-4. Published by MARVEL WORLDWIDE, INC., a subsidiary of MARVEL ENTERTAINMENT, LLC. OFFICE OF PUBLICATION: 1290 Avenue of the Americas, New York, NY 10104. **Printed in Canada.** KEVIN FEIGE, Chief Creative Officer; DAN BUCKLEY, President, Marvel Entertainment; JOHN NEE, Publisher; JOE QUESADA, EVP & Creative Director; TOM BREVOORT, SVP of Publishing; DAVID BOGART, Associate Publisher & SVP of Talent Affairs; Publishing & Partnership; DAVID GABRIEL, VP of Print & Digital Publishing; JEFF YOUNGQUIST, VP of Production & Special Projects; DAN CARR, Executive Director of Publishing Technology; ALEX MORALES, Director of Publishing Operations; DAN EDINGTON, Managing Editor; RICKEY PURDIN, Director of Talent Relations; SUSAN CRESPI, Production Manager; STAN LEE, Chairman Emeritus. For information regarding advertising in Marvel Comics or on Marvel.com, please contact Vit DeBellis, Custom Solutions & Integrated Advertising Manager, at vdebellis@marvel.com. For Marvel subscription inquiries, please call 888-511-5480. **Manufactured between 9/4/2020 and 10/6/2020 by SOLISCO PRINTERS, SCOTT, QC, CANADA.**

10 9 8 7 6 5 4 3 2 1

STAR
BIRTH OF A DRAGON

WRITER
KELLY THOMPSON

ARTISTS
JAVIER PINA WITH **FILIPE ANDRADE** (#1-5) & **JAY LEISTEN** (#4)

COLOR ARTIST
JESUS ABURTOV WITH **CHRIS O'HALLORAN** (#4)

LETTERER
VC'S CLAYTON COWLES

COVER ART
CARMEN CARNERO & JESUS ABURTOV

LOGO DESIGN
SALENA MAHINA

EDITOR
SARAH BRUNSTAD

CONSULTING EDITOR
WIL MOSS

EXECUTIVE EDITOR
TOM BREVOORT

COLLECTION EDITOR JENNIFER GRÜNWALD
ASSISTANT MANAGING EDITOR MAIA LOY
ASSISTANT MANAGING EDITOR LISA MONTALBANO
EDITOR, SPECIAL PROJECTS MARK D. BEAZLEY

VP PRODUCTION & SPECIAL PROJECTS JEFF YOUNGQUIST
BOOK DESIGNER SALENA MAHINA
SVP PRINT, SALES & MARKETING DAVID GABRIEL
EDITOR IN CHIEF C.B. CEBULSKI

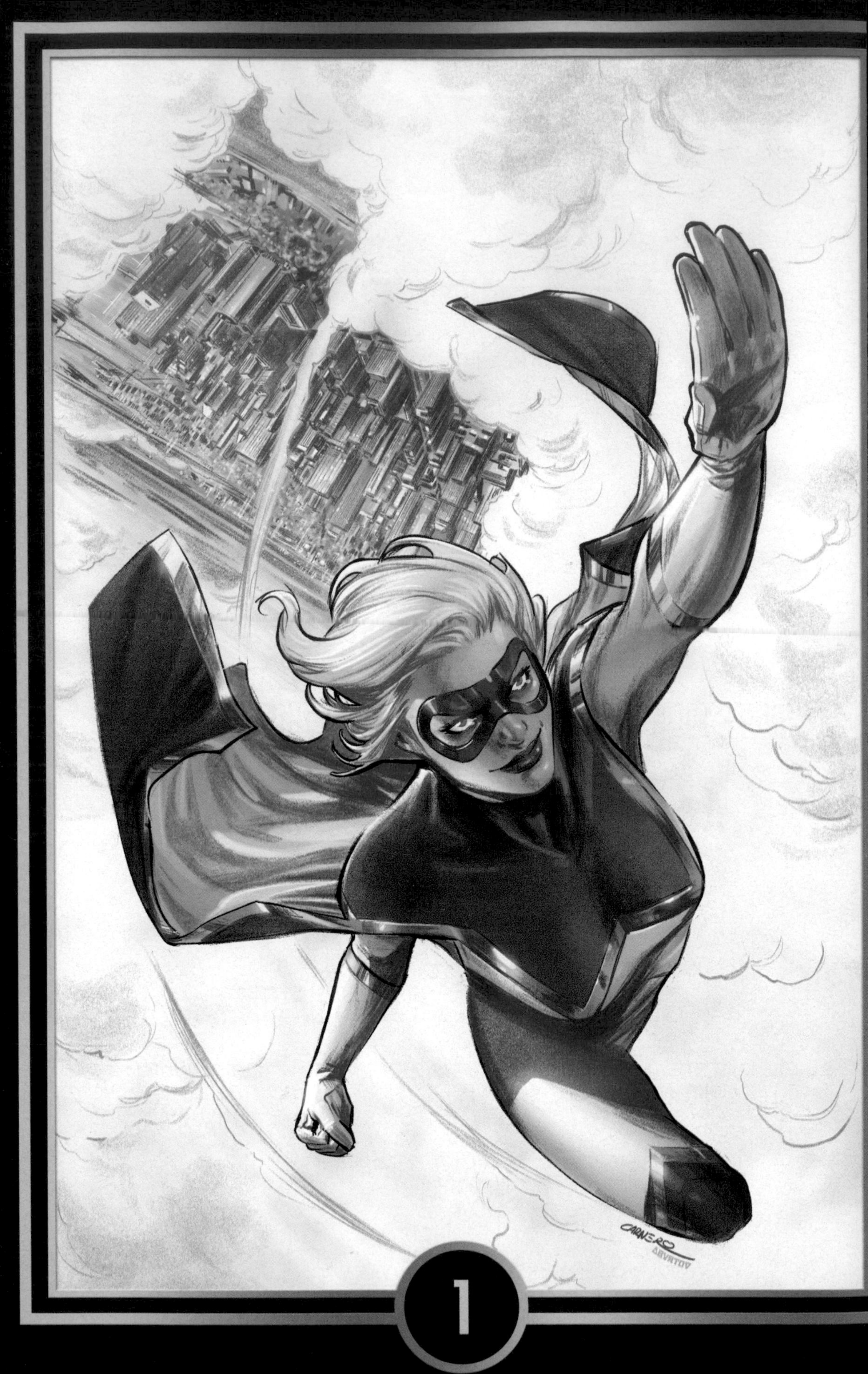
CARNERO
1

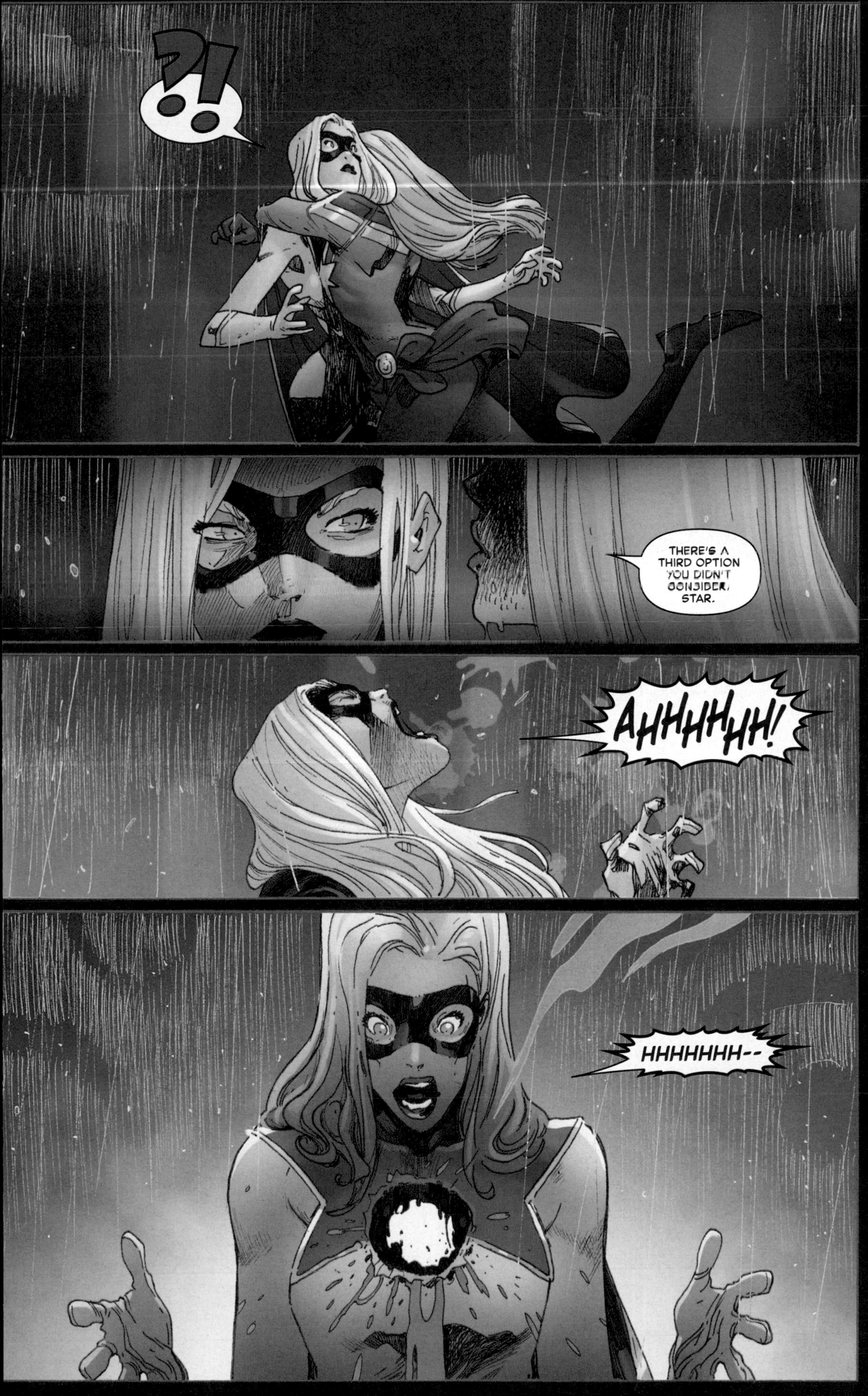
?!
THERE'S A THIRD OPTION YOU DIDN'T CONSIDER, STAR.
AHHHHHH!
HHHHHHH--

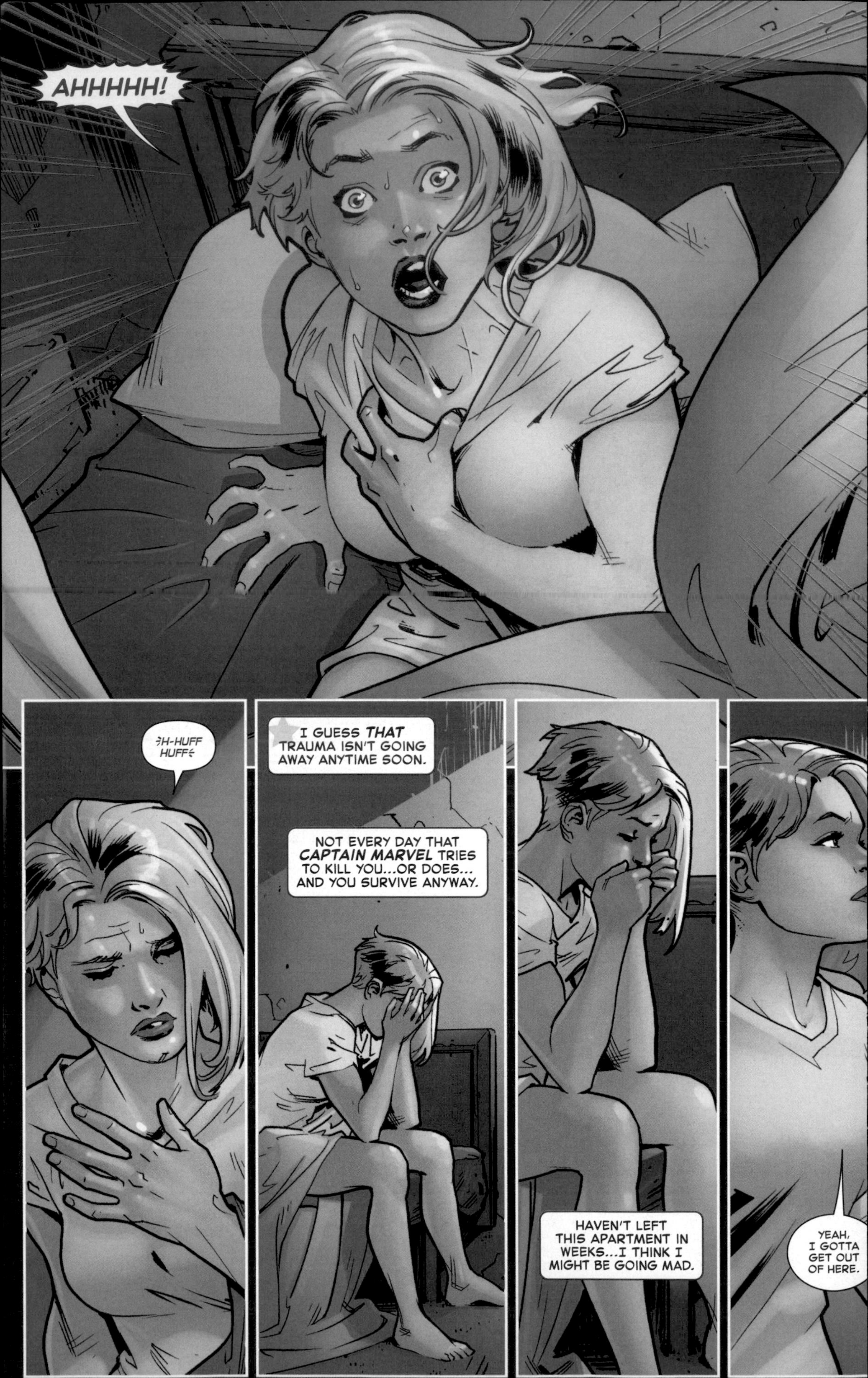
AHHHHH!
H-HUFF HUFF
I GUESS THAT TRAUMA ISN'T GOING AWAY ANYTIME SOON.
NOT EVERY DAY THAT CAPTAIN MARVEL TRIES TO KILL YOU...OR DOES... AND YOU SURVIVE ANYWAY.
HAVEN'T LEFT THIS APARTMENT IN WEEKS...I THINK I MIGHT BE GOING MAD.
YEAH, I GOTTA GET OUT OF HERE.

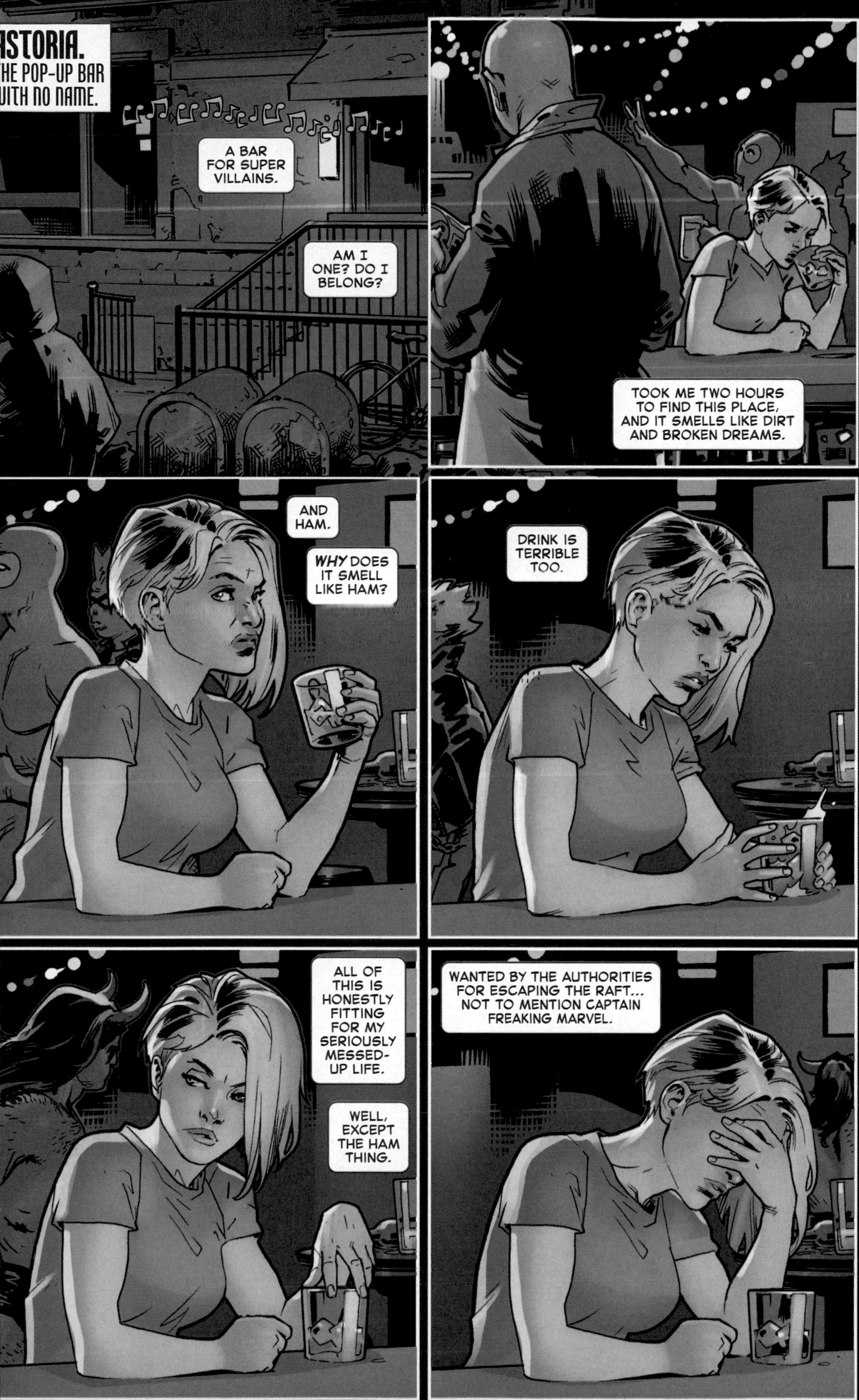

ASTORIA. THE POP-UP BAR WITH NO NAME.
A BAR FOR SUPER VILLAINS.
AM I ONE? DO I BELONG?
TOOK ME TWO HOURS TO FIND THIS PLACE, AND IT SMELLS LIKE DIRT AND BROKEN DREAMS.
AND HAM.
WHY DOES IT SMELL LIKE HAM?
DRINK IS TERRIBLE TOO.
ALL OF THIS IS HONESTLY FITTING FOR MY SERIOUSLY MESSED-UP LIFE.
WELL, EXCEPT THE HAM THING.
WANTED BY THE AUTHORITIES FOR ESCAPING THE RAFT... NOT TO MENTION CAPTAIN FREAKING MARVEL.

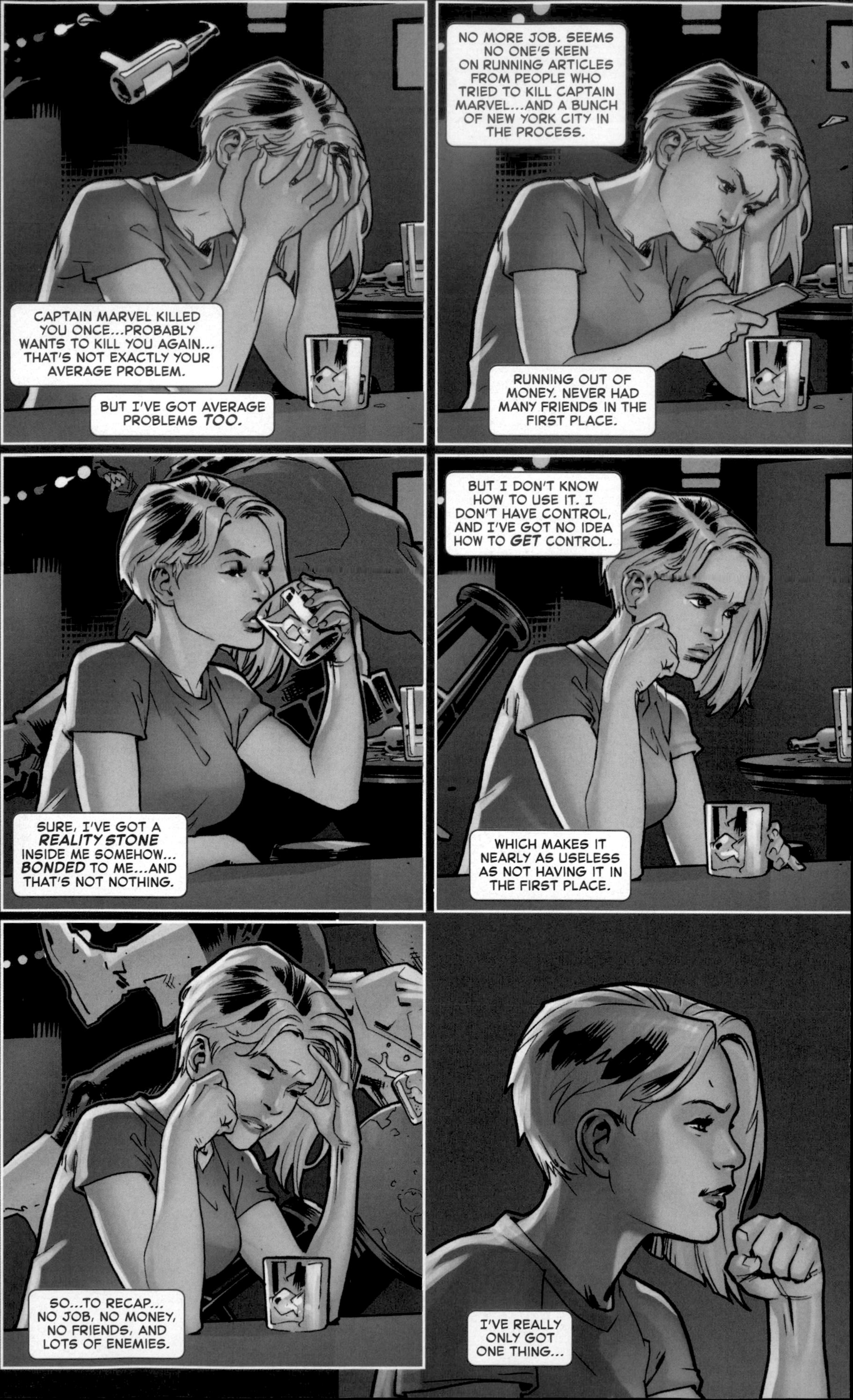
CAPTAIN MARVEL KILLED YOU ONCE...PROBABLY WANTS TO KILL YOU AGAIN... THAT'S NOT EXACTLY YOUR AVERAGE PROBLEM.
BUT I'VE GOT AVERAGE PROBLEMS TOO.
NO MORE JOB. SEEMS NO ONE'S KEEN ON RUNNING ARTICLES FROM PEOPLE WHO TRIED TO KILL CAPTAIN MARVEL...AND A BUNCH OF NEW YORK CITY IN THE PROCESS.
RUNNING OUT OF MONEY. NEVER HAD MANY FRIENDS IN THE FIRST PLACE.
SURE, I'VE GOT A REALITY STONE INSIDE ME SOMEHOW... BONDED TO ME...AND THAT'S NOT NOTHING.
BUT I DON'T KNOW HOW TO USE IT. I DON'T HAVE CONTROL, AND I'VE GOT NO IDEA HOW TO GET CONTROL.
WHICH MAKES IT NEARLY AS USELESS AS NOT HAVING IT IN THE FIRST PLACE.
SO...TO RECAP... NO JOB, NO MONEY, NO FRIENDS, AND LOTS OF ENEMIES.
I'VE REALLY ONLY GOT ONE THING...

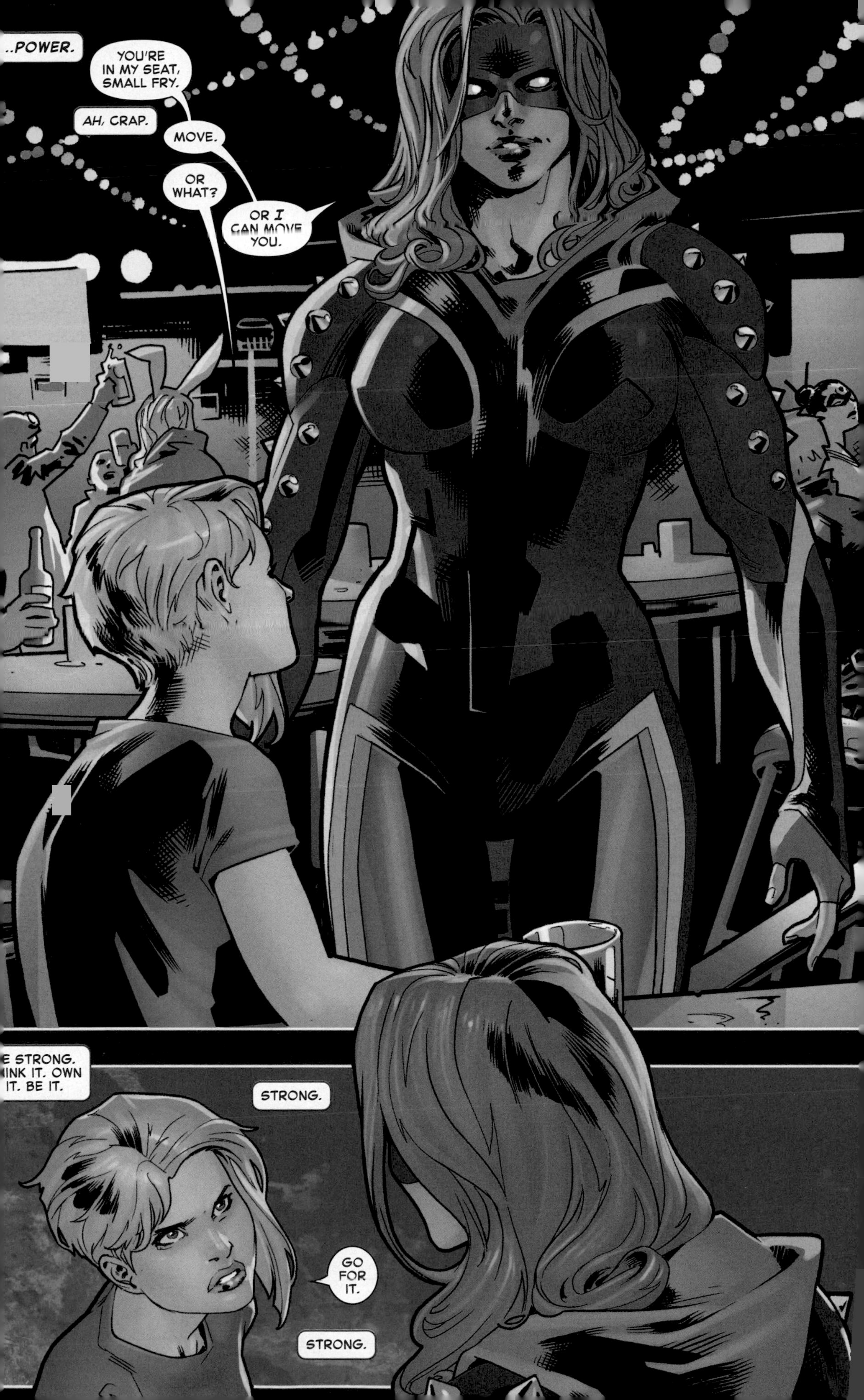
..POWER.
YOU'RE IN MY SEAT, SMALL FRY.
AH, CRAP.
MOVE.
OR WHAT?
OR I CAN MOVE YOU.
E STRONG. INK IT. OWN IT. BE IT.
STRONG.
GO FOR IT.
STRONG.

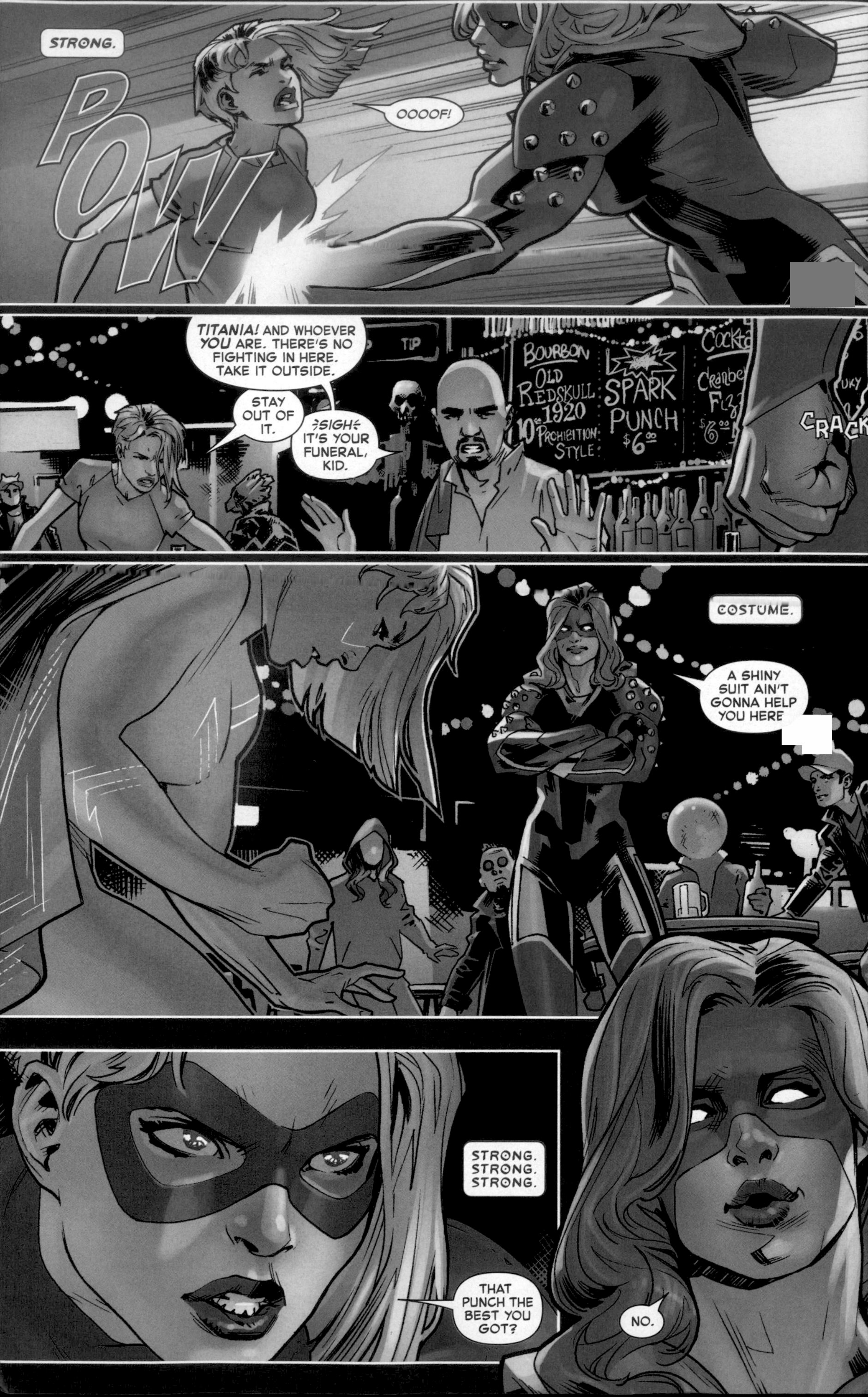
STRONG.
POW
OOOOF!
TITANIA! AND WHOEVER YOU ARE. THERE'S NO FIGHTING IN HERE. TAKE IT OUTSIDE.
STAY OUT OF IT.
SIGH IT'S YOUR FUNERAL, KID.
BOURBON
OLD REDSKULL 1920
PROHIBITION STYLE
SPARK PUNCH $6.00
CRACK
COSTUME.
A SHINY SUIT AIN'T GONNA HELP YOU HERE
STRONG. STRONG. STRONG.
THAT PUNCH THE BEST YOU GOT?
NO.

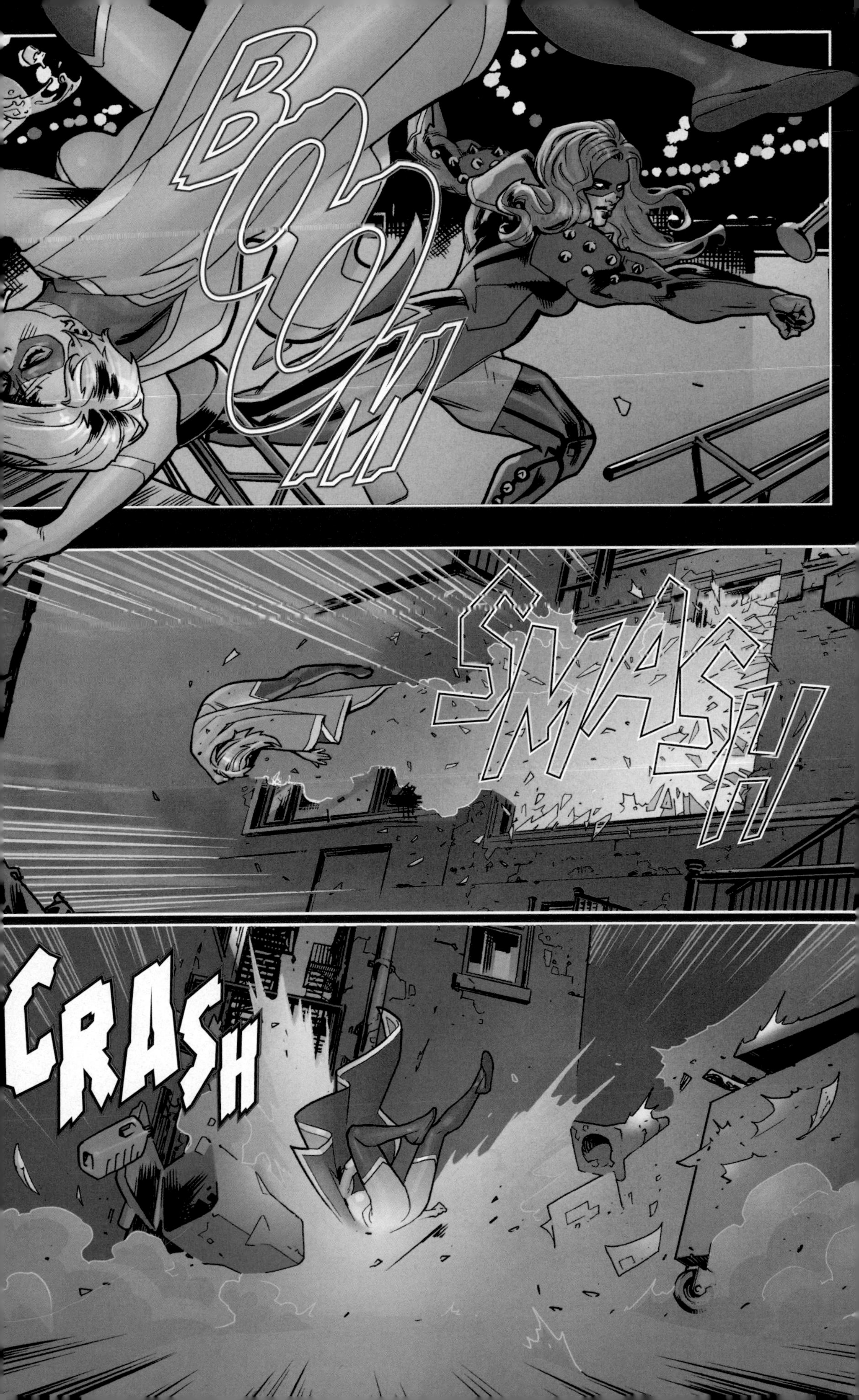
BOOM
SMASH
CRASH

NGH.

IDIOT. STRONG ISN'T "THE STRONGEST" OR "STRONGER THAN HER" OR EVEN "INVULNERABLE" OR "IMMOVABLE." I GOTTA BE SMARTER THAN THAT.

AND MORE... PRECISE.

I ALSO SHOULDN'T THINK SO SMALL. IN FACT, MAYBE...

THIS WHOLE BUILDING SHOULD BE IN FLAM--

AH, AH, AH-- LET'S NOT.

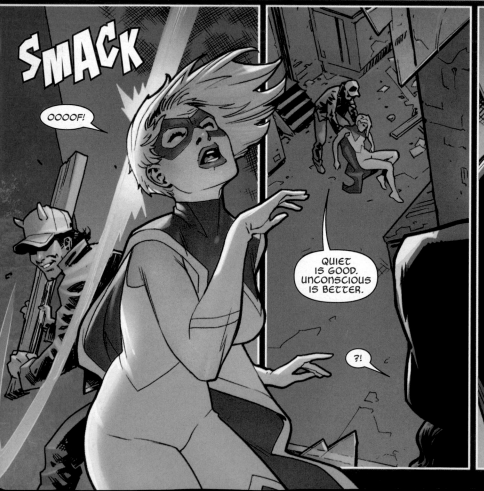

SMACK

OOOOF!

QUIET IS GOOD. UNCONSCIOUS IS BETTER.

?!

THAT'S... INTERESTING.

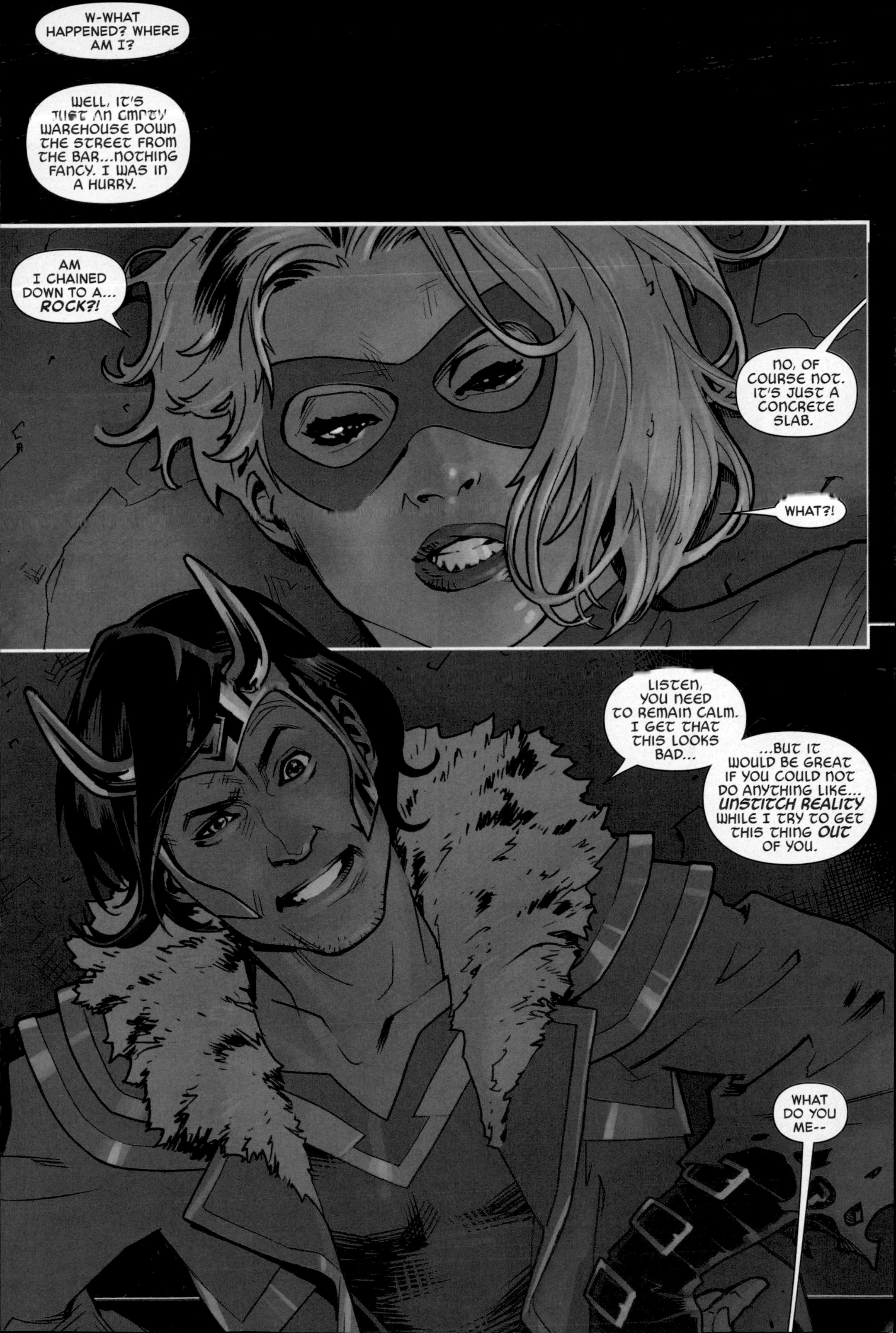
W-WHAT HAPPENED? WHERE AM I?
WELL, IT'S JUST AN EMPTY WAREHOUSE DOWN THE STREET FROM THE BAR...NOTHING FANCY. I WAS IN A HURRY.
AM I CHAINED DOWN TO A... ROCK?!
NO, OF COURSE NOT. IT'S JUST A CONCRETE SLAB.
WHAT?!
LISTEN, YOU NEED TO REMAIN CALM. I GET THAT THIS LOOKS BAD...
...BUT IT WOULD BE GREAT IF YOU COULD NOT DO ANYTHING LIKE... UNSTITCH REALITY WHILE I TRY TO GET THIS THING OUT OF YOU.
WHAT DO YOU ME--

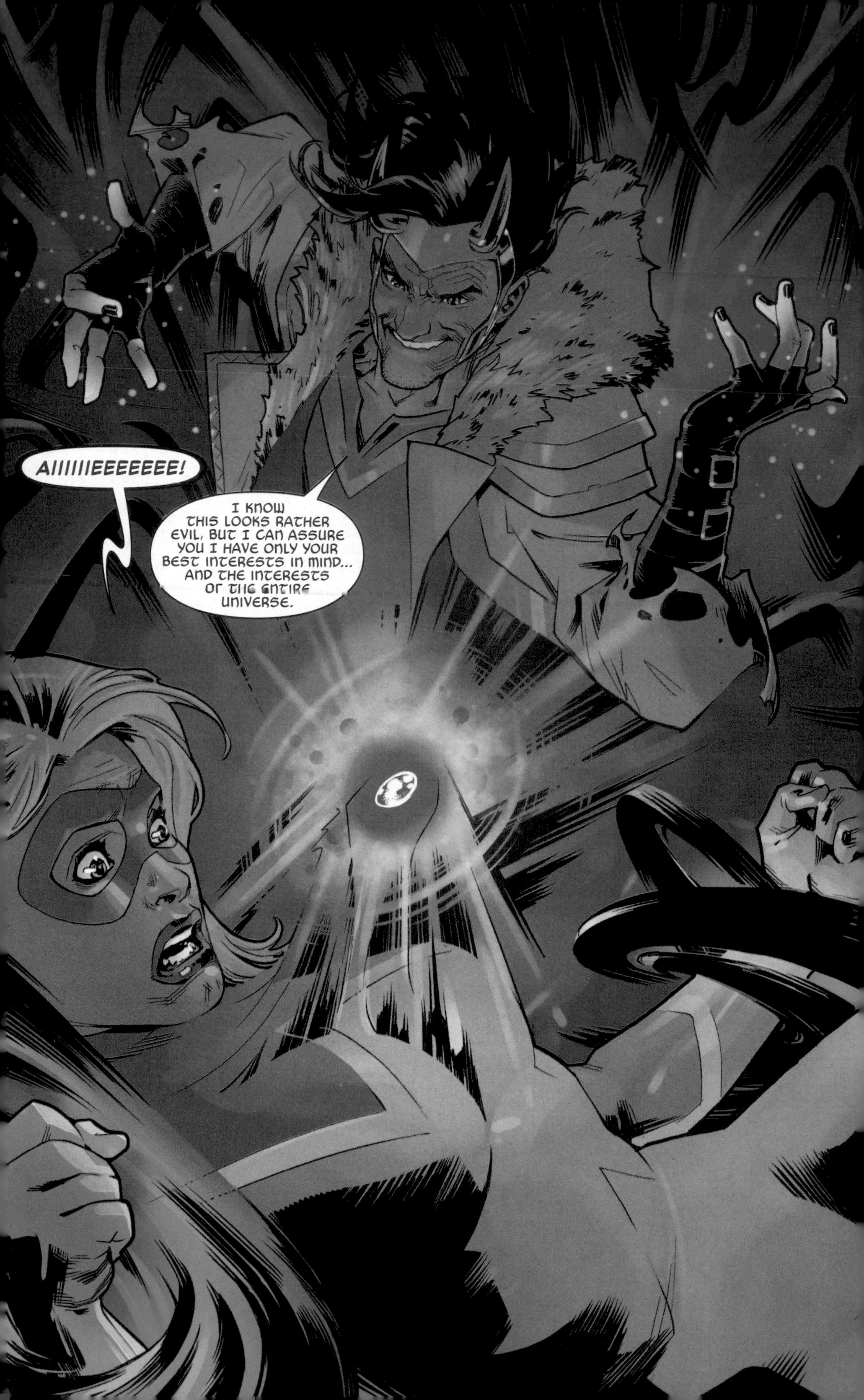
AIIIIIIEEEEEEE!
I KNOW THIS LOOKS RATHER EVIL, BUT I CAN ASSURE YOU I HAVE ONLY YOUR BEST INTERESTS IN MIND... AND THE INTERESTS OF THE ENTIRE UNIVERSE.

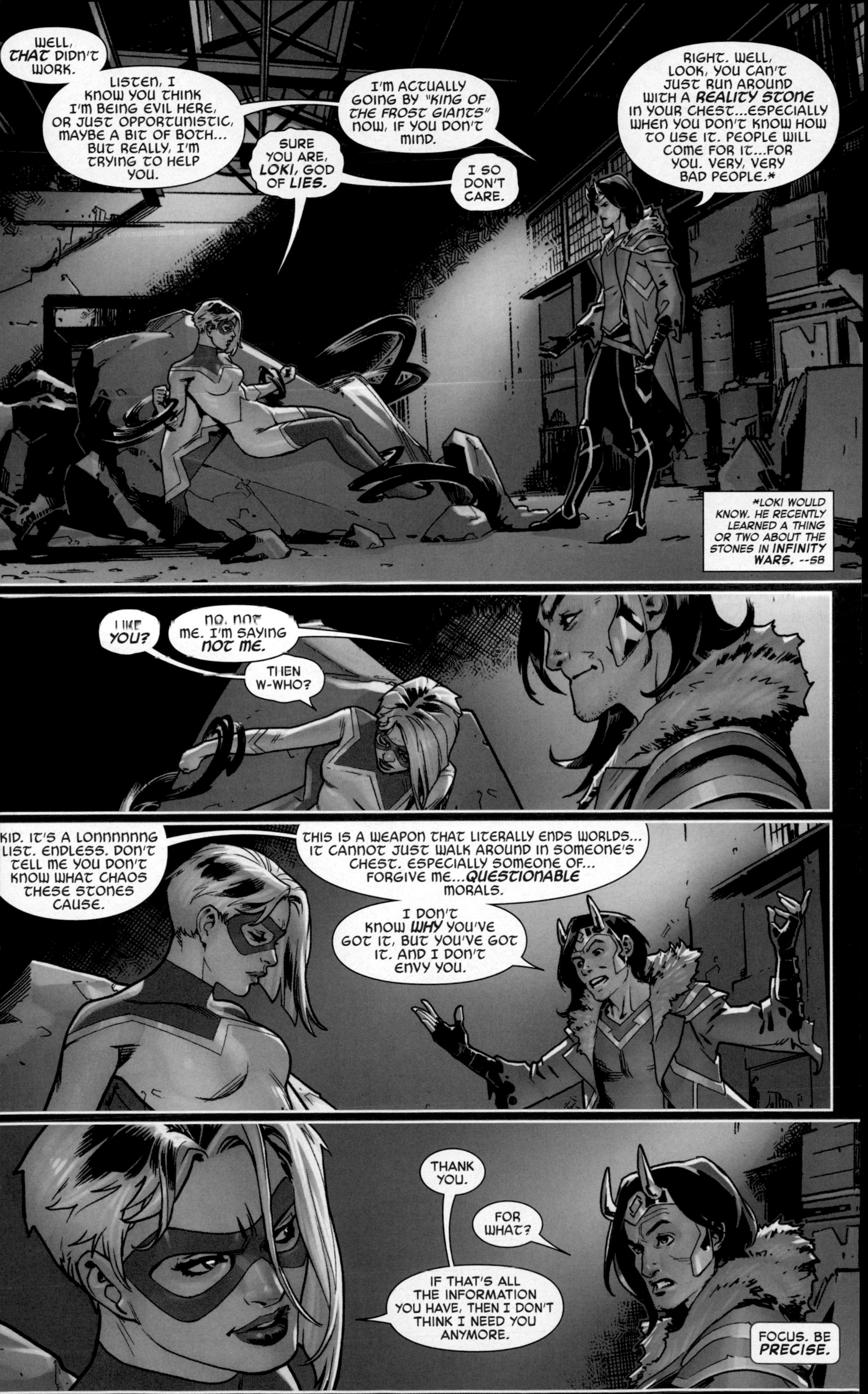

WELL, THAT DIDN'T WORK.
LISTEN, I KNOW YOU THINK I'M BEING EVIL HERE, OR JUST OPPORTUNISTIC, MAYBE A BIT OF BOTH... BUT REALLY, I'M TRYING TO HELP YOU.
SURE YOU ARE, LOKI, GOD OF LIES.
I'M ACTUALLY GOING BY "KING OF THE FROST GIANTS" NOW, IF YOU DON'T MIND.
I SO DON'T CARE.
RIGHT. WELL, LOOK, YOU CAN'T JUST RUN AROUND WITH A REALITY STONE IN YOUR CHEST...ESPECIALLY WHEN YOU DON'T KNOW HOW TO USE IT. PEOPLE WILL COME FOR IT...FOR YOU. VERY, VERY BAD PEOPLE.*
*LOKI WOULD KNOW. HE RECENTLY LEARNED A THING OR TWO ABOUT THE STONES IN INFINITY WARS. --SB
LIKE YOU?
NO, NOT ME. I'M SAYING NOT ME.
THEN W-WHO?
KID. IT'S A LONNNNNNG LIST. ENDLESS. DON'T TELL ME YOU DON'T KNOW WHAT CHAOS THESE STONES CAUSE.
THIS IS A WEAPON THAT LITERALLY ENDS WORLDS... IT CANNOT JUST WALK AROUND IN SOMEONE'S CHEST. ESPECIALLY SOMEONE OF... FORGIVE ME...QUESTIONABLE MORALS.
I DON'T KNOW WHY YOU'VE GOT IT, BUT YOU'VE GOT IT. AND I DON'T ENVY YOU.
THANK YOU.
FOR WHAT?
IF THAT'S ALL THE INFORMATION YOU HAVE, THEN I DON'T THINK I NEED YOU ANYMORE.
FOCUS. BE PRECISE.

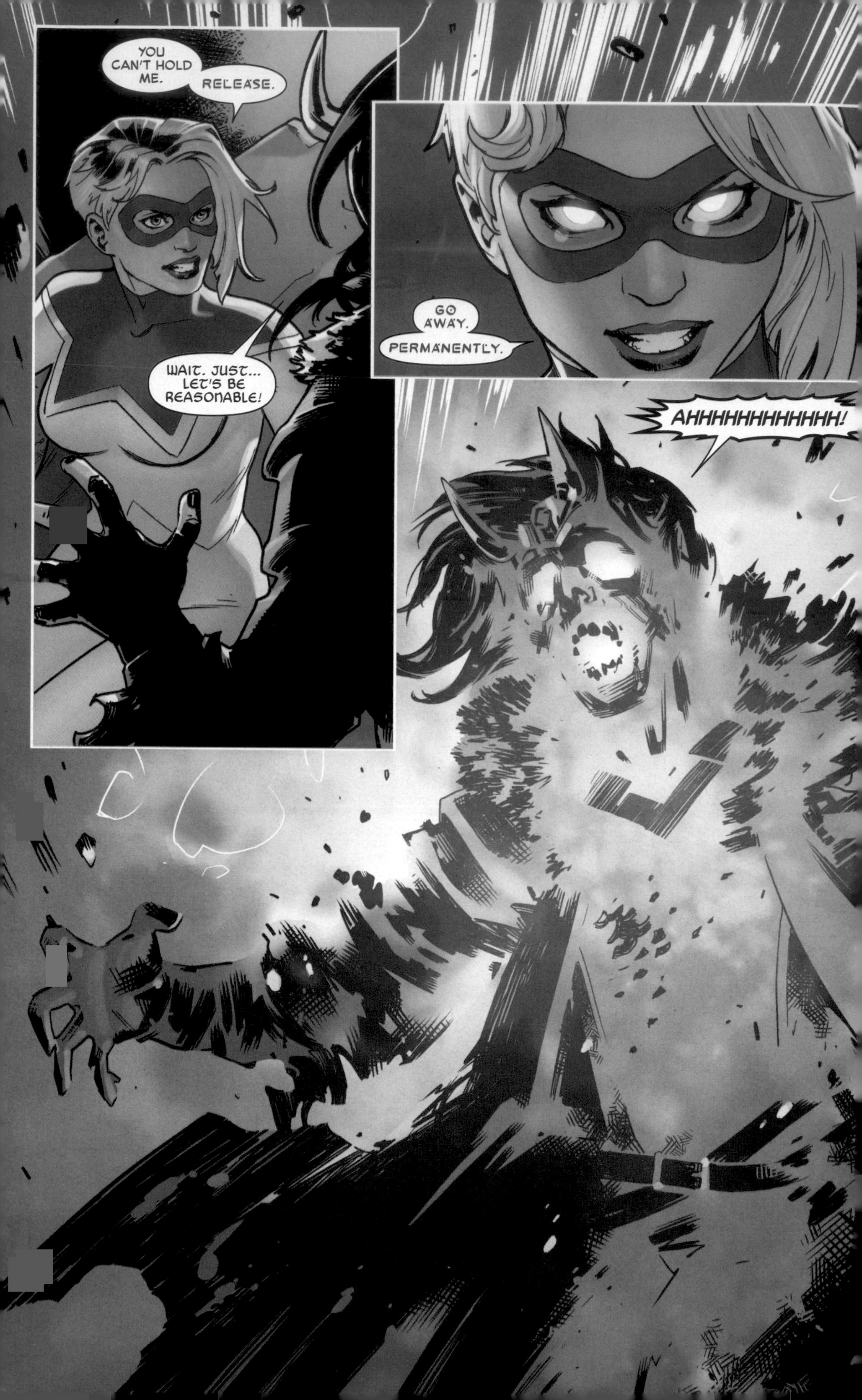
YOU CAN'T HOLD ME.
RELEASE.
WAIT. JUST... LET'S BE REASONABLE!
GO AWAY.
PERMANENTLY.
AHHHHHHHHHHHH!

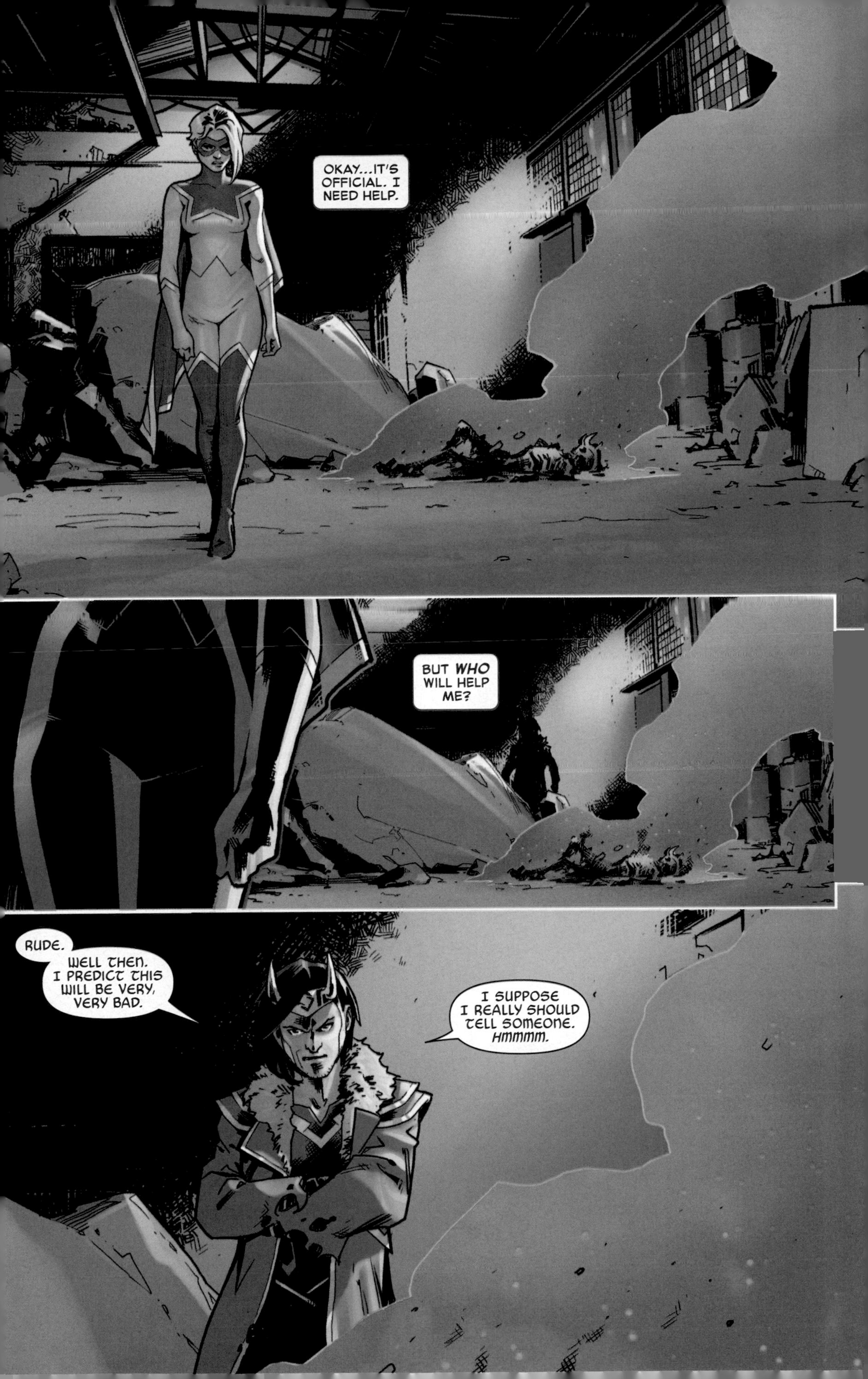
OKAY...IT'S OFFICIAL. I NEED HELP.
BUT WHO WILL HELP ME?
RUDE.
WELL THEN. I PREDICT THIS WILL BE VERY, VERY BAD.
I SUPPOSE I REALLY SHOULD TELL SOMEONE. Hmmmm.

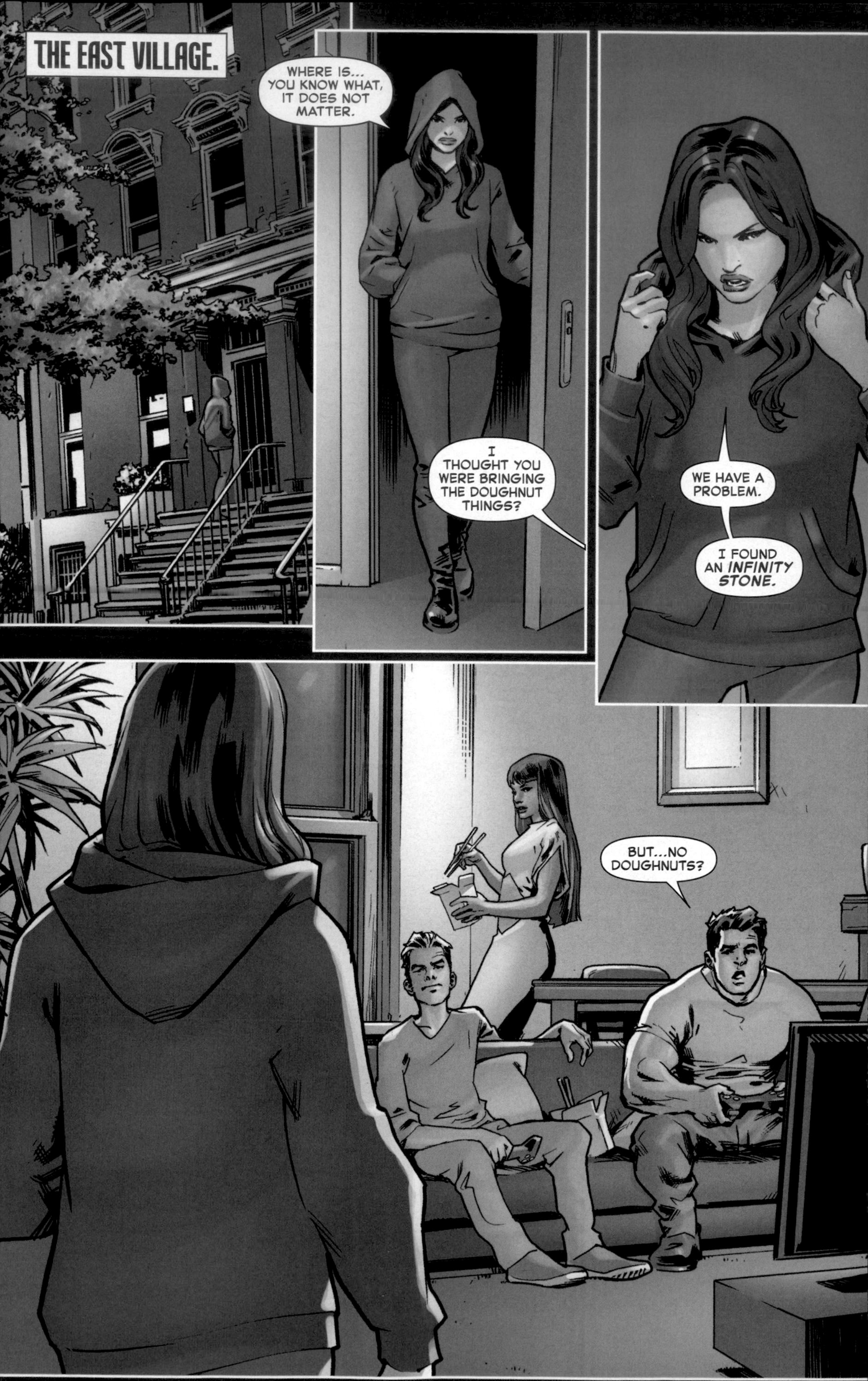
THE EAST VILLAGE.
WHERE IS... YOU KNOW WHAT, IT DOES NOT MATTER.
I THOUGHT YOU WERE BRINGING THE DOUGHNUT THINGS?
WE HAVE A PROBLEM.
I FOUND AN INFINITY STONE.
BUT...NO DOUGHNUTS?

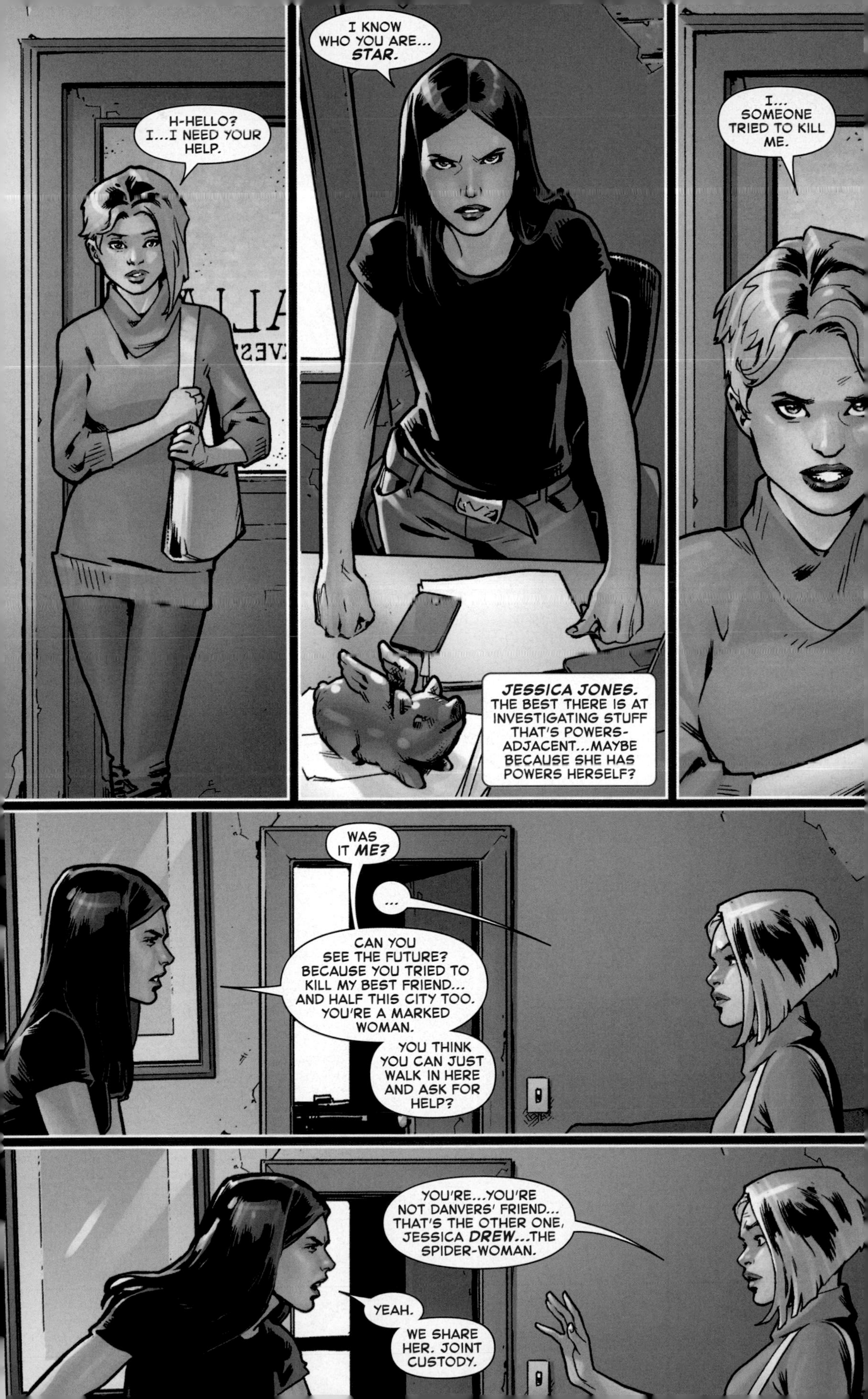
H-HELLO? I...I NEED YOUR HELP.
I KNOW WHO YOU ARE... STAR.
JESSICA JONES. THE BEST THERE IS AT INVESTIGATING STUFF THAT'S POWERS-ADJACENT...MAYBE BECAUSE SHE HAS POWERS HERSELF?
I... SOMEONE TRIED TO KILL ME.
WAS IT ME?
...
CAN YOU SEE THE FUTURE? BECAUSE YOU TRIED TO KILL MY BEST FRIEND... AND HALF THIS CITY TOO. YOU'RE A MARKED WOMAN.
YOU THINK YOU CAN JUST WALK IN HERE AND ASK FOR HELP?
YOU'RE...YOU'RE NOT DANVERS' FRIEND... THAT'S THE OTHER ONE, JESSICA DREW...THE SPIDER-WOMAN.
YEAH.
WE SHARE HER. JOINT CUSTODY.

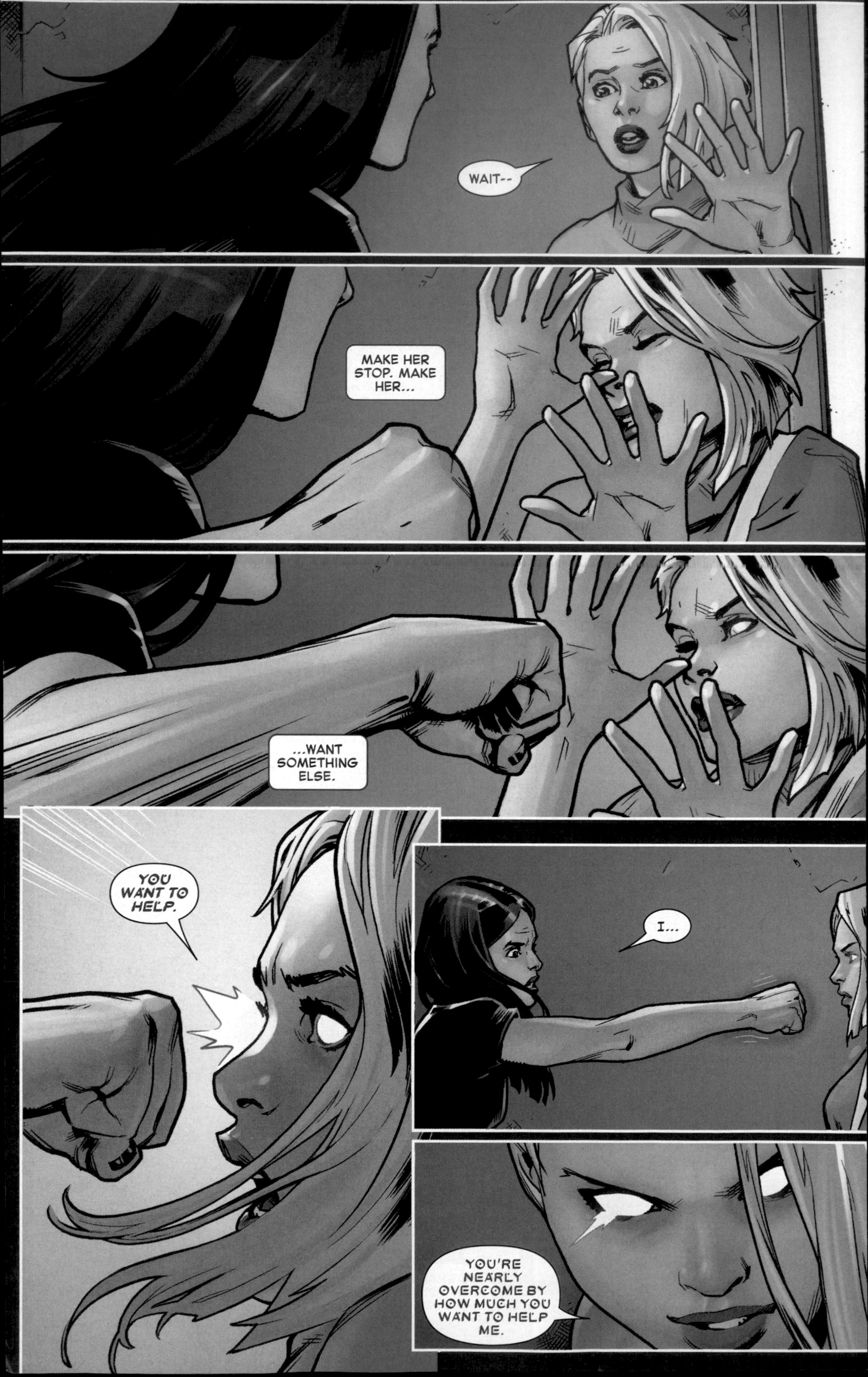
WAIT--
MAKE HER STOP. MAKE HER...
...WANT SOMETHING ELSE.
YOU WANT TO HELP.
I...
YOU'RE NEARLY OVERCOME BY HOW MUCH YOU WANT TO HELP ME.

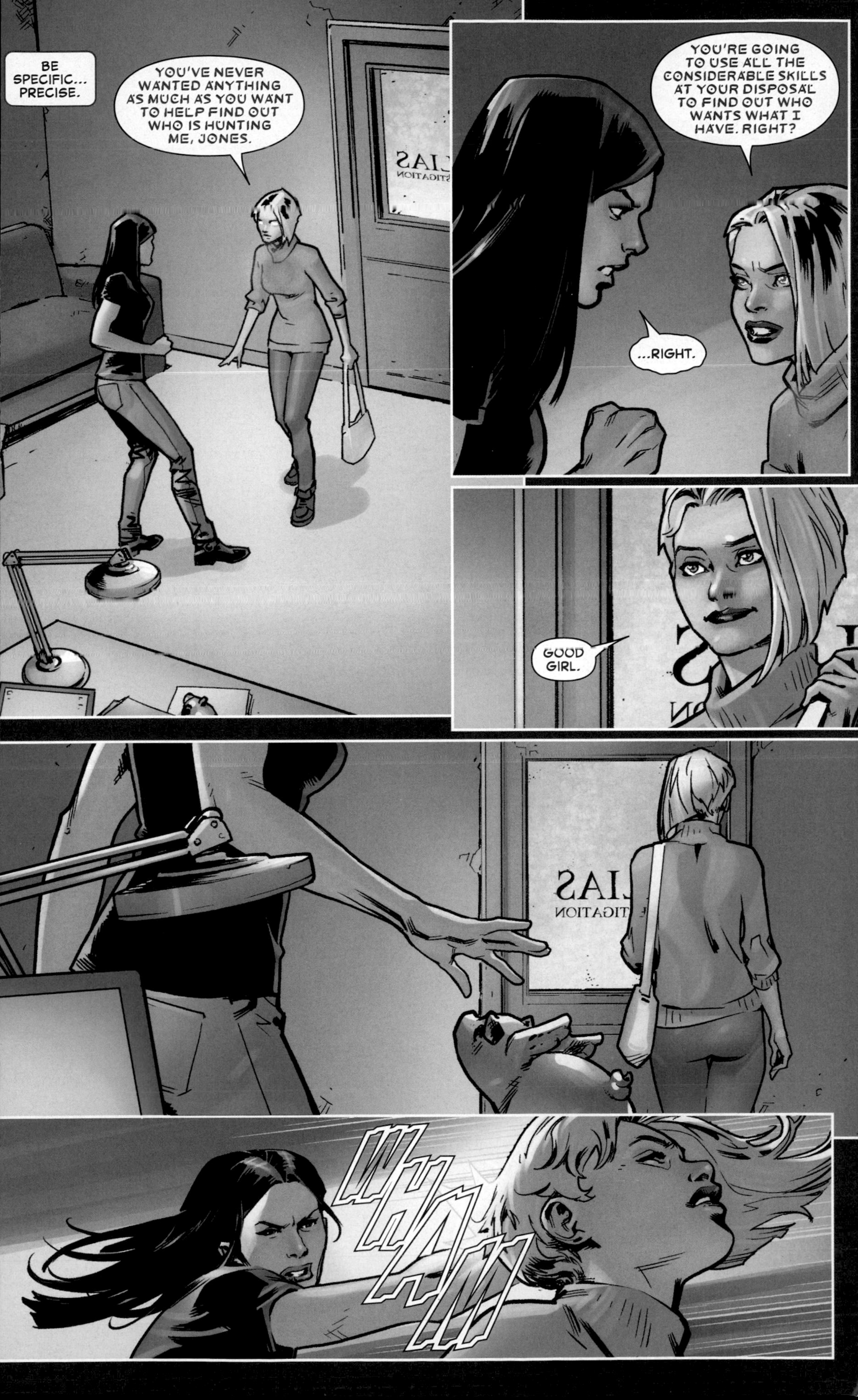
BE SPECIFIC... PRECISE.
YOU'VE NEVER WANTED ANYTHING AS MUCH AS YOU WANT TO HELP FIND OUT WHO IS HUNTING ME, JONES.
YOU'RE GOING TO USE ALL THE CONSIDERABLE SKILLS AT YOUR DISPOSAL TO FIND OUT WHO WANTS WHAT I HAVE. RIGHT?
...RIGHT.
GOOD GIRL.
WHAM

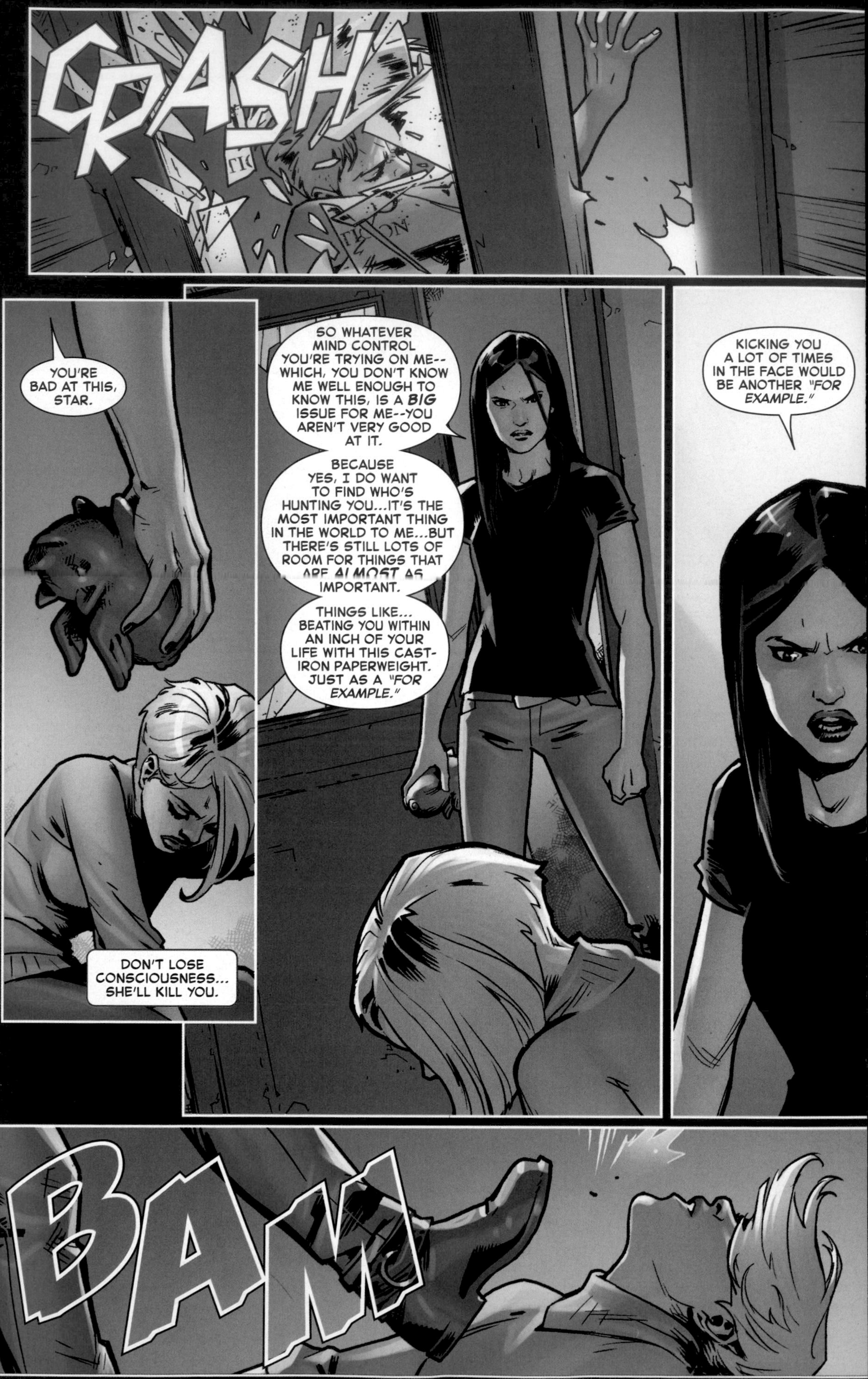
CRASH
YOU'RE BAD AT THIS, STAR.
DON'T LOSE CONSCIOUSNESS... SHE'LL KILL YOU.
SO WHATEVER MIND CONTROL YOU'RE TRYING ON ME--WHICH, YOU DON'T KNOW ME WELL ENOUGH TO KNOW THIS, IS A BIG ISSUE FOR ME--YOU AREN'T VERY GOOD AT IT.
BECAUSE YES, I DO WANT TO FIND WHO'S HUNTING YOU...IT'S THE MOST IMPORTANT THING IN THE WORLD TO ME...BUT THERE'S STILL LOTS OF ROOM FOR THINGS THAT ARE ALMOST AS IMPORTANT.
THINGS LIKE... BEATING YOU WITHIN AN INCH OF YOUR LIFE WITH THIS CAST-IRON PAPERWEIGHT. JUST AS A "FOR EXAMPLE."
KICKING YOU A LOT OF TIMES IN THE FACE WOULD BE ANOTHER "FOR EXAMPLE."
BAM

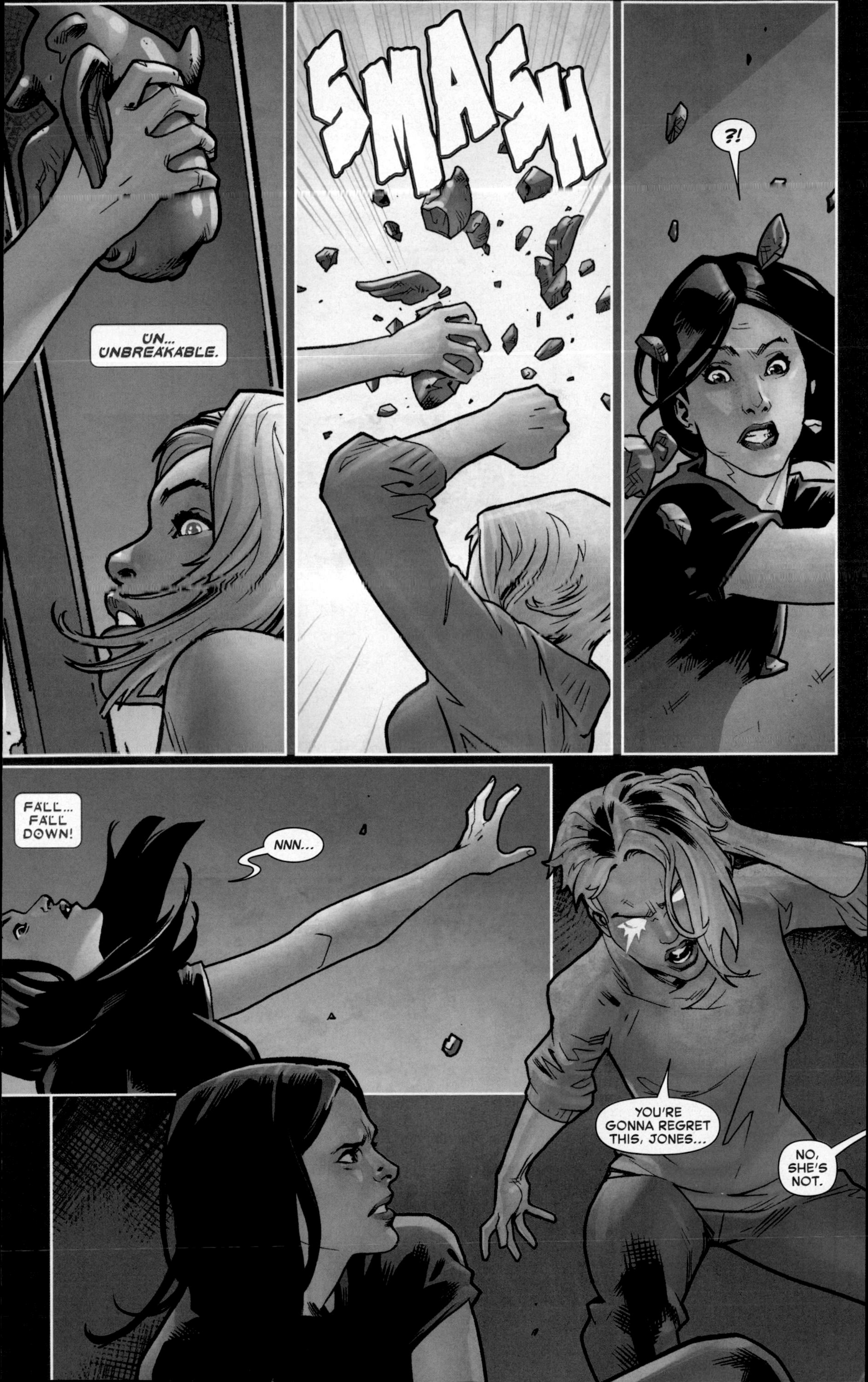
UN... UNBREAKABLE.
SMASH
?!
FALL... FALL DOWN!
NNN...
YOU'RE GONNA REGRET THIS, JONES...
NO, SHE'S NOT.

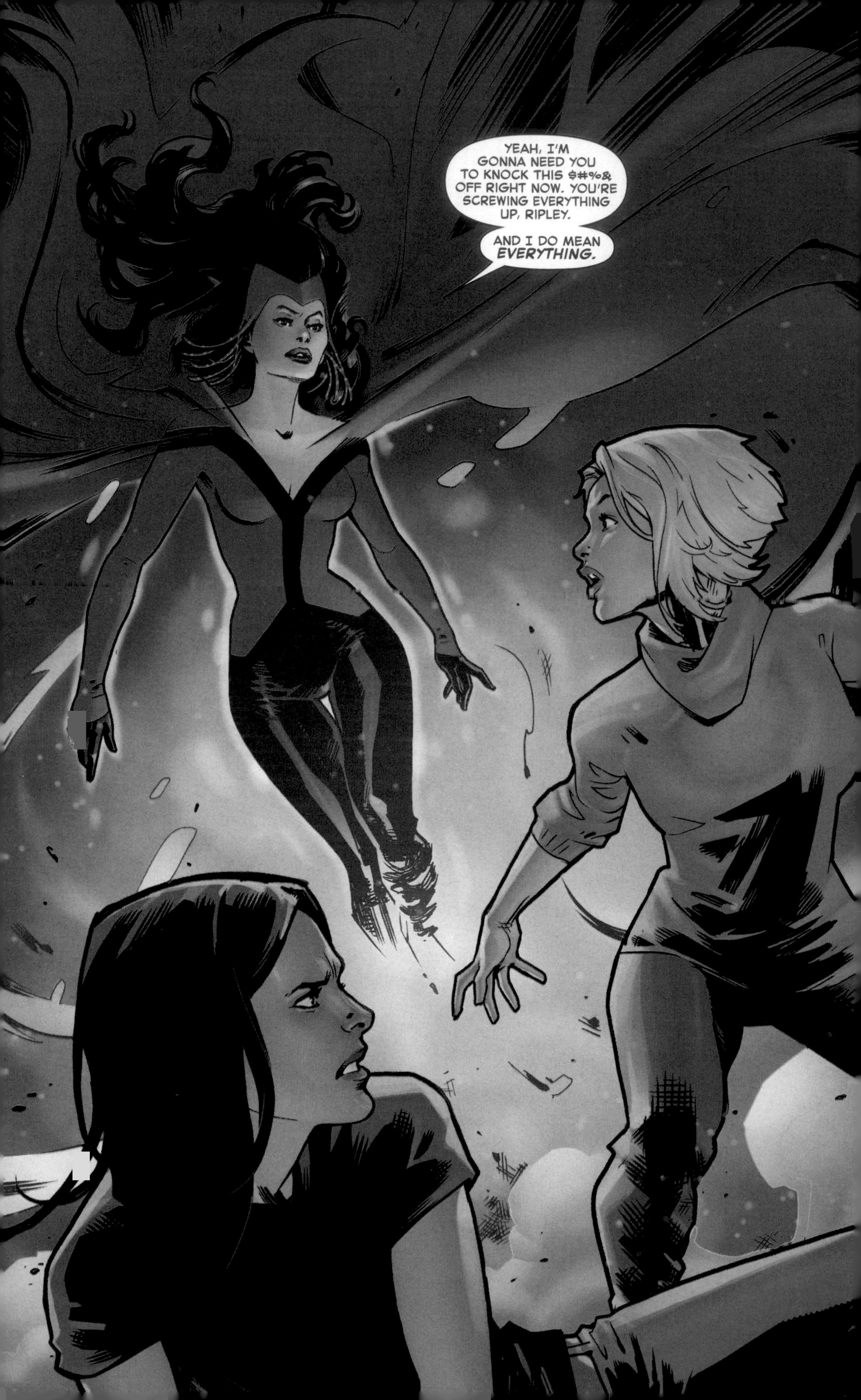
YEAH, I'M GONNA NEED YOU TO KNOCK THIS $#%& OFF RIGHT NOW. YOU'RE SCREWING EVERYTHING UP, RIPLEY.
AND I DO MEAN *EVERYTHING.*

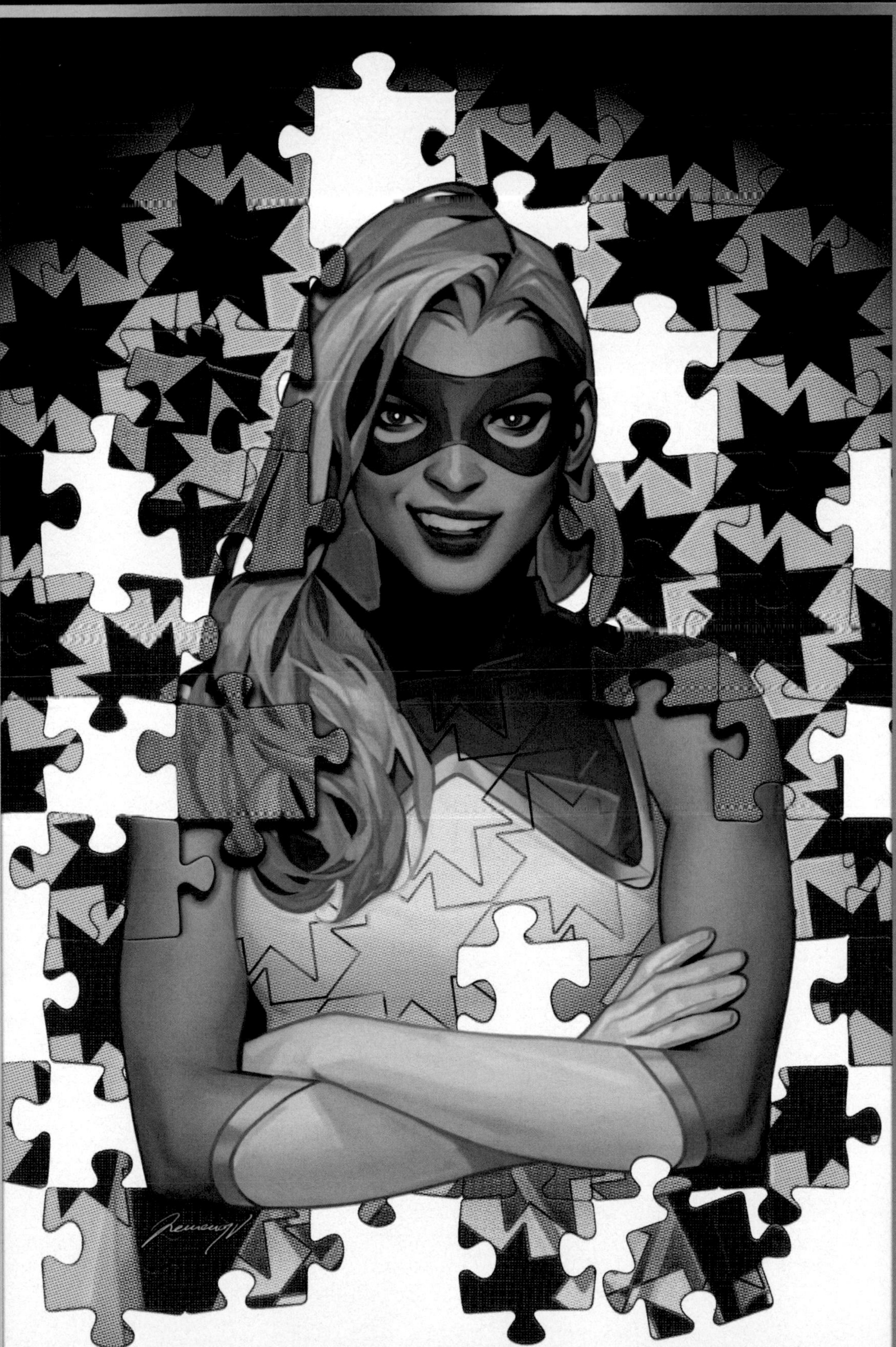

#1 VARIANT BY
VALENTINA REMENAR

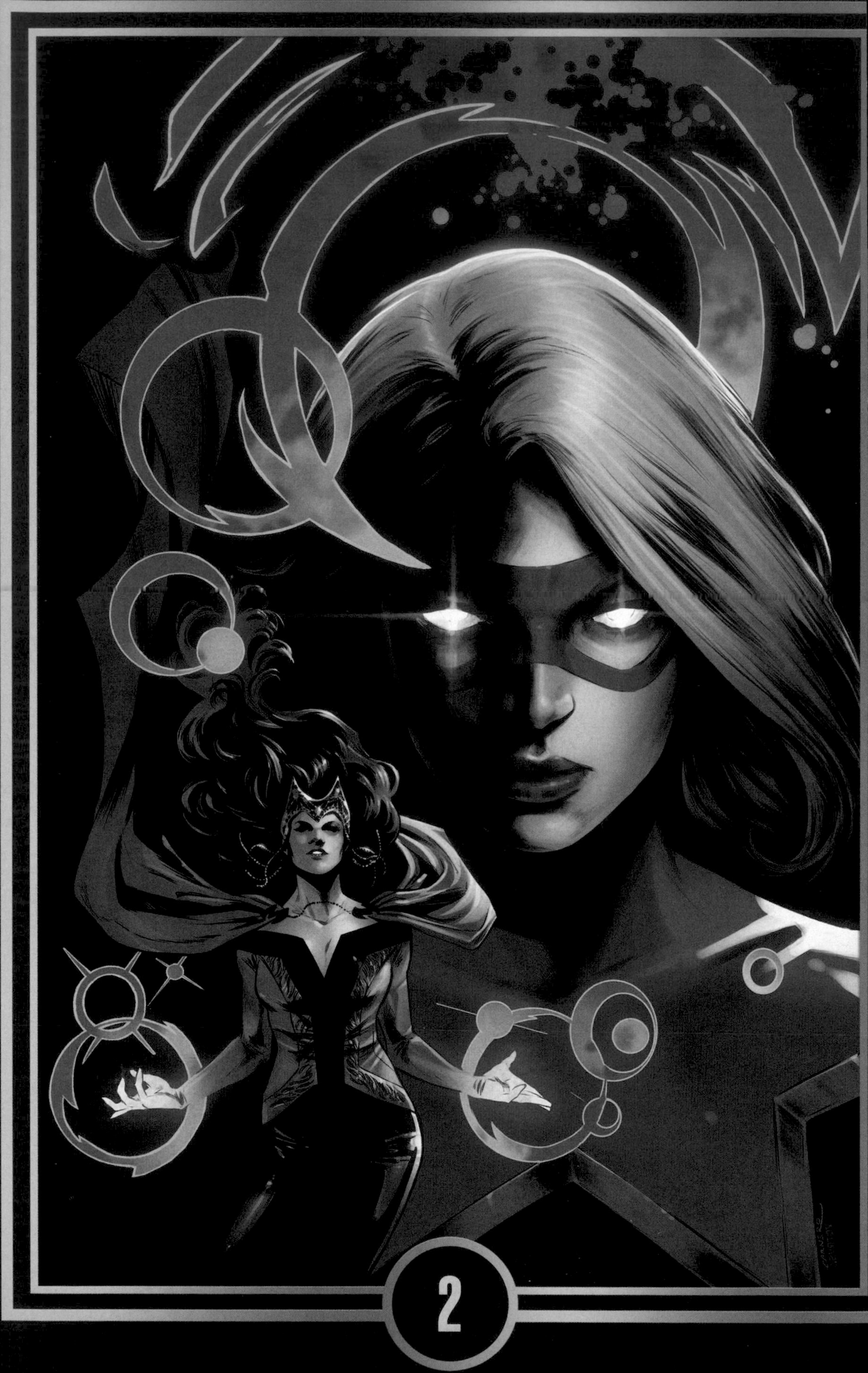
2

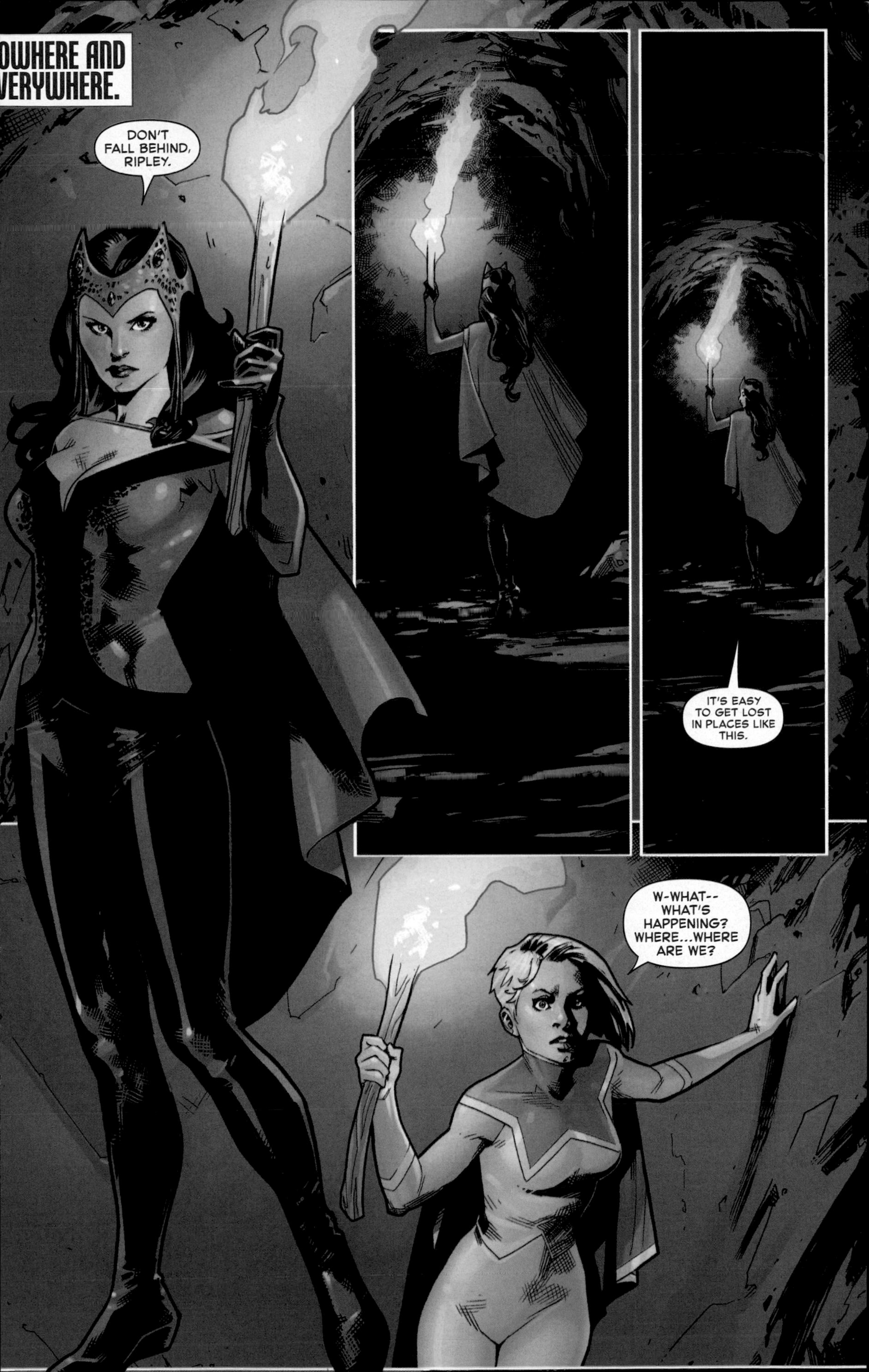
OWHERE AND
VERYWHERE.
DON'T FALL BEHIND, RIPLEY.
IT'S EASY TO GET LOST IN PLACES LIKE THIS.
W-WHAT-- WHAT'S HAPPENING? WHERE...WHERE ARE WE?

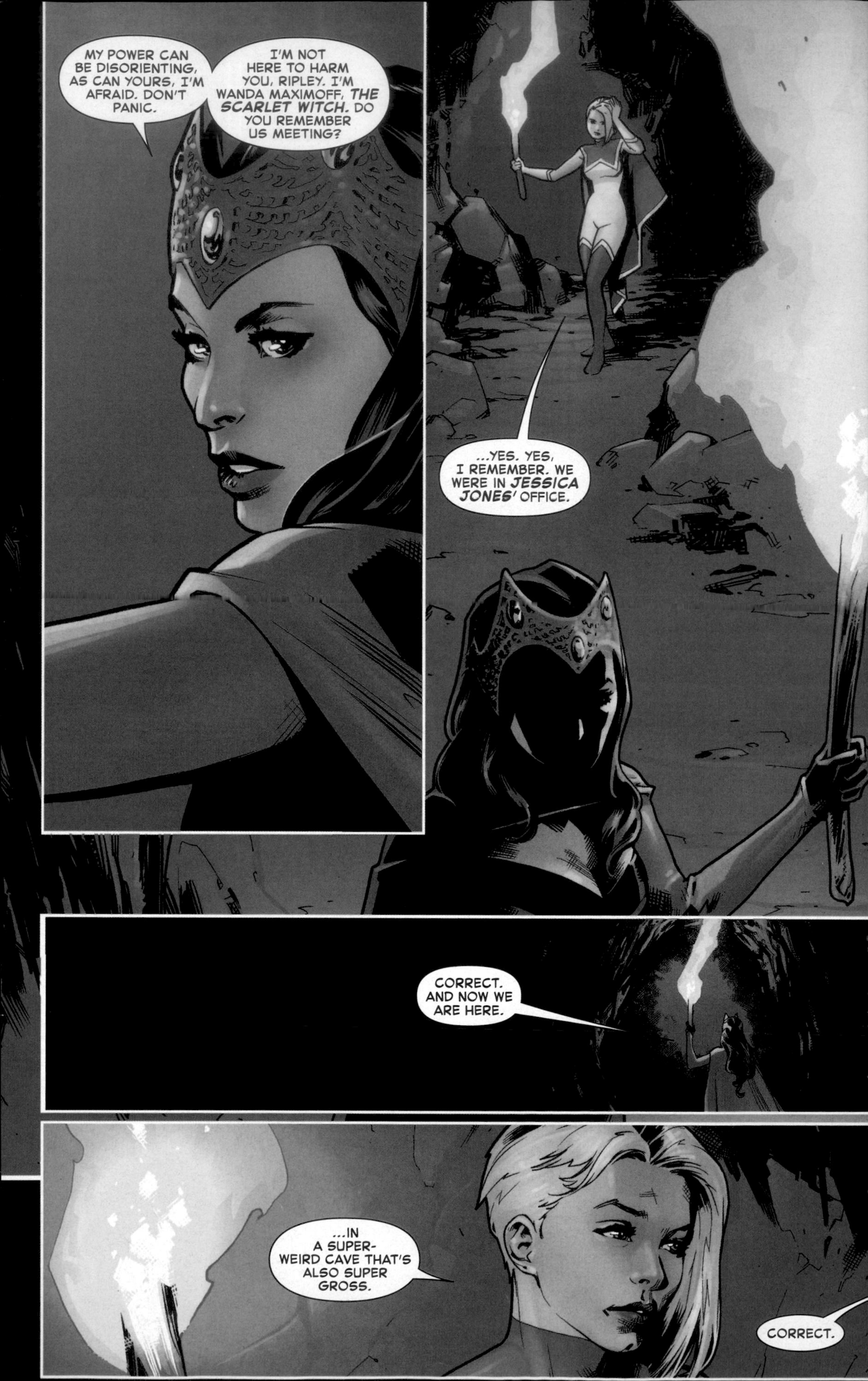
MY POWER CAN BE DISORIENTING, AS CAN YOURS, I'M AFRAID. DON'T PANIC.
I'M NOT HERE TO HARM YOU, RIPLEY. I'M WANDA MAXIMOFF, THE SCARLET WITCH. DO YOU REMEMBER US MEETING?
...YES. YES, I REMEMBER. WE WERE IN JESSICA JONES' OFFICE.
CORRECT. AND NOW WE ARE HERE.
...IN A SUPER-WEIRD CAVE THAT'S ALSO SUPER GROSS.
CORRECT.

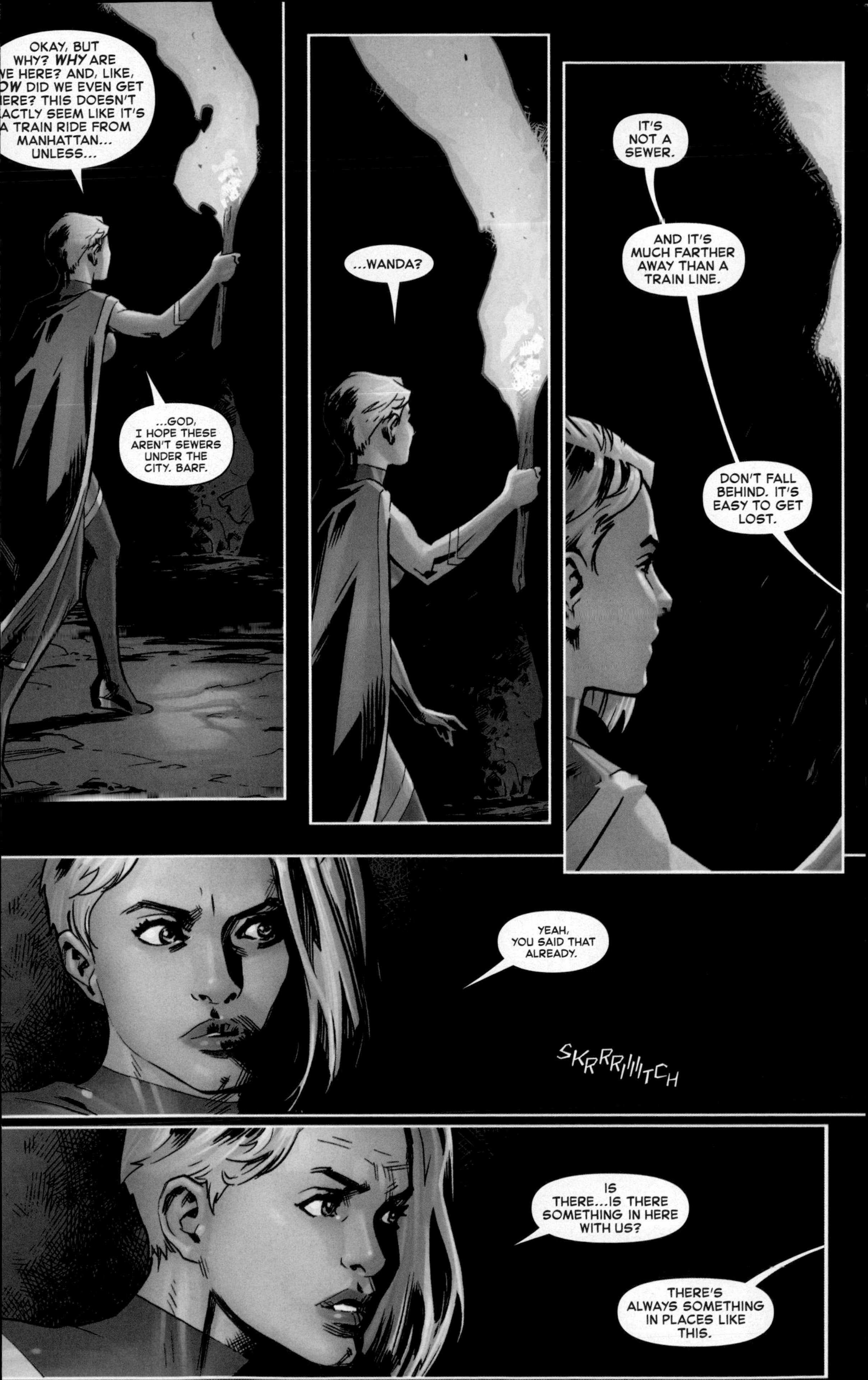
OKAY, BUT WHY? *WHY* ARE E HERE? AND, LIKE, OW DID WE EVEN GET ERE? THIS DOESN'T ACTLY SEEM LIKE IT'S A TRAIN RIDE FROM MANHATTAN... UNLESS...
...GOD, I HOPE THESE AREN'T SEWERS UNDER THE CITY. BARF.
...WANDA?
IT'S NOT A SEWER.
AND IT'S MUCH FARTHER AWAY THAN A TRAIN LINE.
DON'T FALL BEHIND. IT'S EASY TO GET LOST.
YEAH, YOU SAID THAT ALREADY.
SKRRRIIIITCH
IS THERE...IS THERE SOMETHING IN HERE WITH US?
THERE'S ALWAYS SOMETHING IN PLACES LIKE THIS.

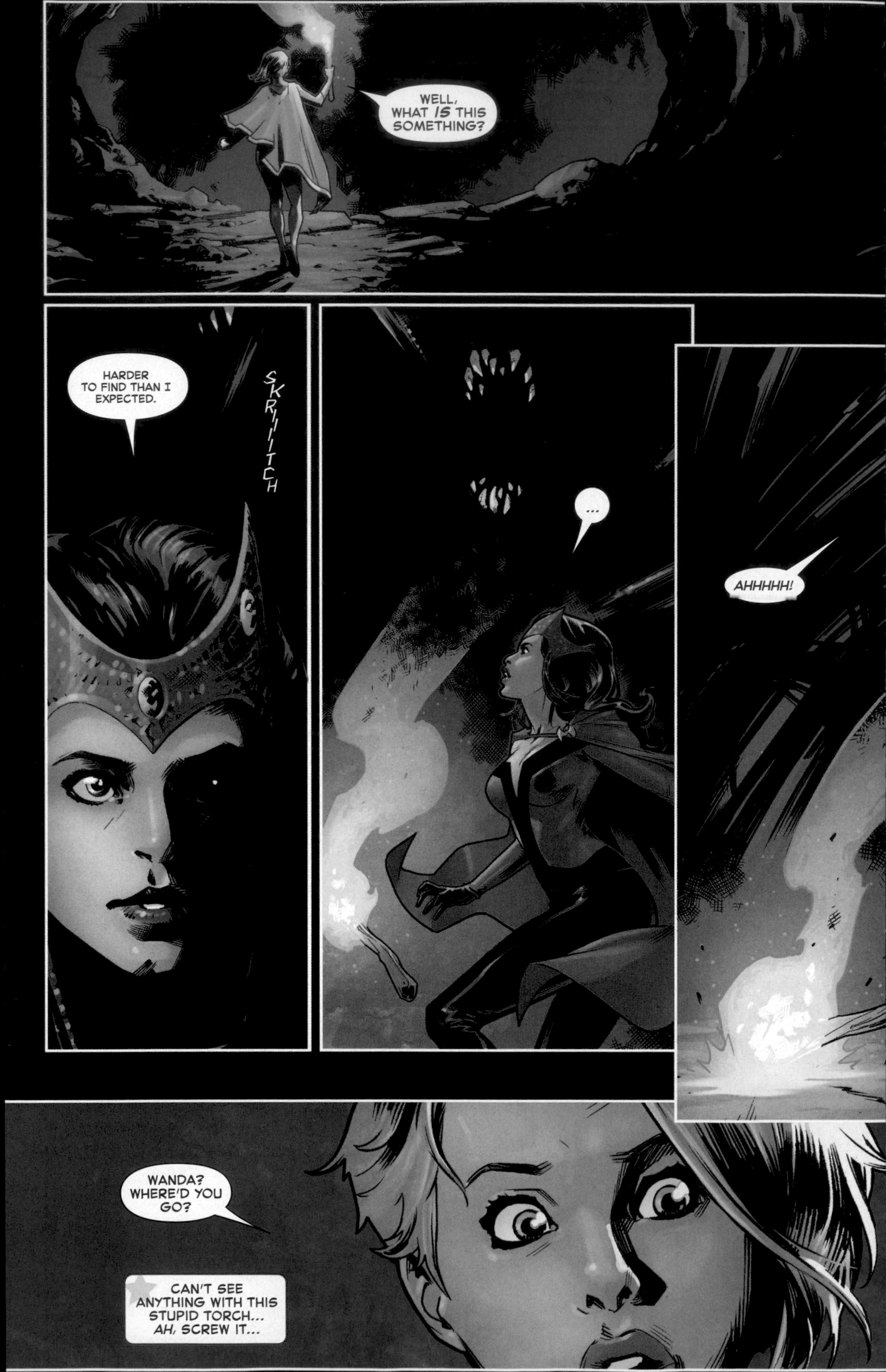
WELL, WHAT *IS* THIS SOMETHING?
HARDER TO FIND THAN I EXPECTED.
SKRIIIITCH
...
AHHHHH!
WANDA? WHERE'D YOU GO?
CAN'T SEE ANYTHING WITH THIS STUPID TORCH... *AH,* SCREW IT...

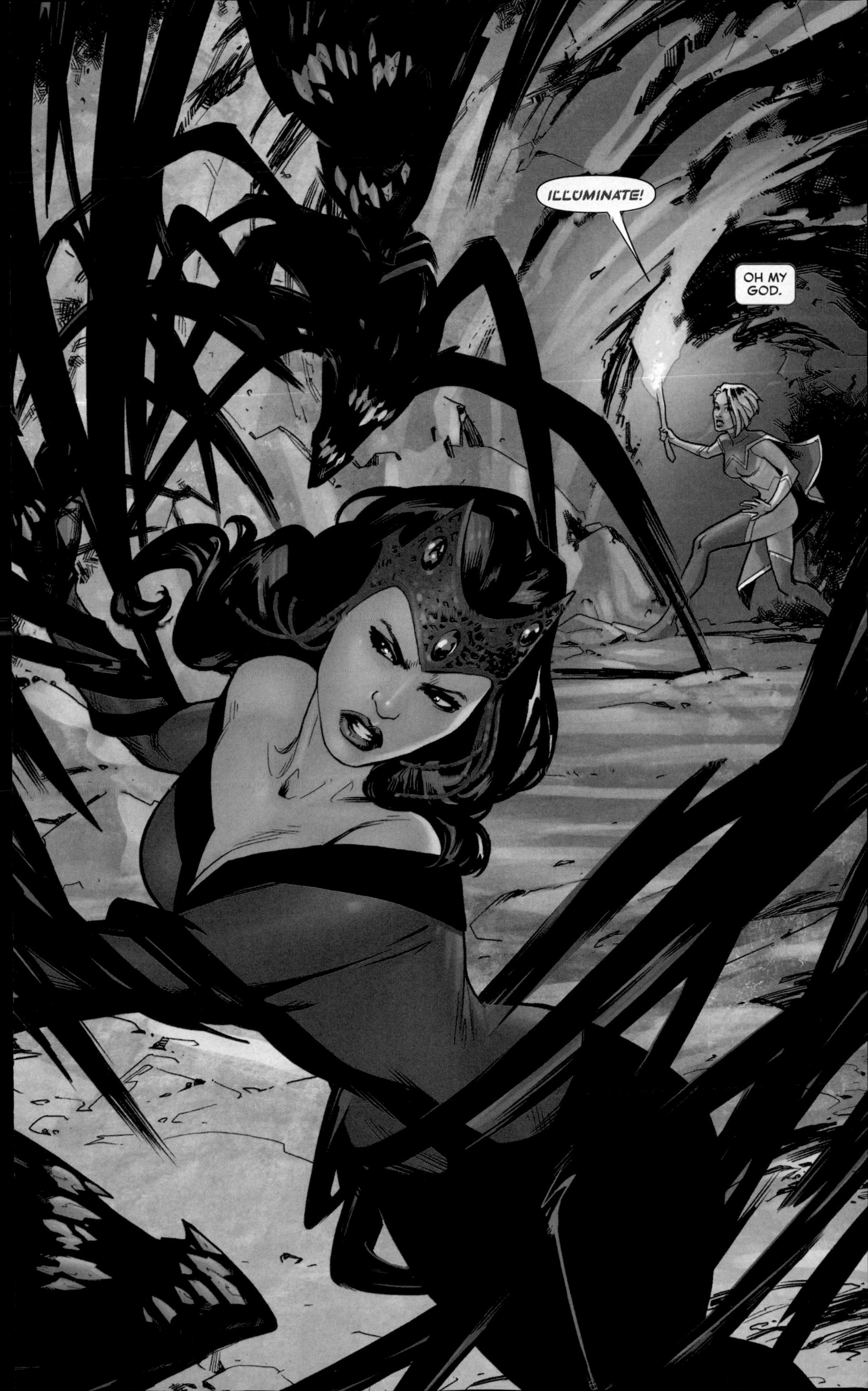
ILLUMINATE!
OH MY GOD.

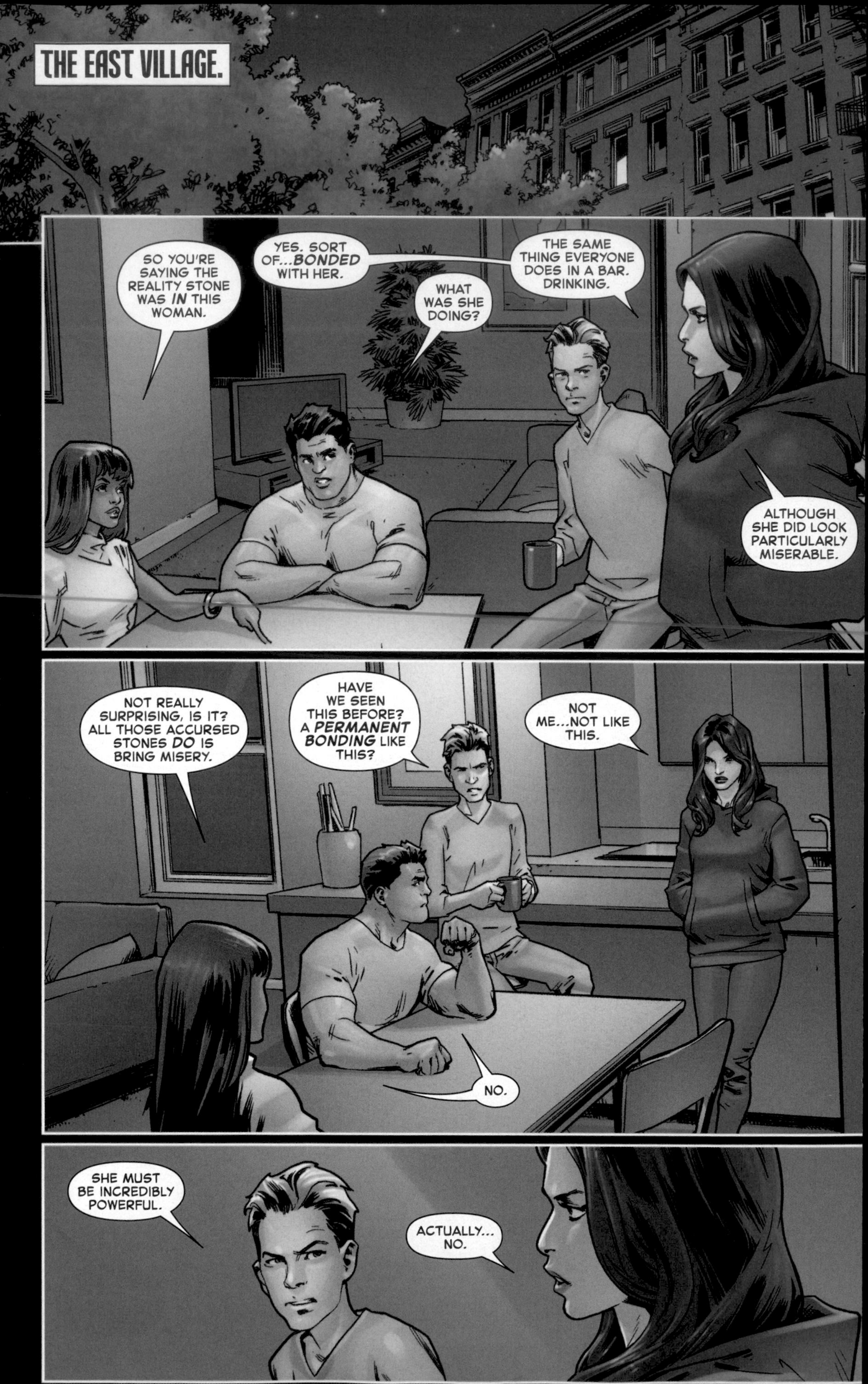
THE EAST VILLAGE.
SO YOU'RE SAYING THE REALITY STONE WAS IN THIS WOMAN.
YES. SORT OF...BONDED WITH HER.
WHAT WAS SHE DOING?
THE SAME THING EVERYONE DOES IN A BAR. DRINKING.
ALTHOUGH SHE DID LOOK PARTICULARLY MISERABLE.
NOT REALLY SURPRISING, IS IT? ALL THOSE ACCURSED STONES DO IS BRING MISERY.
HAVE WE SEEN THIS BEFORE? A PERMANENT BONDING LIKE THIS?
NOT ME...NOT LIKE THIS.
NO.
SHE MUST BE INCREDIBLY POWERFUL.
ACTUALLY... NO.

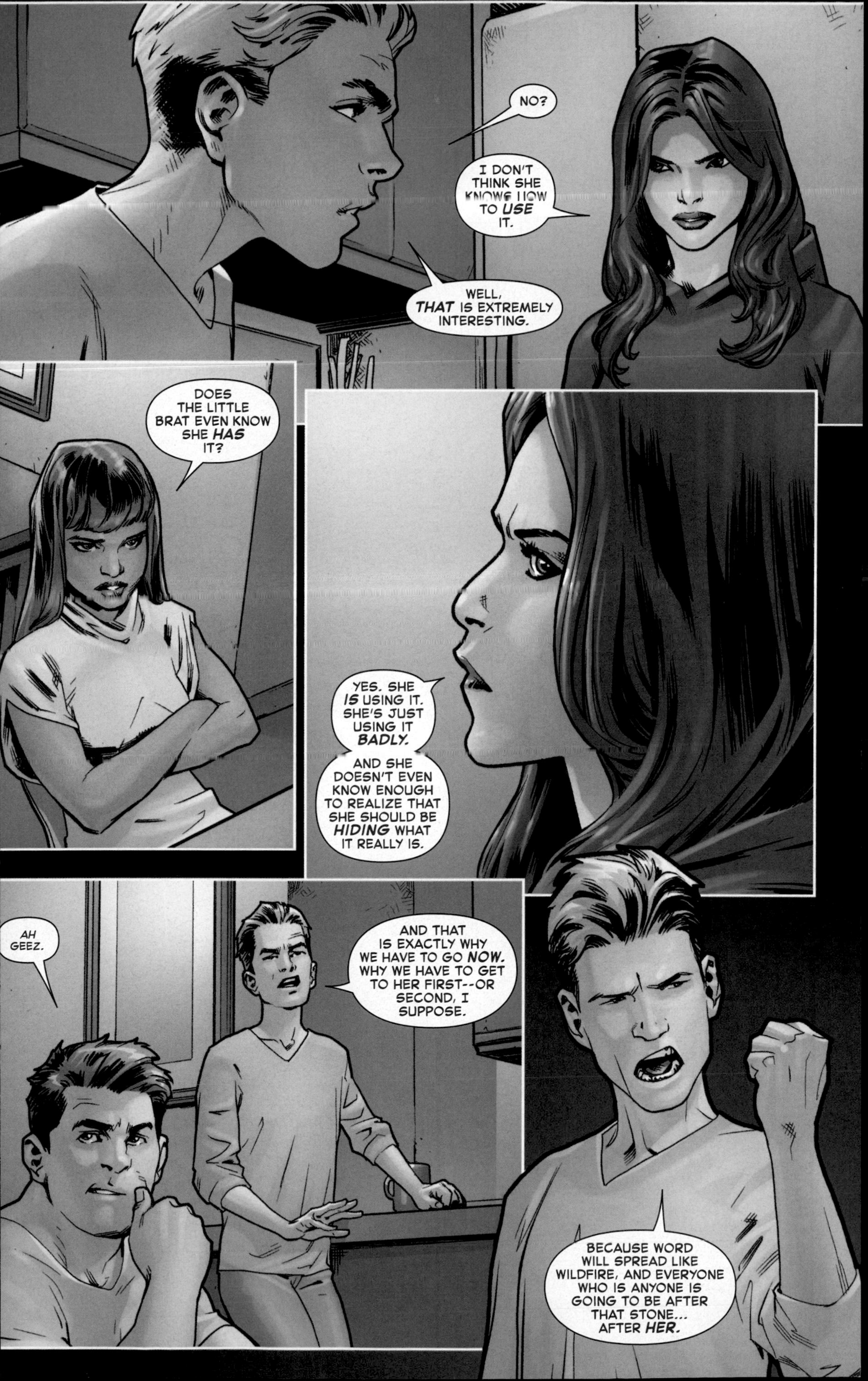
NO?
I DON'T THINK SHE KNOWS HOW TO USE IT.
WELL, THAT IS EXTREMELY INTERESTING.
DOES THE LITTLE BRAT EVEN KNOW SHE HAS IT?
YES. SHE IS USING IT. SHE'S JUST USING IT BADLY.
AND SHE DOESN'T EVEN KNOW ENOUGH TO REALIZE THAT SHE SHOULD BE HIDING WHAT IT REALLY IS.
AH GEEZ.
AND THAT IS EXACTLY WHY WE HAVE TO GO NOW. WHY WE HAVE TO GET TO HER FIRST--OR SECOND, I SUPPOSE.
BECAUSE WORD WILL SPREAD LIKE WILDFIRE, AND EVERYONE WHO IS ANYONE IS GOING TO BE AFTER THAT STONE... AFTER HER.

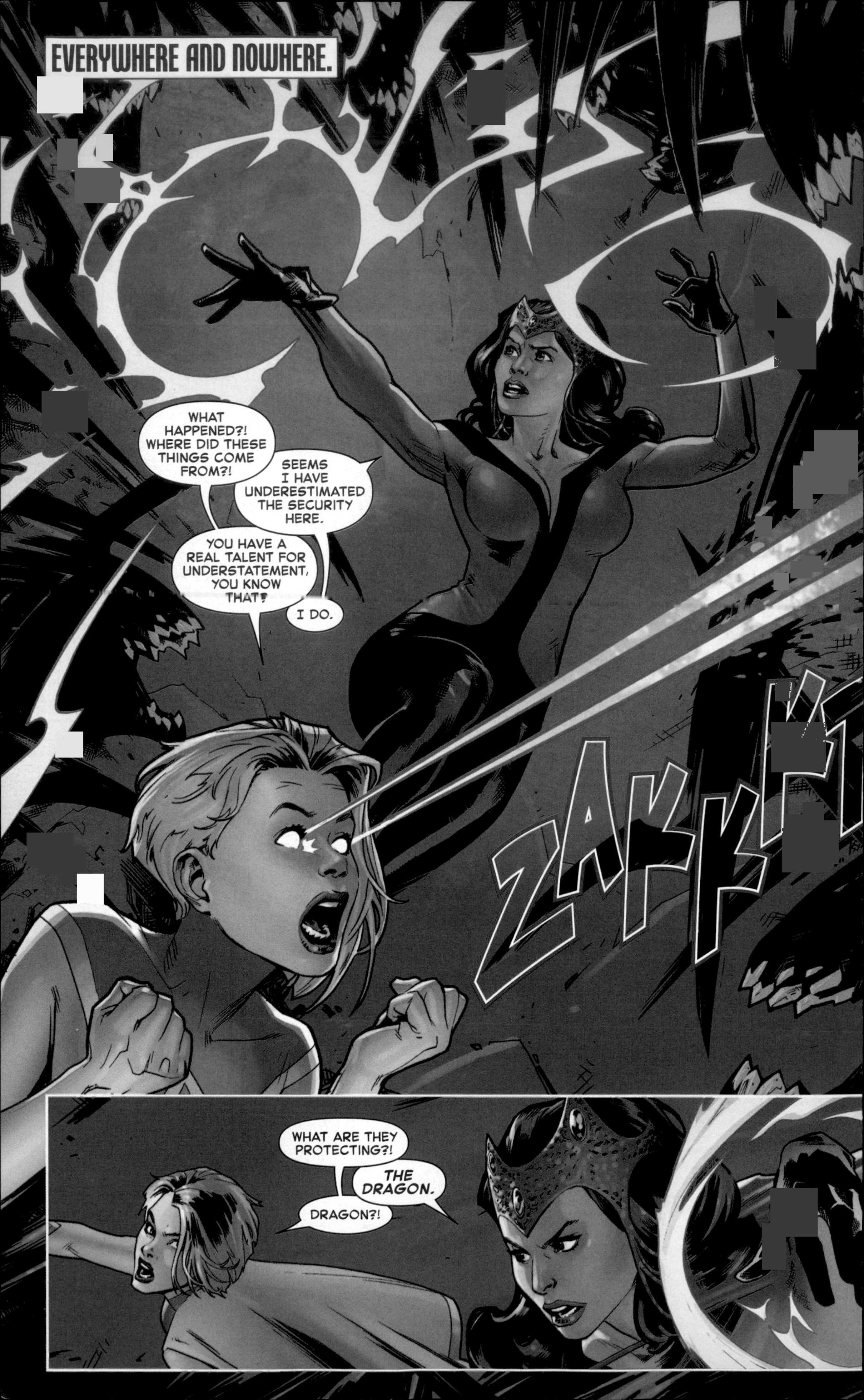
EVERYWHERE AND NOWHERE.
WHAT HAPPENED?! WHERE DID THESE THINGS COME FROM?!
SEEMS I HAVE UNDERESTIMATED THE SECURITY HERE.
YOU HAVE A REAL TALENT FOR UNDERSTATEMENT, YOU KNOW THAT?
I DO.
ZAKK
WHAT ARE THEY PROTECTING?!
THE DRAGON.
DRAGON?!

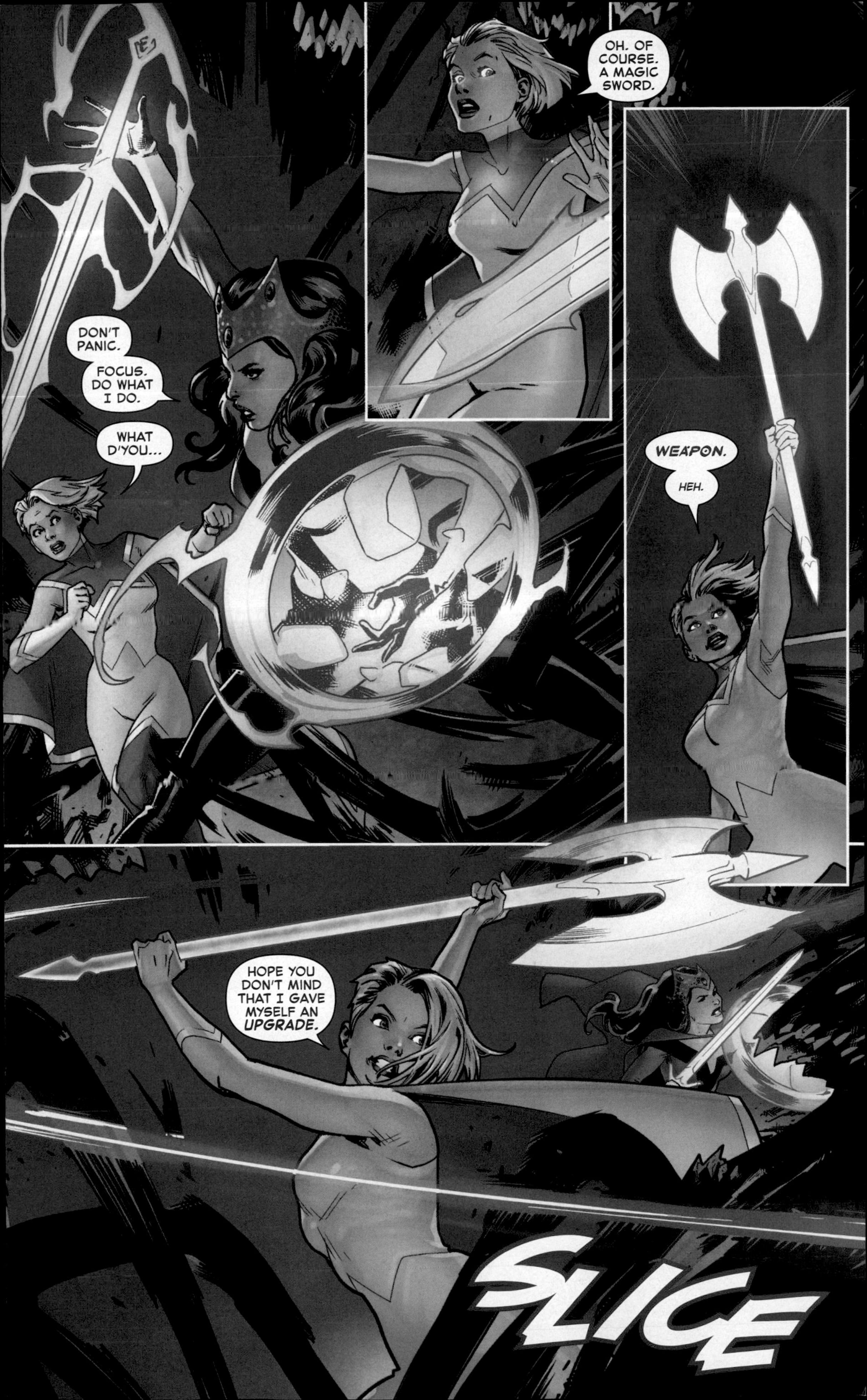
DON'T PANIC.
FOCUS. DO WHAT I DO.
WHAT D'YOU...
OH. OF COURSE. A MAGIC SWORD.
WEAPON.
HEH.
HOPE YOU DON'T MIND THAT I GAVE MYSELF AN UPGRADE.
SLICE

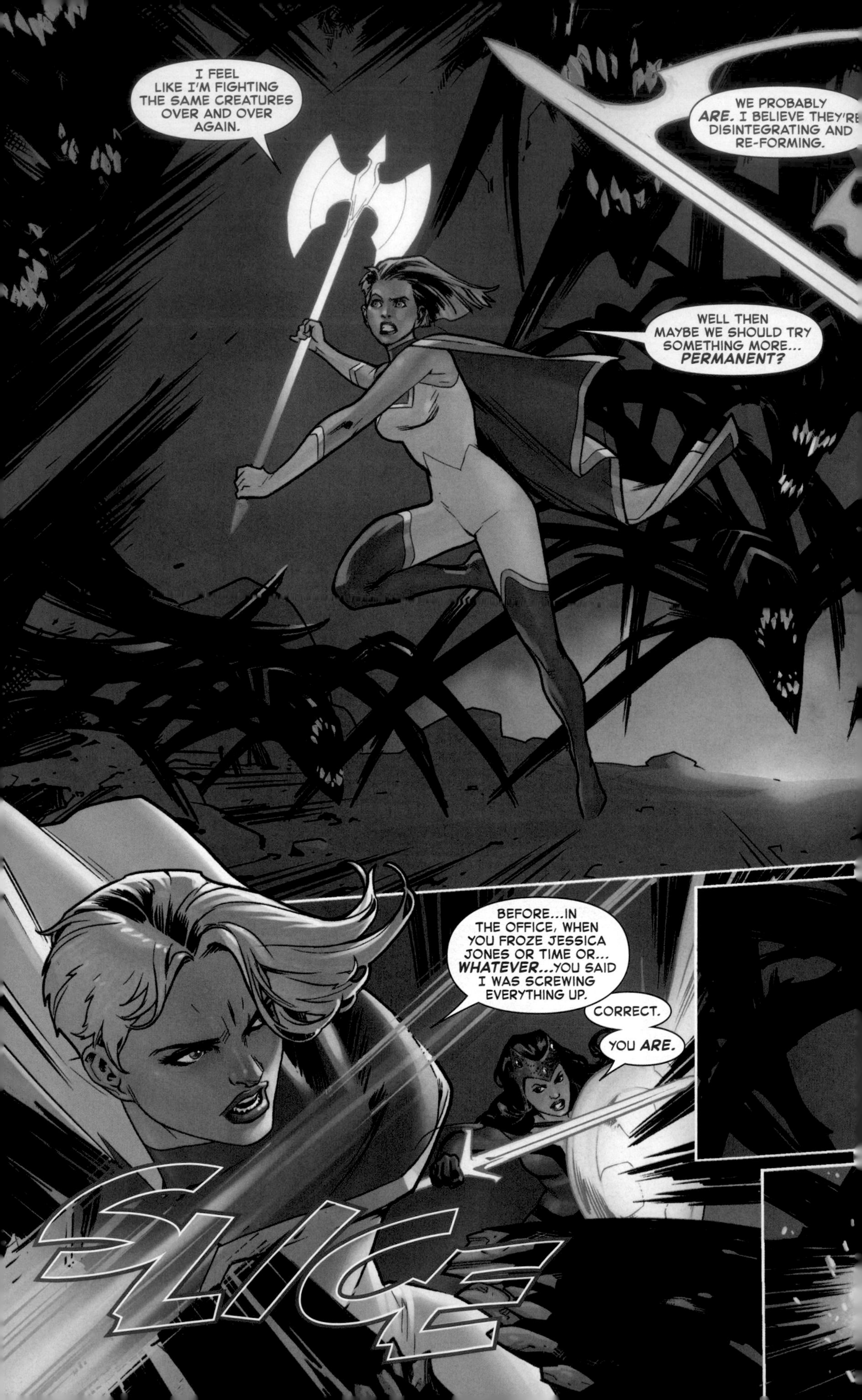
I FEEL LIKE I'M FIGHTING THE SAME CREATURES OVER AND OVER AGAIN.
WE PROBABLY ARE. I BELIEVE THEY'RE DISINTEGRATING AND RE-FORMING.
WELL THEN MAYBE WE SHOULD TRY SOMETHING MORE... PERMANENT?
BEFORE...IN THE OFFICE, WHEN YOU FROZE JESSICA JONES OR TIME OR... WHATEVER...YOU SAID I WAS SCREWING EVERYTHING UP.
CORRECT.
YOU ARE.
SLICE

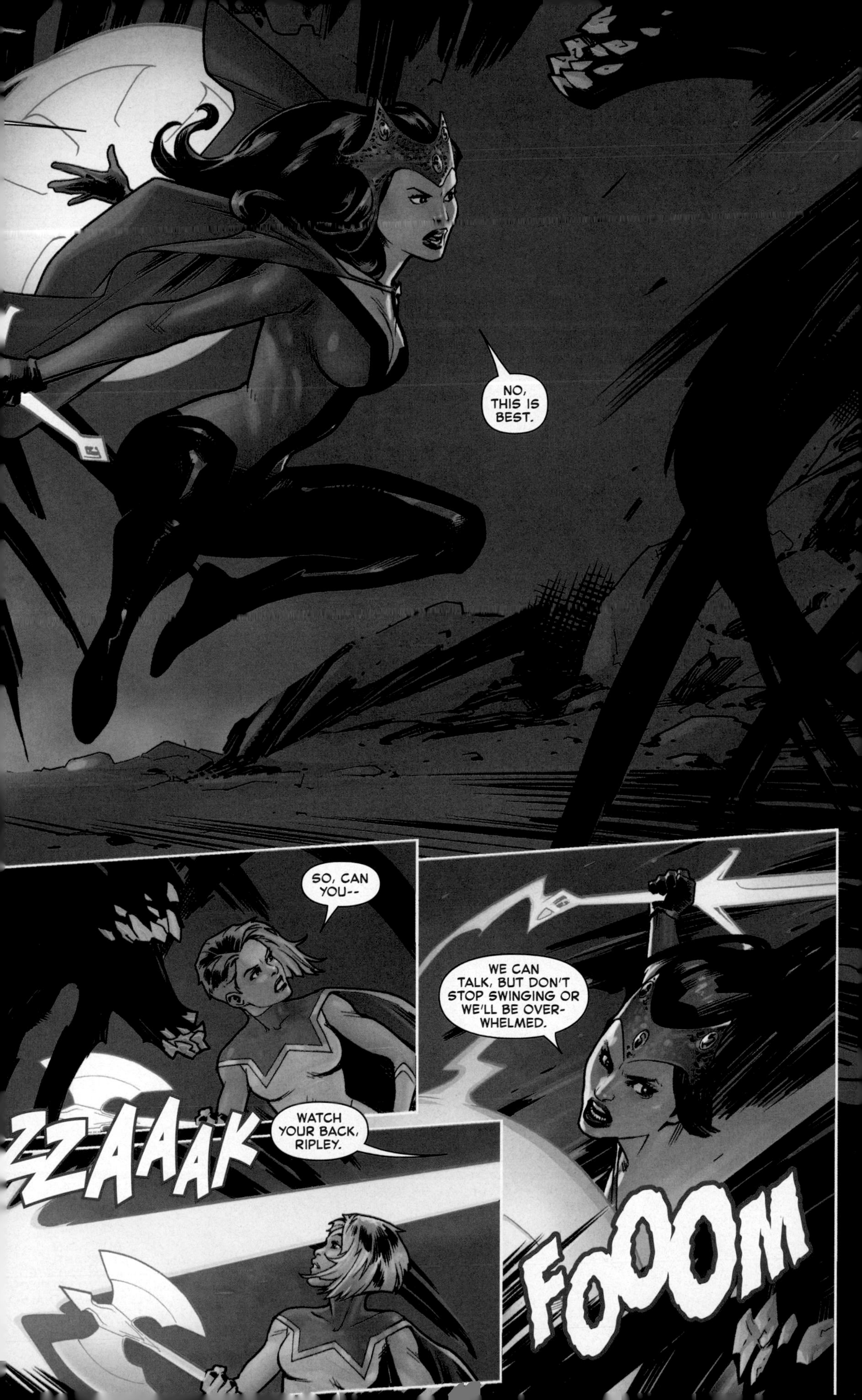
NO, THIS IS BEST.
SO, CAN YOU--
WE CAN TALK, BUT DON'T STOP SWINGING OR WE'LL BE OVER-WHELMED.
ZZAAAK
WATCH YOUR BACK, RIPLEY.
FOOOM

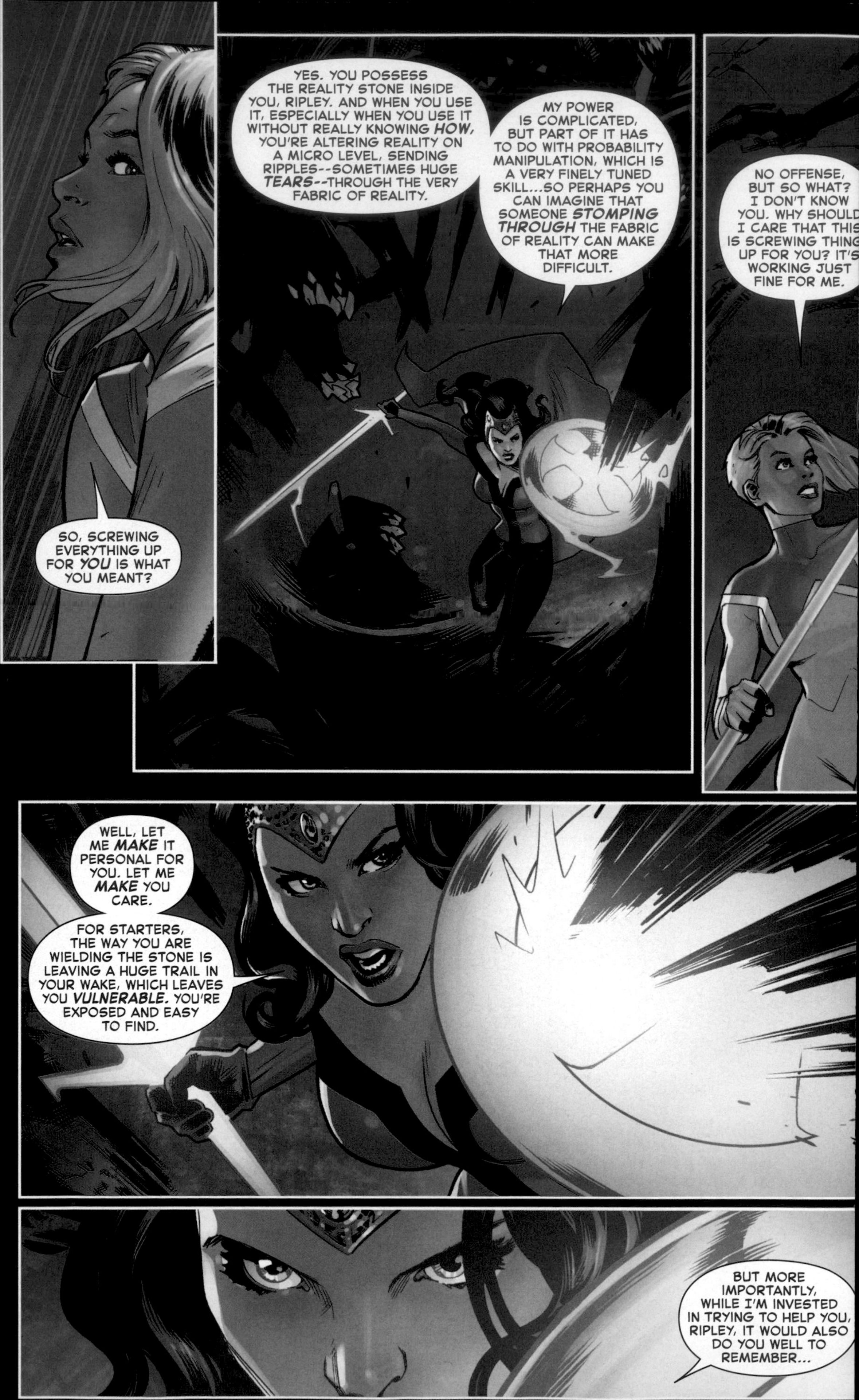

YES. YOU POSSESS THE REALITY STONE INSIDE YOU, RIPLEY. AND WHEN YOU USE IT, ESPECIALLY WHEN YOU USE IT WITHOUT REALLY KNOWING *HOW*, YOU'RE ALTERING REALITY ON A MICRO LEVEL, SENDING RIPPLES--SOMETIMES HUGE *TEARS*--THROUGH THE VERY FABRIC OF REALITY.
MY POWER IS COMPLICATED, BUT PART OF IT HAS TO DO WITH PROBABILITY MANIPULATION, WHICH IS A VERY FINELY TUNED SKILL...SO PERHAPS YOU CAN IMAGINE THAT SOMEONE *STOMPING THROUGH* THE FABRIC OF REALITY CAN MAKE THAT MORE DIFFICULT.
SO, SCREWING EVERYTHING UP FOR *YOU* IS WHAT YOU MEANT?
NO OFFENSE, BUT SO WHAT? I DON'T KNOW YOU. WHY SHOULD I CARE THAT THIS IS SCREWING THING UP FOR YOU? IT'S WORKING JUST FINE FOR ME.
WELL, LET ME *MAKE* IT PERSONAL FOR YOU. LET ME *MAKE* YOU CARE.
FOR STARTERS, THE WAY YOU ARE WIELDING THE STONE IS LEAVING A HUGE TRAIL IN YOUR WAKE, WHICH LEAVES YOU *VULNERABLE*. YOU'RE EXPOSED AND EASY TO FIND.
BUT MORE IMPORTANTLY, WHILE I'M INVESTED IN TRYING TO HELP YOU, RIPLEY, IT WOULD ALSO DO YOU WELL TO REMEMBER...

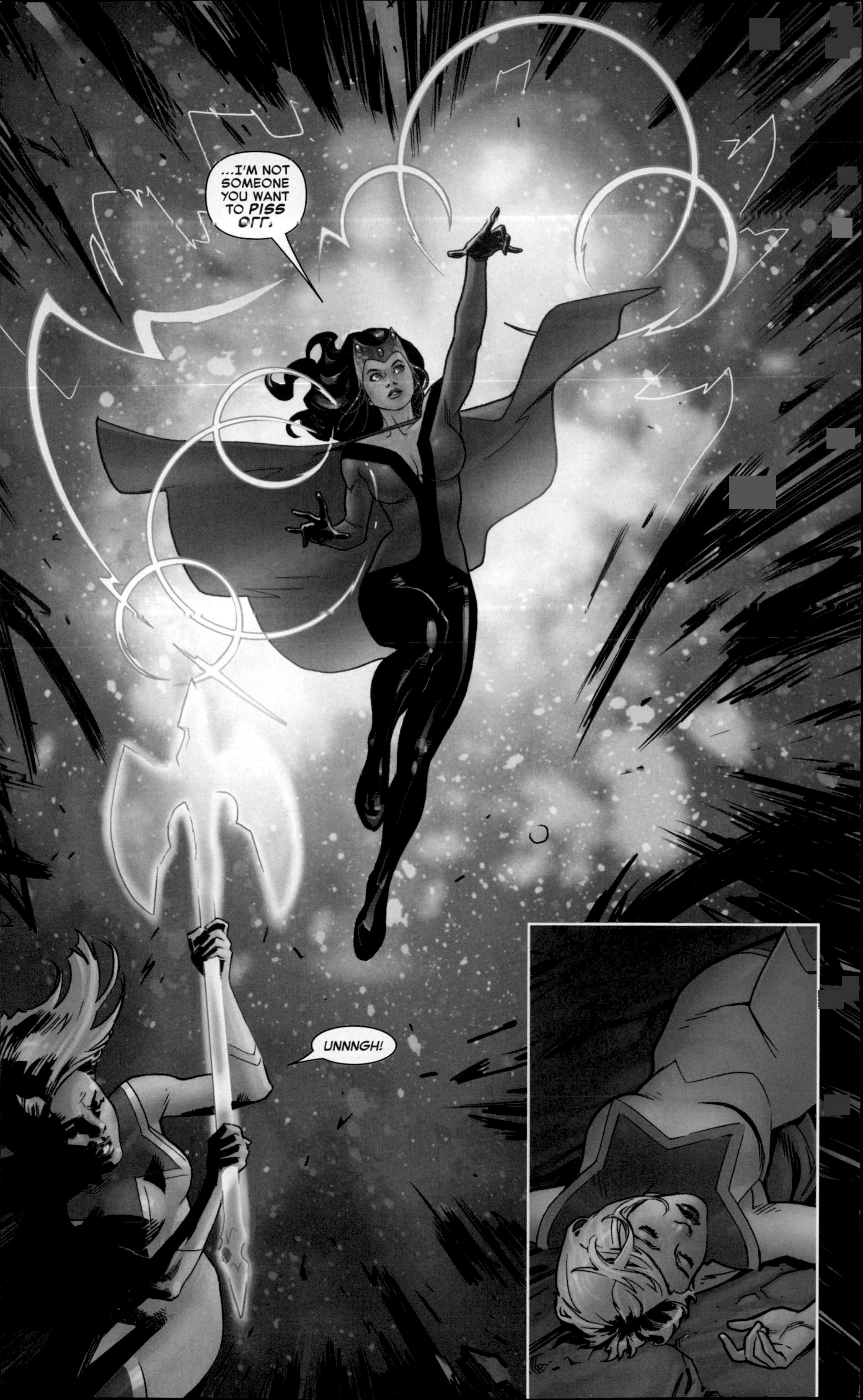
...I'M NOT SOMEONE YOU WANT TO PISS OFF.
UNNNGH!

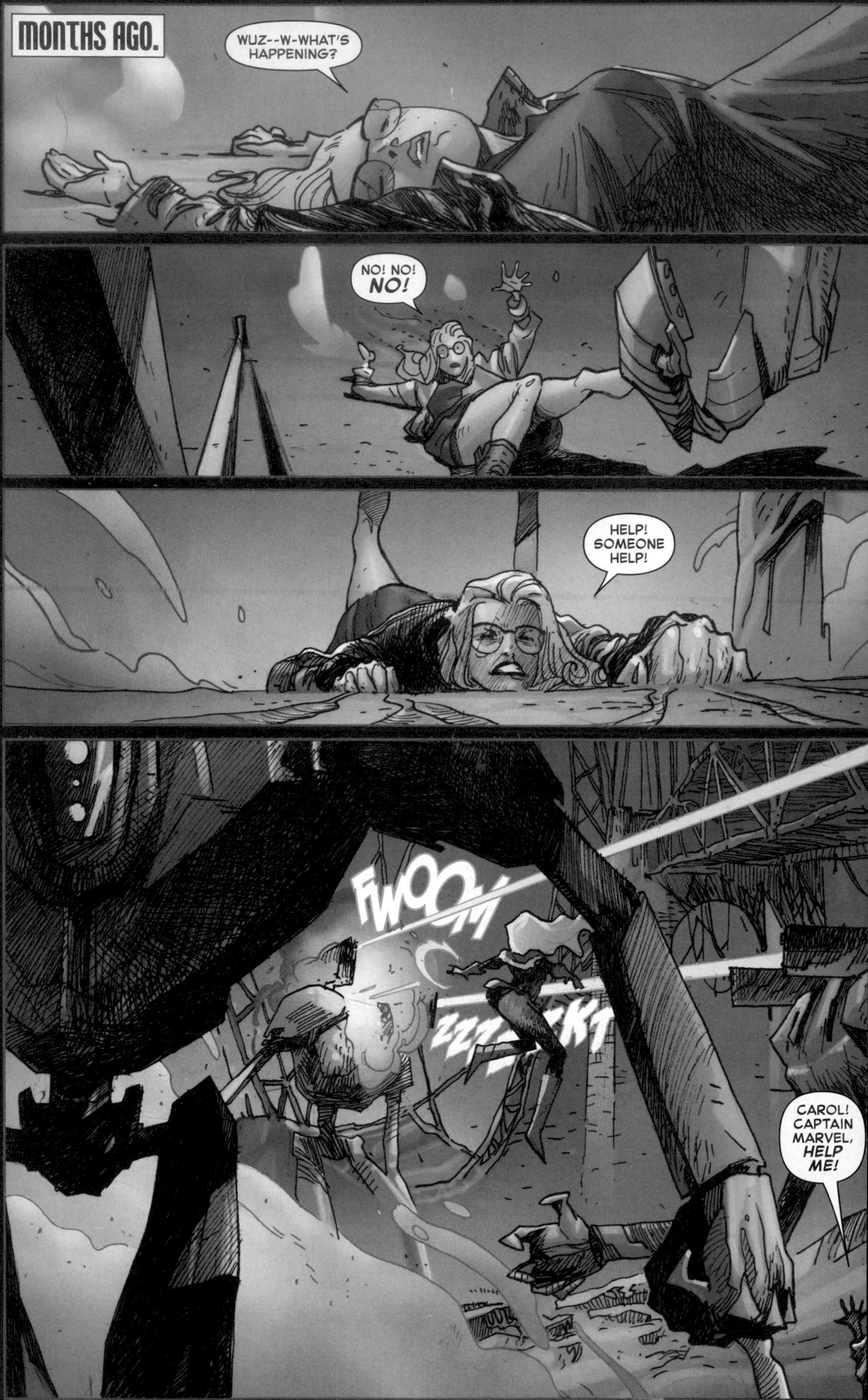
MONTHS AGO.
WUZ--W-WHAT'S HAPPENING?
NO! NO! NO!
HELP! SOMEONE HELP!
FWOOM
ZZZZAKT
CAROL! CAPTAIN MARVEL, HELP ME!

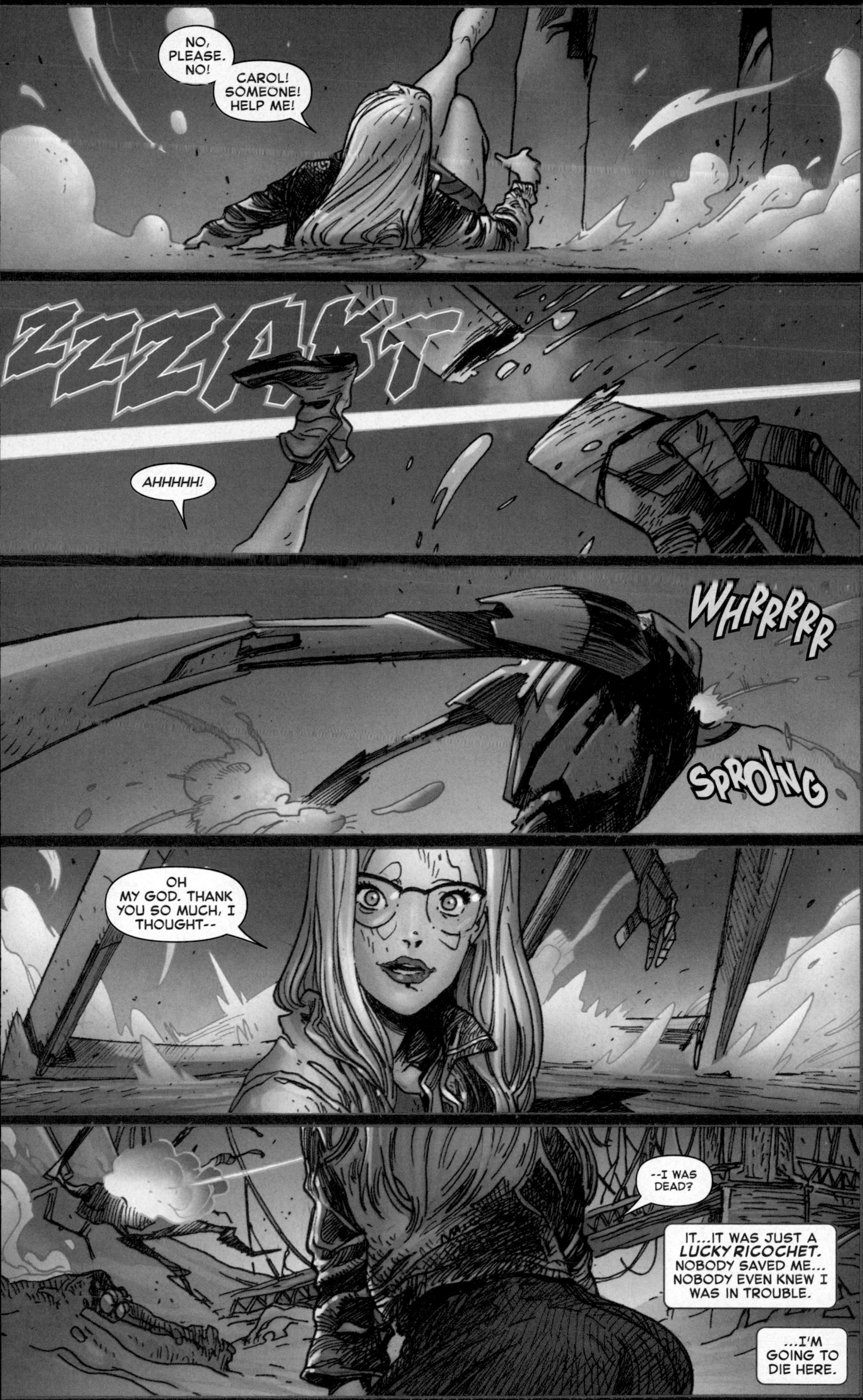
NO, PLEASE. NO!
CAROL! SOMEONE! HELP ME!
ZZZAKT
AHHHHH!
WHRRRRR
SPROING
OH MY GOD. THANK YOU SO MUCH, I THOUGHT--
--I WAS DEAD?
IT...IT WAS JUST A LUCKY RICOCHET. NOBODY SAVED ME... NOBODY EVEN KNEW I WAS IN TROUBLE.
...I'M GOING TO DIE HERE.

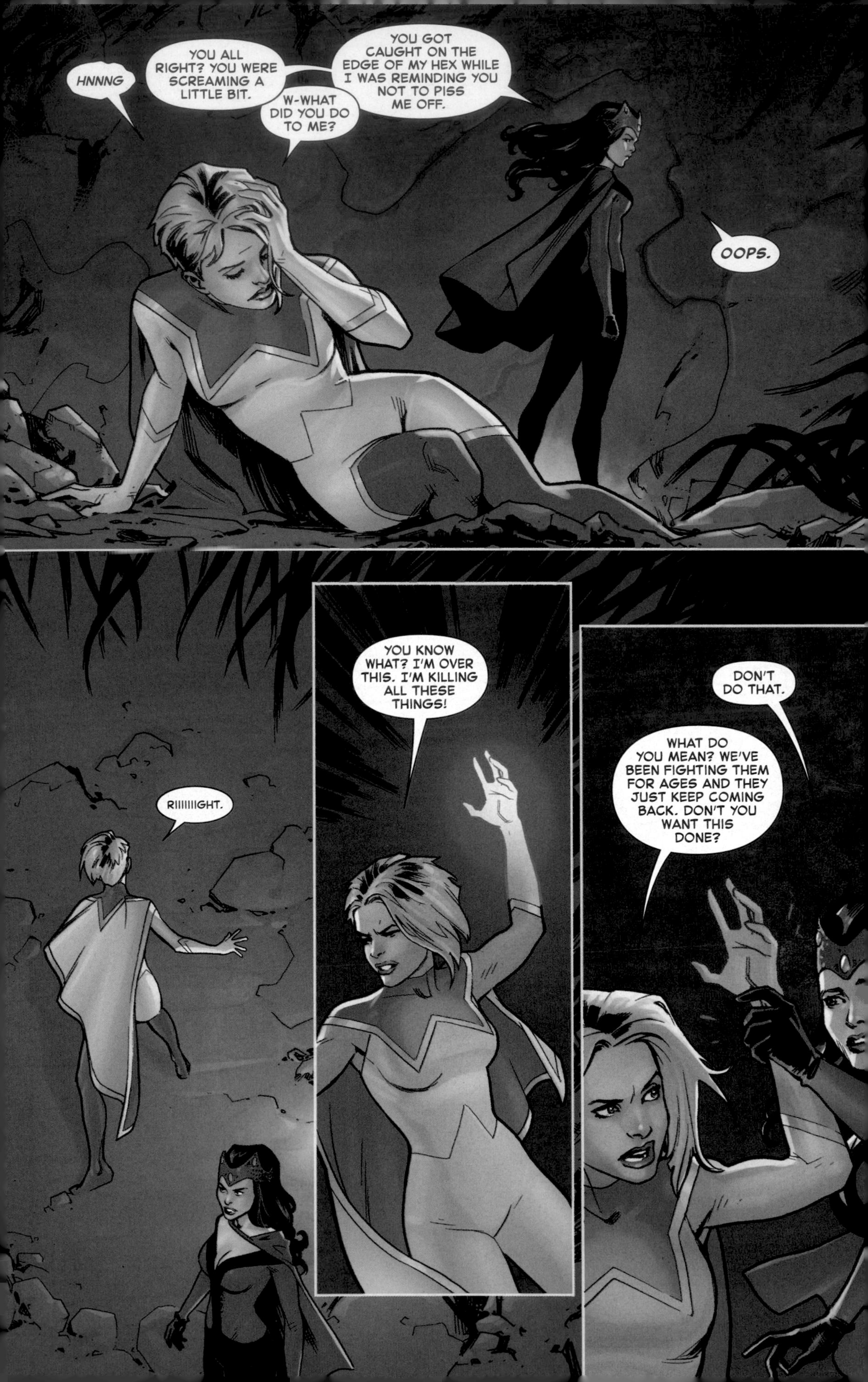
HNNNG
YOU ALL RIGHT? YOU WERE SCREAMING A LITTLE BIT.
W-WHAT DID YOU DO TO ME?
YOU GOT CAUGHT ON THE EDGE OF MY HEX WHILE I WAS REMINDING YOU NOT TO PISS ME OFF.
OOPS.
RIIIIIIGHT.
YOU KNOW WHAT? I'M OVER THIS. I'M KILLING ALL THESE THINGS!
DON'T DO THAT.
WHAT DO YOU MEAN? WE'VE BEEN FIGHTING THEM FOR AGES AND THEY JUST KEEP COMING BACK. DON'T YOU WANT THIS DONE?

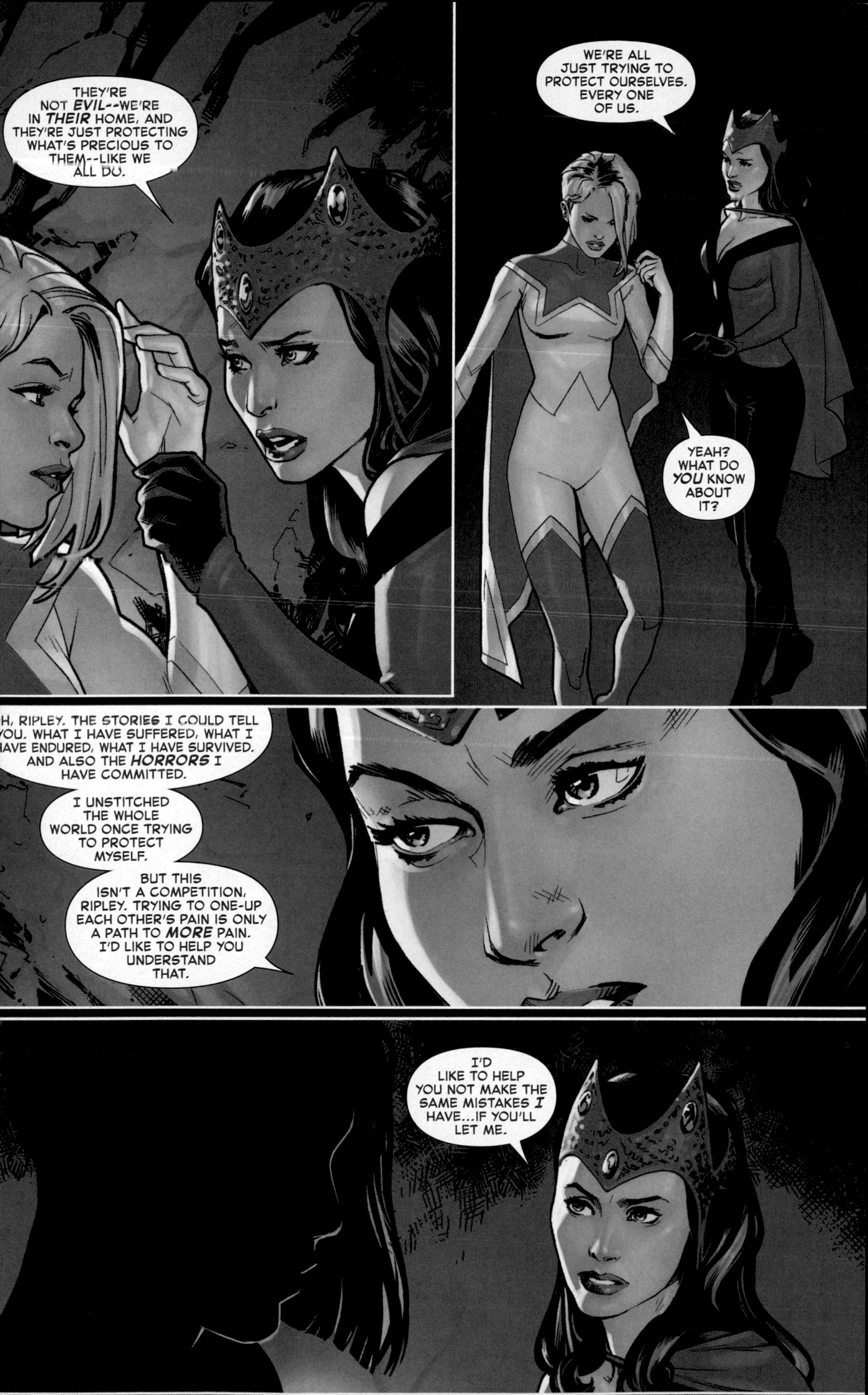
THEY'RE NOT EVIL--WE'RE IN THEIR HOME, AND THEY'RE JUST PROTECTING WHAT'S PRECIOUS TO THEM--LIKE WE ALL DO.
WE'RE ALL JUST TRYING TO PROTECT OURSELVES. EVERY ONE OF US.
YEAH? WHAT DO YOU KNOW ABOUT IT?
H, RIPLEY. THE STORIES I COULD TELL YOU. WHAT I HAVE SUFFERED, WHAT I HAVE ENDURED, WHAT I HAVE SURVIVED. AND ALSO THE HORRORS I HAVE COMMITTED.
I UNSTITCHED THE WHOLE WORLD ONCE TRYING TO PROTECT MYSELF.
BUT THIS ISN'T A COMPETITION, RIPLEY. TRYING TO ONE-UP EACH OTHER'S PAIN IS ONLY A PATH TO MORE PAIN. I'D LIKE TO HELP YOU UNDERSTAND THAT.
I'D LIKE TO HELP YOU NOT MAKE THE SAME MISTAKES I HAVE...IF YOU'LL LET ME.

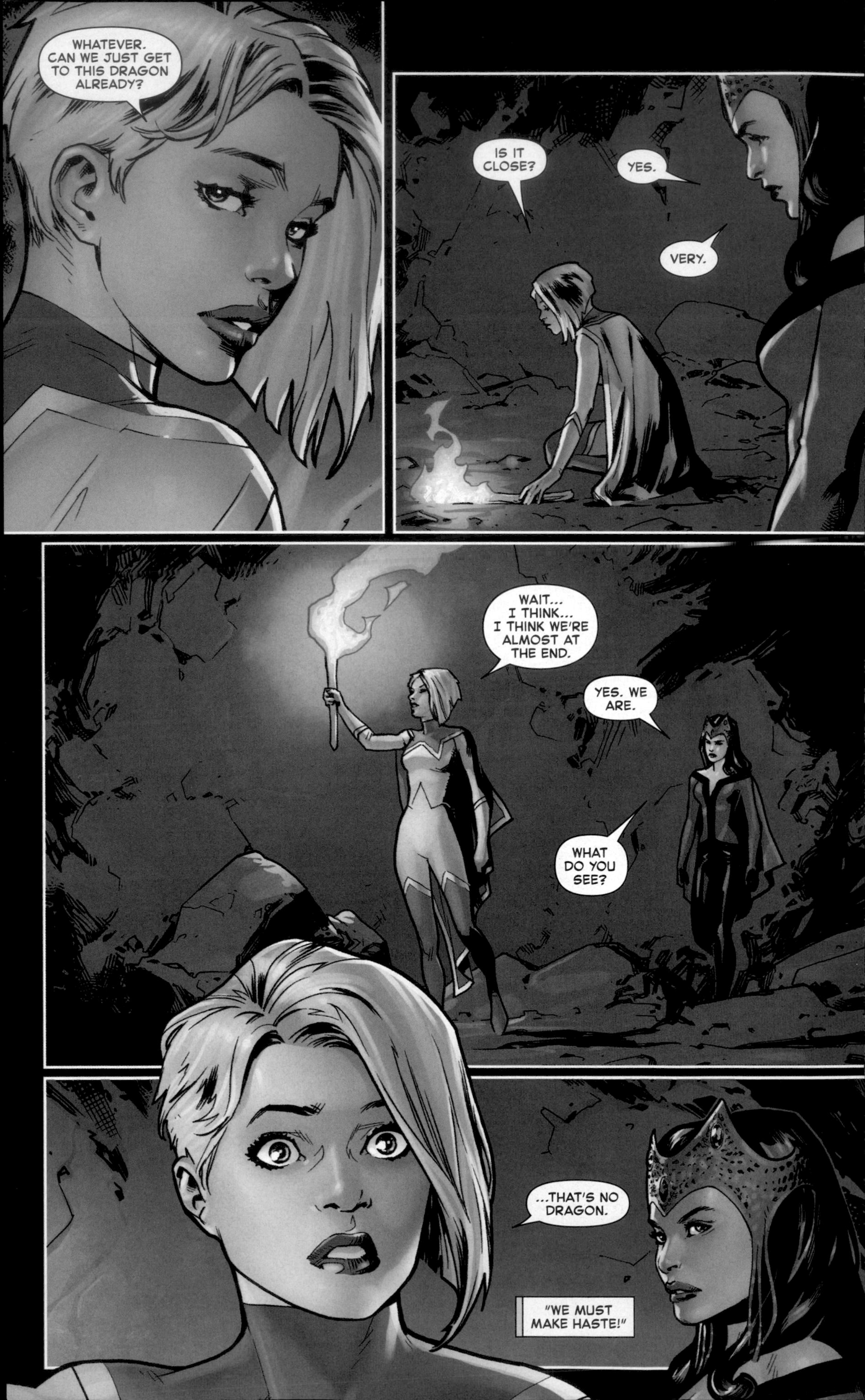
WHATEVER. CAN WE JUST GET TO THIS DRAGON ALREADY?
IS IT CLOSE?
YES.
VERY.
WAIT... I THINK... I THINK WE'RE ALMOST AT THE END.
YES. WE ARE.
WHAT DO YOU SEE?
...THAT'S NO DRAGON.
"WE MUST MAKE HASTE!"

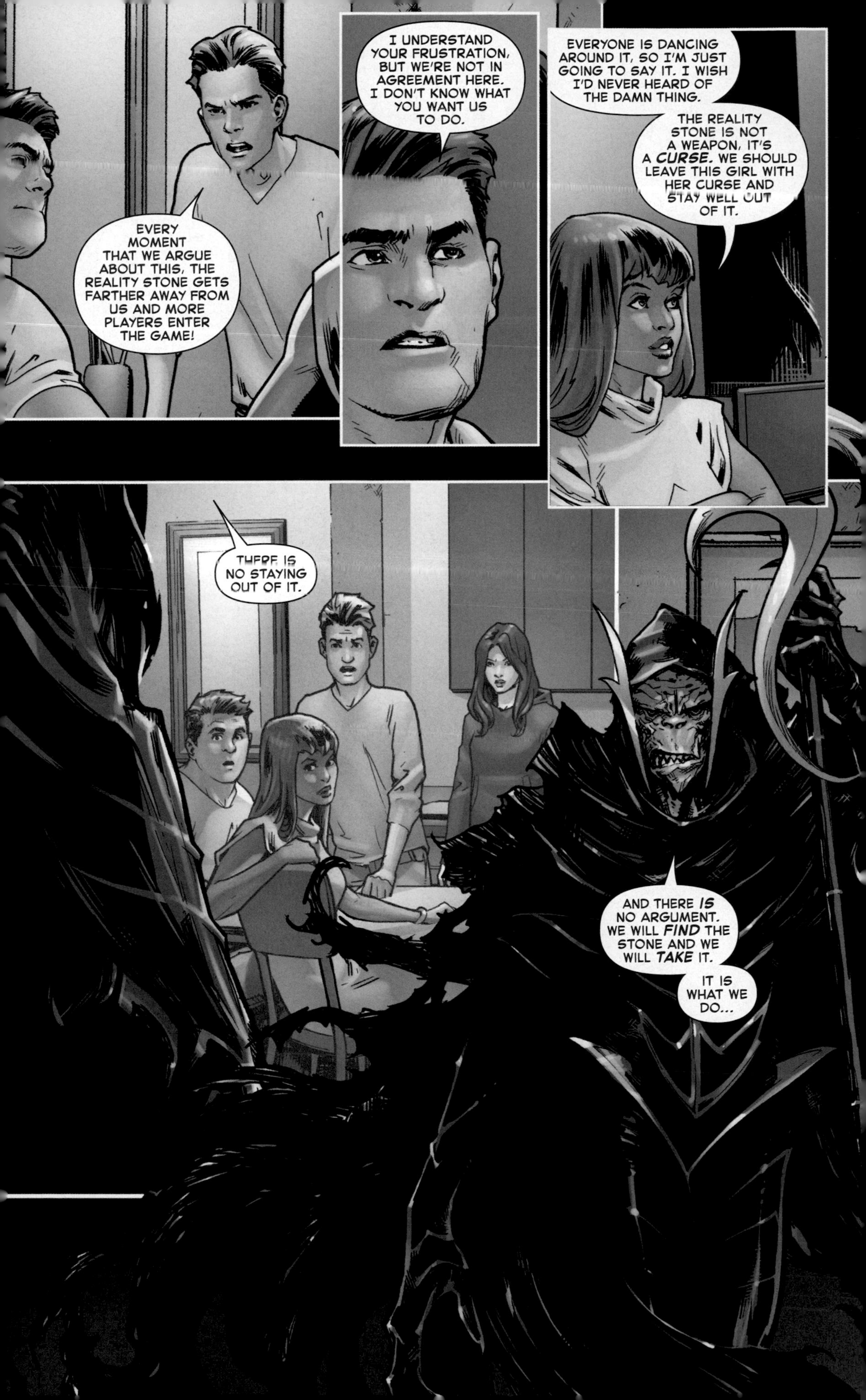
EVERY MOMENT THAT WE ARGUE ABOUT THIS, THE REALITY STONE GETS FARTHER AWAY FROM US AND MORE PLAYERS ENTER THE GAME!
I UNDERSTAND YOUR FRUSTRATION, BUT WE'RE NOT IN AGREEMENT HERE. I DON'T KNOW WHAT YOU WANT US TO DO.
EVERYONE IS DANCING AROUND IT, SO I'M JUST GOING TO SAY IT. I WISH I'D NEVER HEARD OF THE DAMN THING.
THE REALITY STONE IS NOT A WEAPON, IT'S A CURSE. WE SHOULD LEAVE THIS GIRL WITH HER CURSE AND STAY WELL OUT OF IT.
THERE IS NO STAYING OUT OF IT.
AND THERE IS NO ARGUMENT. WE WILL FIND THE STONE AND WE WILL TAKE IT.
IT IS WHAT WE DO...

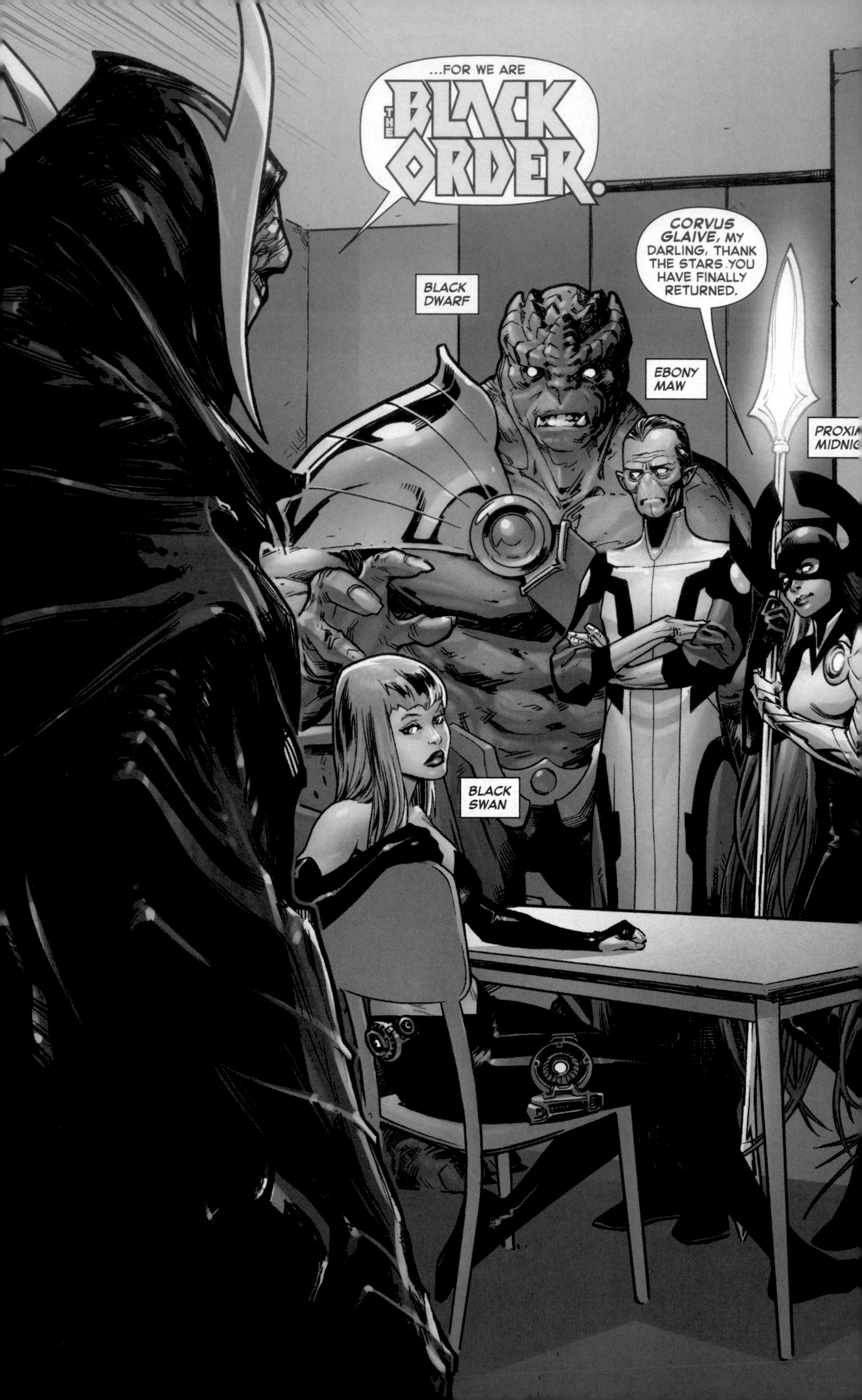
...FOR WE ARE
THE BLACK ORDER.
BLACK DWARF
CORVUS GLAIVE, MY DARLING, THANK THE STARS YOU HAVE FINALLY RETURNED.
EBONY MAW
PROXI
MIDNI
BLACK SWAN

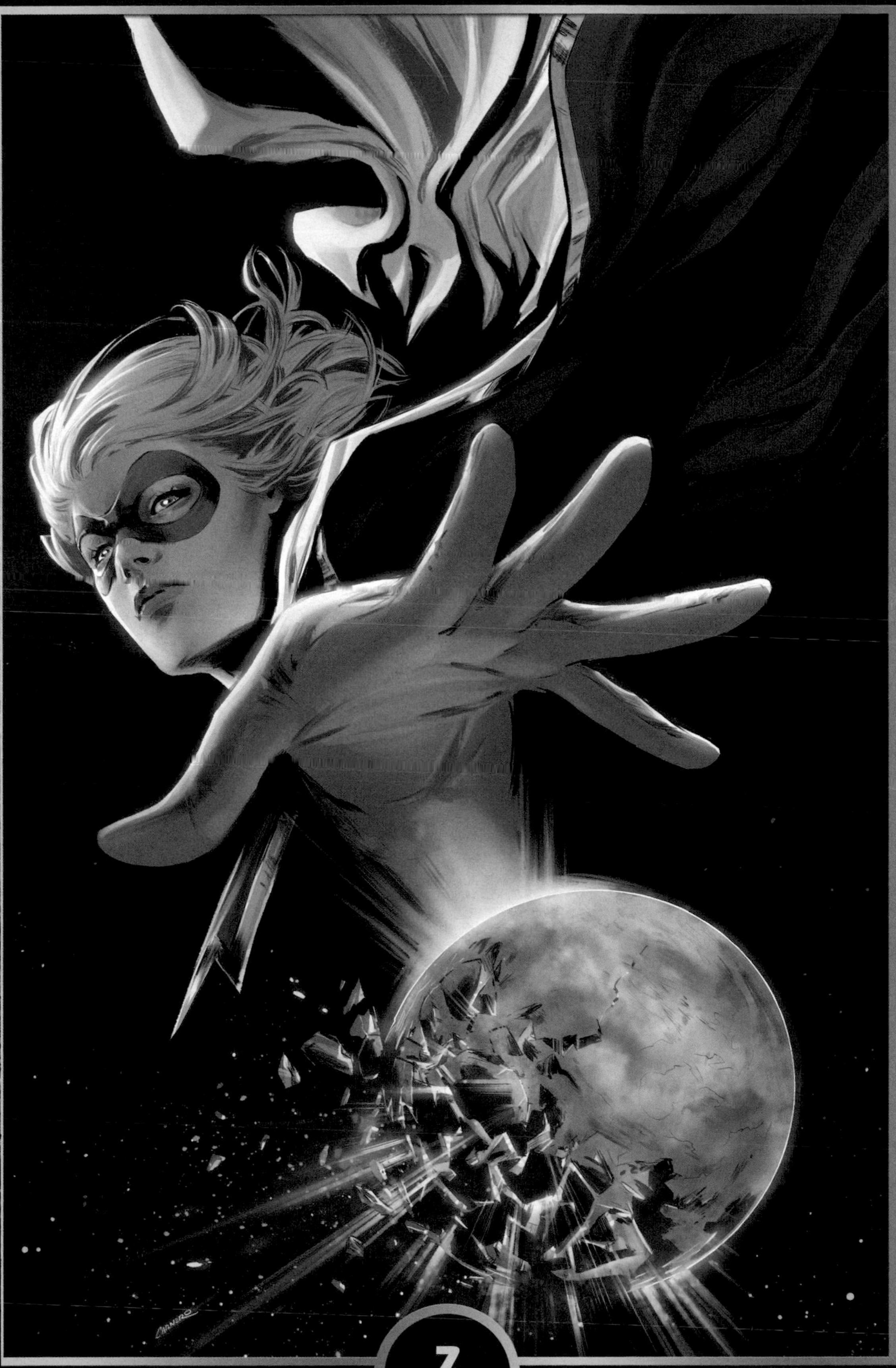

3

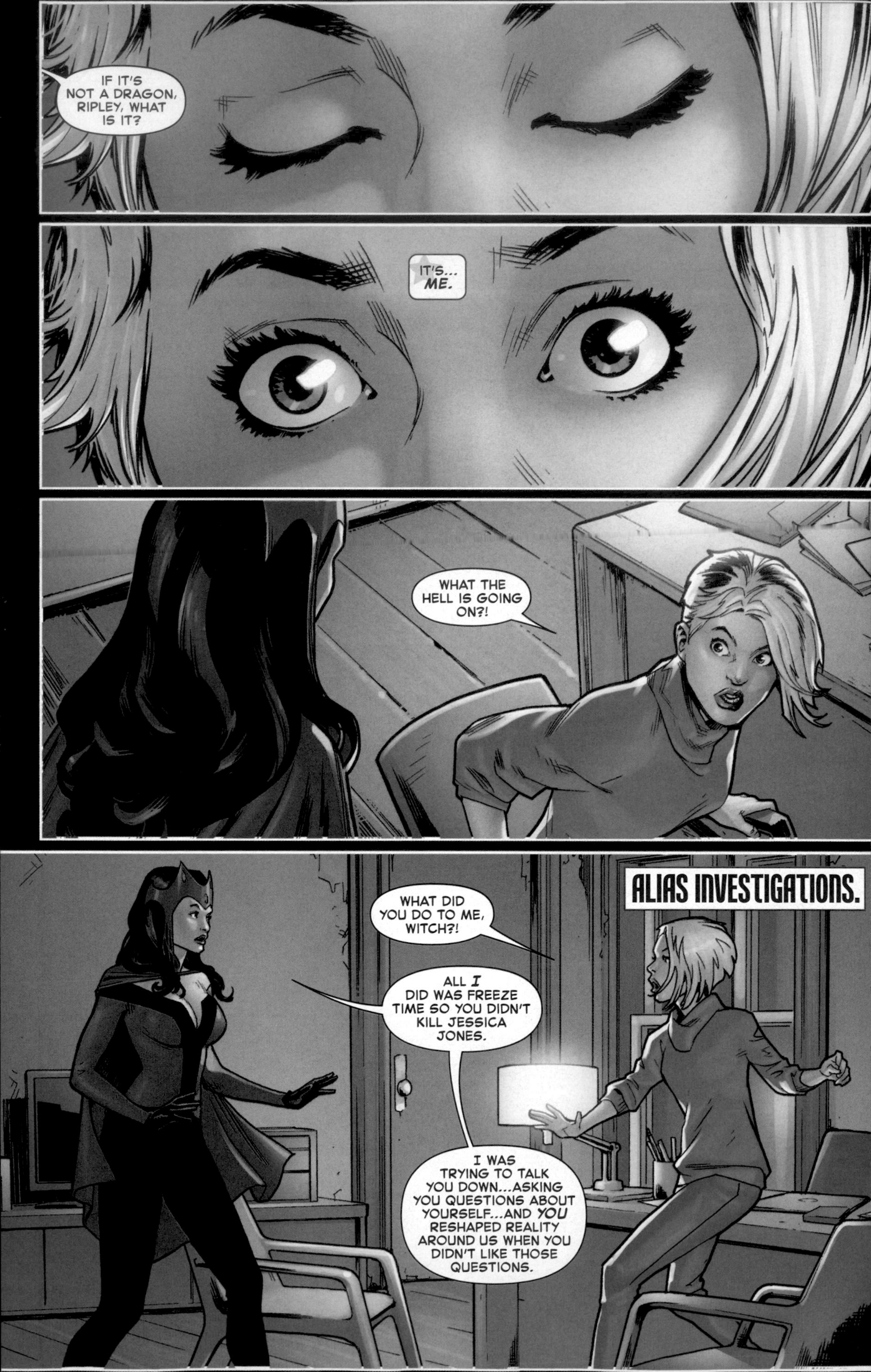
IF IT'S NOT A DRAGON, RIPLEY, WHAT IS IT?
IT'S... ME.
WHAT THE HELL IS GOING ON?!
ALIAS INVESTIGATIONS.
WHAT DID YOU DO TO ME, WITCH?!
ALL I DID WAS FREEZE TIME SO YOU DIDN'T KILL JESSICA JONES.
I WAS TRYING TO TALK YOU DOWN...ASKING YOU QUESTIONS ABOUT YOURSELF...AND YOU RESHAPED REALITY AROUND US WHEN YOU DIDN'T LIKE THOSE QUESTIONS.

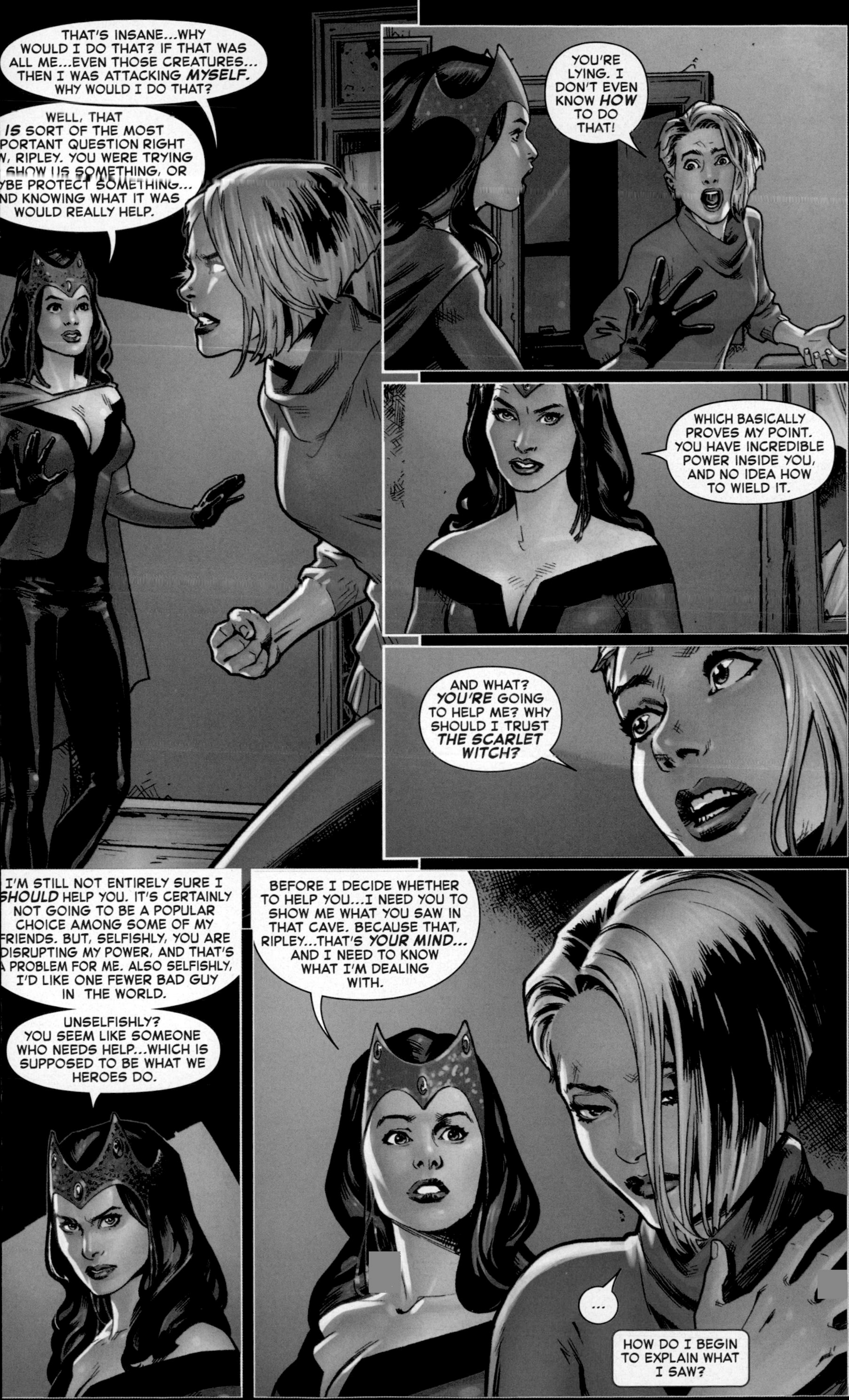
THAT'S INSANE...WHY WOULD I DO THAT? IF THAT WAS ALL ME...EVEN THOSE CREATURES... THEN I WAS ATTACKING *MYSELF.* WHY WOULD I DO THAT?
WELL, THAT *IS* SORT OF THE MOST PORTANT QUESTION RIGHT W, RIPLEY. YOU WERE TRYING SHOW US SOMETHING, OR YBE PROTECT SOMETHING... ND KNOWING WHAT IT WAS WOULD REALLY HELP.
YOU'RE LYING. I DON'T EVEN KNOW *HOW* TO DO THAT!
WHICH BASICALLY PROVES MY POINT. YOU HAVE INCREDIBLE POWER INSIDE YOU, AND NO IDEA HOW TO WIELD IT.
AND WHAT? *YOU'RE* GOING TO HELP ME? WHY SHOULD I TRUST *THE SCARLET WITCH?*
I'M STILL NOT ENTIRELY SURE I *SHOULD* HELP YOU. IT'S CERTAINLY NOT GOING TO BE A POPULAR CHOICE AMONG SOME OF MY FRIENDS. BUT, SELFISHLY, YOU ARE DISRUPTING MY POWER, AND THAT'S A PROBLEM FOR ME. ALSO SELFISHLY, I'D LIKE ONE FEWER BAD GUY IN THE WORLD.
UNSELFISHLY? YOU SEEM LIKE SOMEONE WHO NEEDS HELP...WHICH IS SUPPOSED TO BE WHAT WE HEROES DO.
BEFORE I DECIDE WHETHER TO HELP YOU...I NEED YOU TO SHOW ME WHAT YOU SAW IN THAT CAVE. BECAUSE THAT, RIPLEY...THAT'S *YOUR MIND...* AND I NEED TO KNOW WHAT I'M DEALING WITH.
...
HOW DO I BEGIN TO EXPLAIN WHAT I SAW?

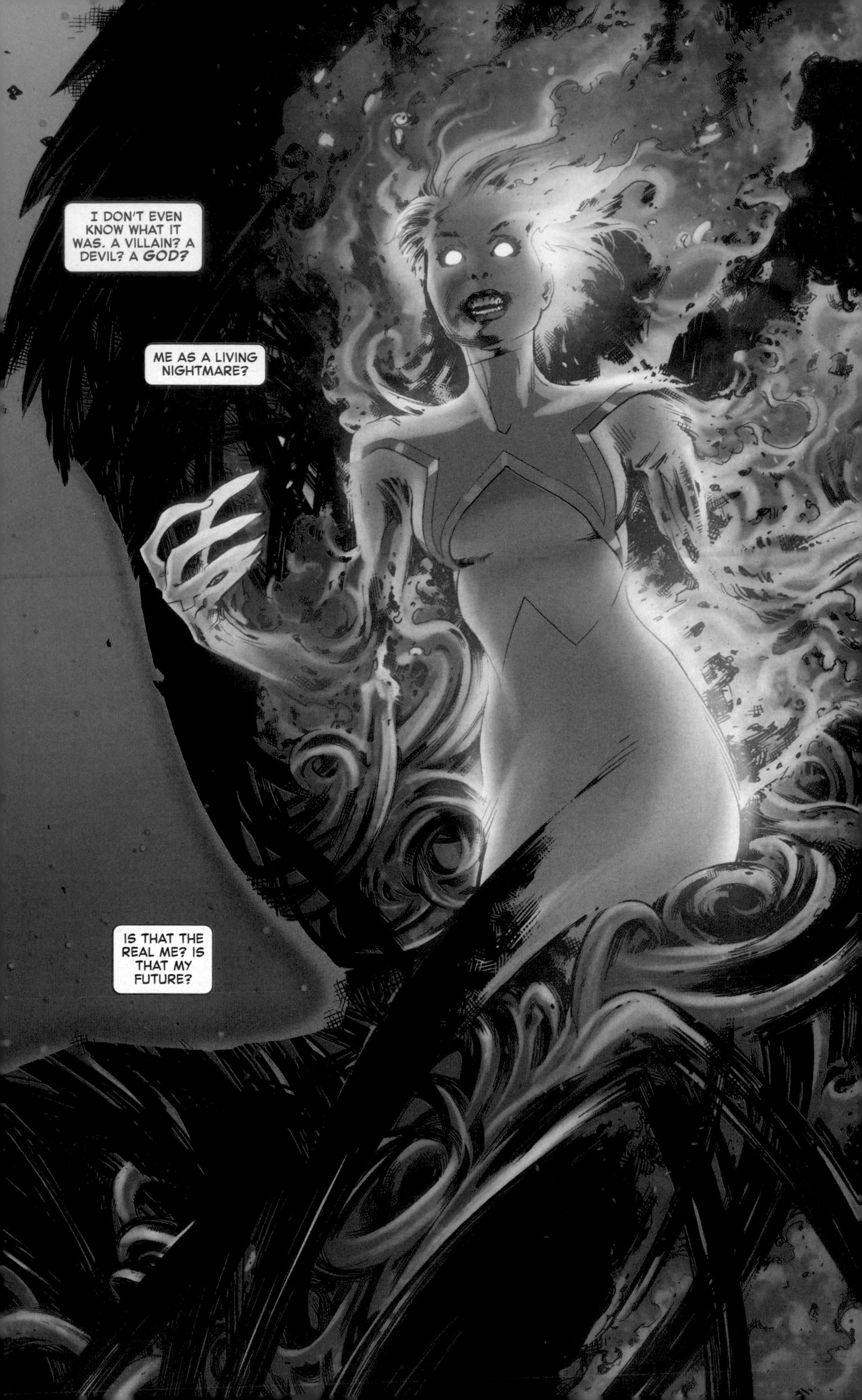
I DON'T EVEN KNOW WHAT IT WAS. A VILLAIN? A DEVIL? A *GOD?*
ME AS A LIVING NIGHTMARE?
IS THAT THE REAL ME? IS THAT MY FUTURE?

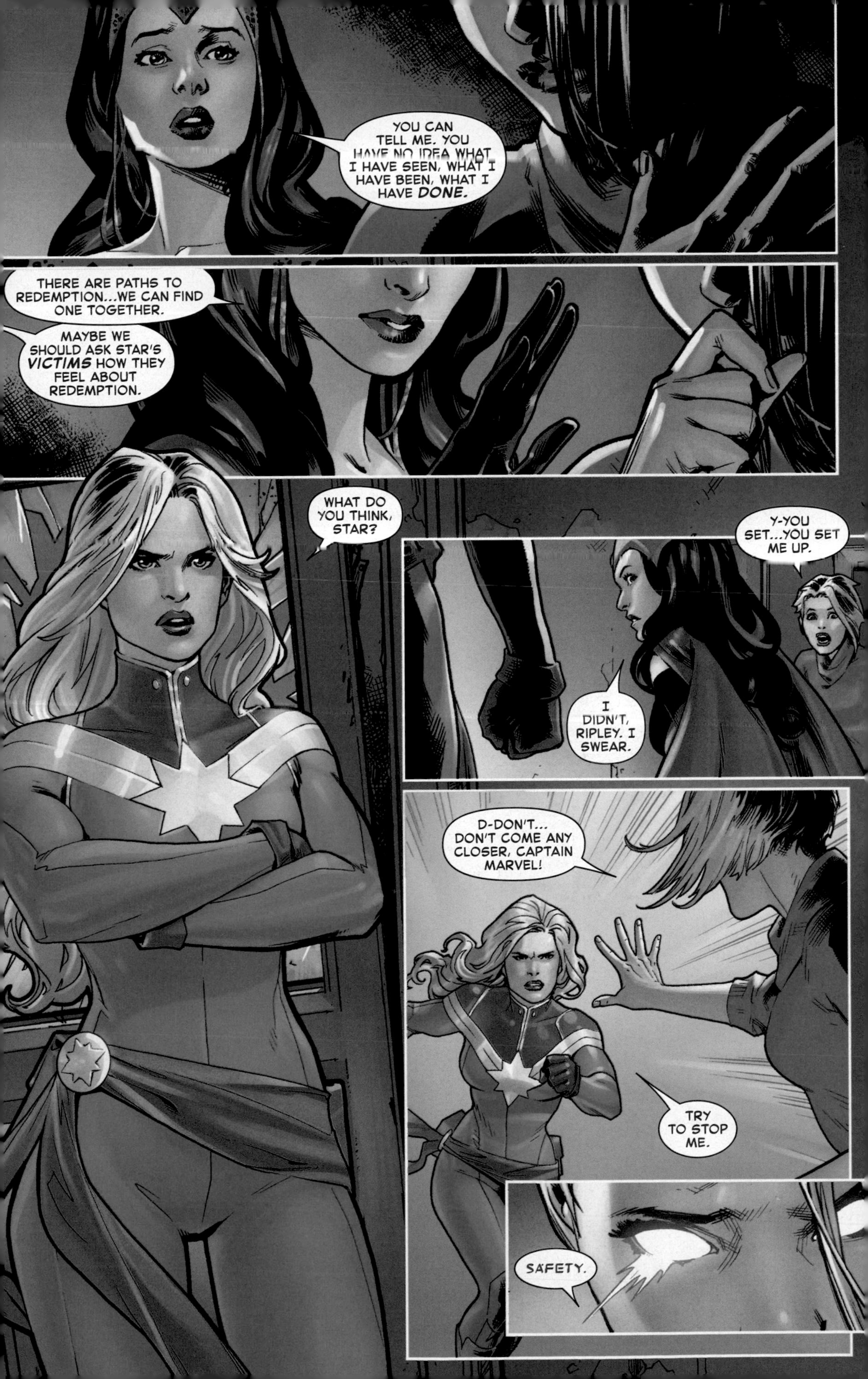
YOU CAN TELL ME. YOU HAVE NO IDEA WHAT I HAVE SEEN, WHAT I HAVE BEEN, WHAT I HAVE DONE.
THERE ARE PATHS TO REDEMPTION...WE CAN FIND ONE TOGETHER.
MAYBE WE SHOULD ASK STAR'S VICTIMS HOW THEY FEEL ABOUT REDEMPTION.
WHAT DO YOU THINK, STAR?
Y-YOU SET...YOU SET ME UP.
I DIDN'T, RIPLEY. I SWEAR.
D-DON'T... DON'T COME ANY CLOSER, CAPTAIN MARVEL!
TRY TO STOP ME.
SAFETY.

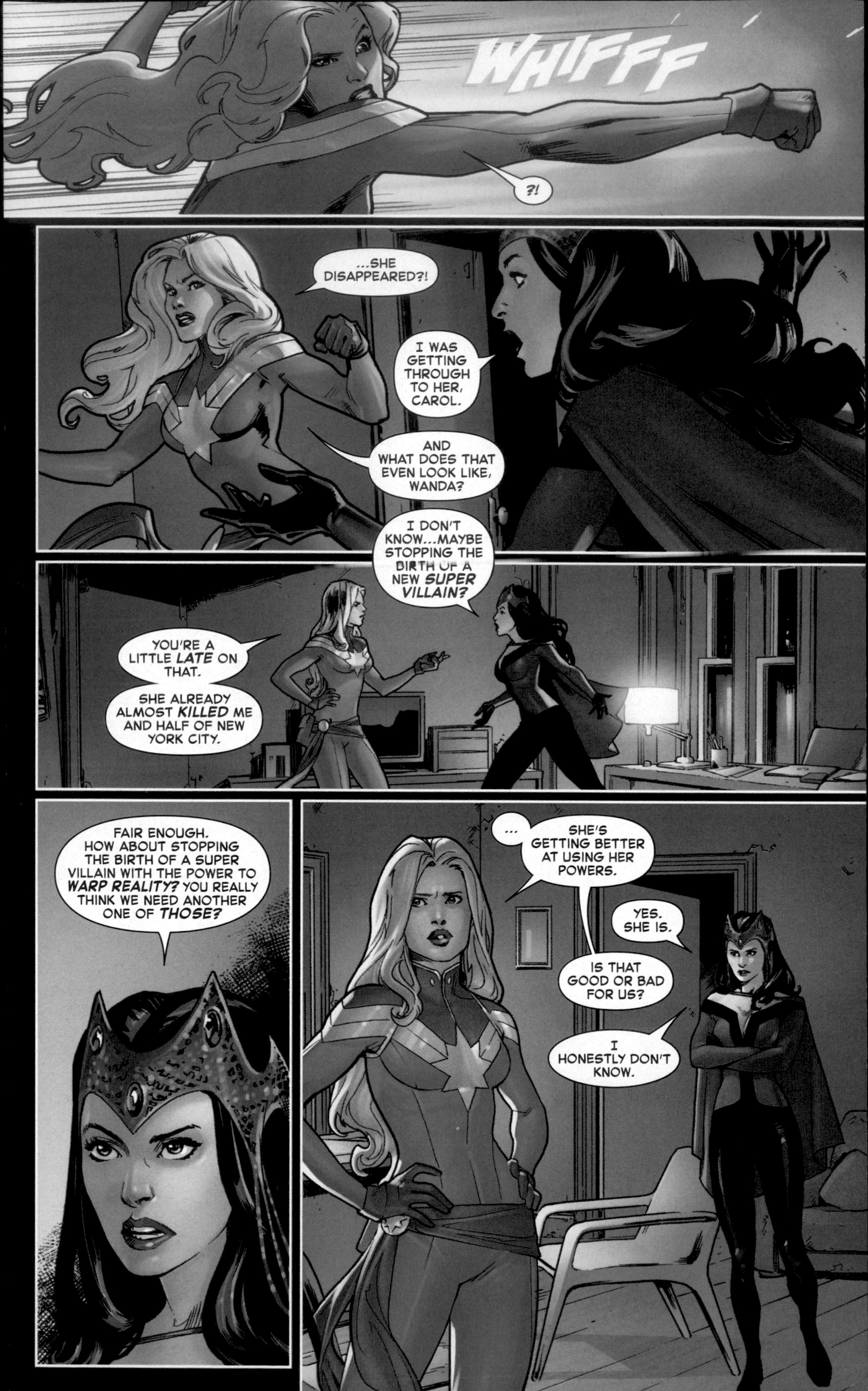
WHIFFF
?!
...SHE DISAPPEARED?!
I WAS GETTING THROUGH TO HER, CAROL.
AND WHAT DOES THAT EVEN LOOK LIKE, WANDA?
I DON'T KNOW...MAYBE STOPPING THE BIRTH OF A NEW SUPER VILLAIN?
YOU'RE A LITTLE LATE ON THAT.
SHE ALREADY ALMOST KILLED ME AND HALF OF NEW YORK CITY.
FAIR ENOUGH. HOW ABOUT STOPPING THE BIRTH OF A SUPER VILLAIN WITH THE POWER TO WARP REALITY? YOU REALLY THINK WE NEED ANOTHER ONE OF THOSE?
...
SHE'S GETTING BETTER AT USING HER POWERS.
YES. SHE IS.
IS THAT GOOD OR BAD FOR US?
I HONESTLY DON'T KNOW.

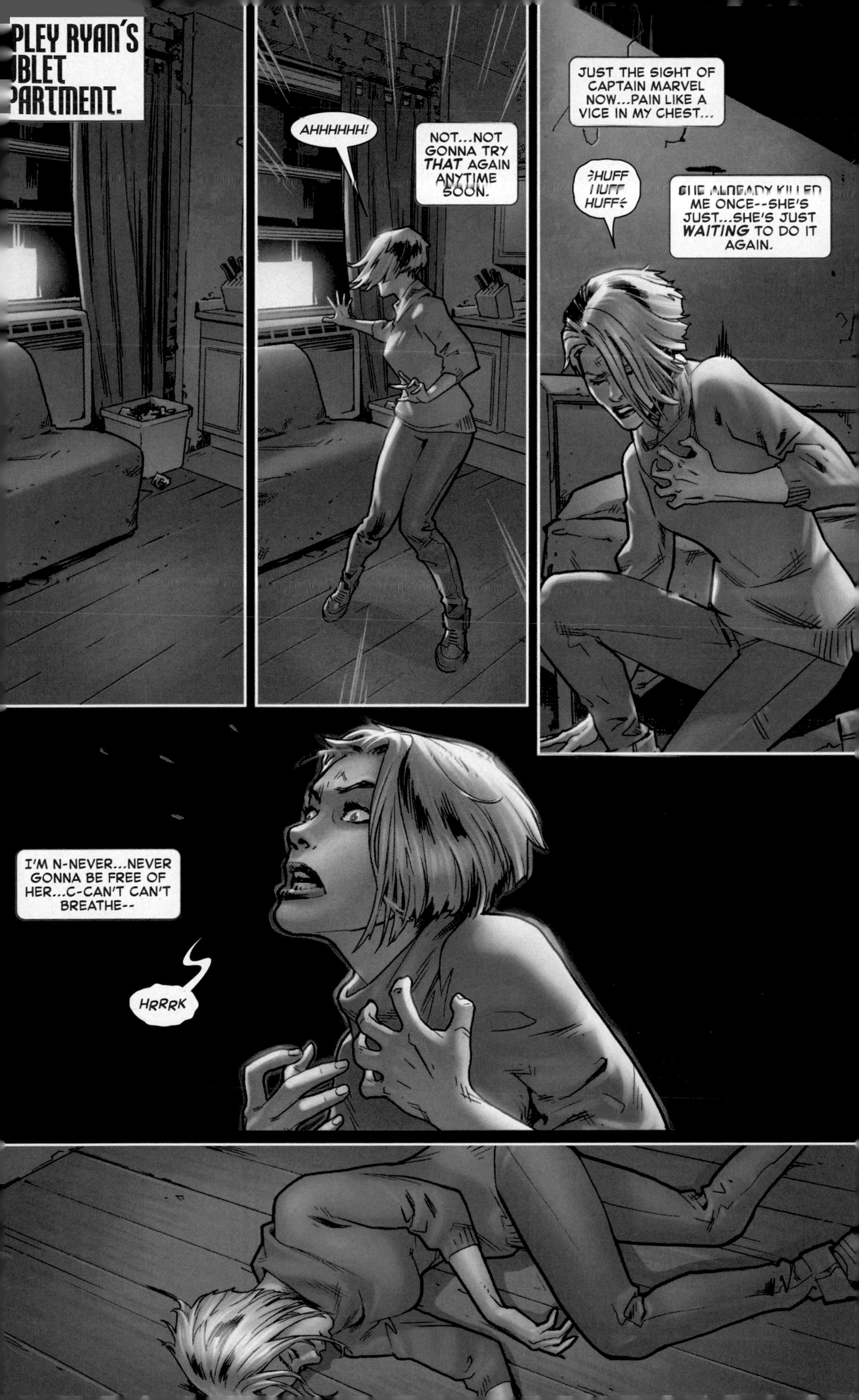
PLEY RYAN'S
BLET
PARTMENT.
AHHHHHH!
NOT...NOT GONNA TRY THAT AGAIN ANYTIME SOON.
JUST THE SIGHT OF CAPTAIN MARVEL NOW...PAIN LIKE A VICE IN MY CHEST...
HUFF HUFF HUFF
SHE ALREADY KILLED ME ONCE--SHE'S JUST...SHE'S JUST WAITING TO DO IT AGAIN.
I'M N-NEVER...NEVER GONNA BE FREE OF HER...C-CAN'T CAN'T BREATHE--
HRRRK

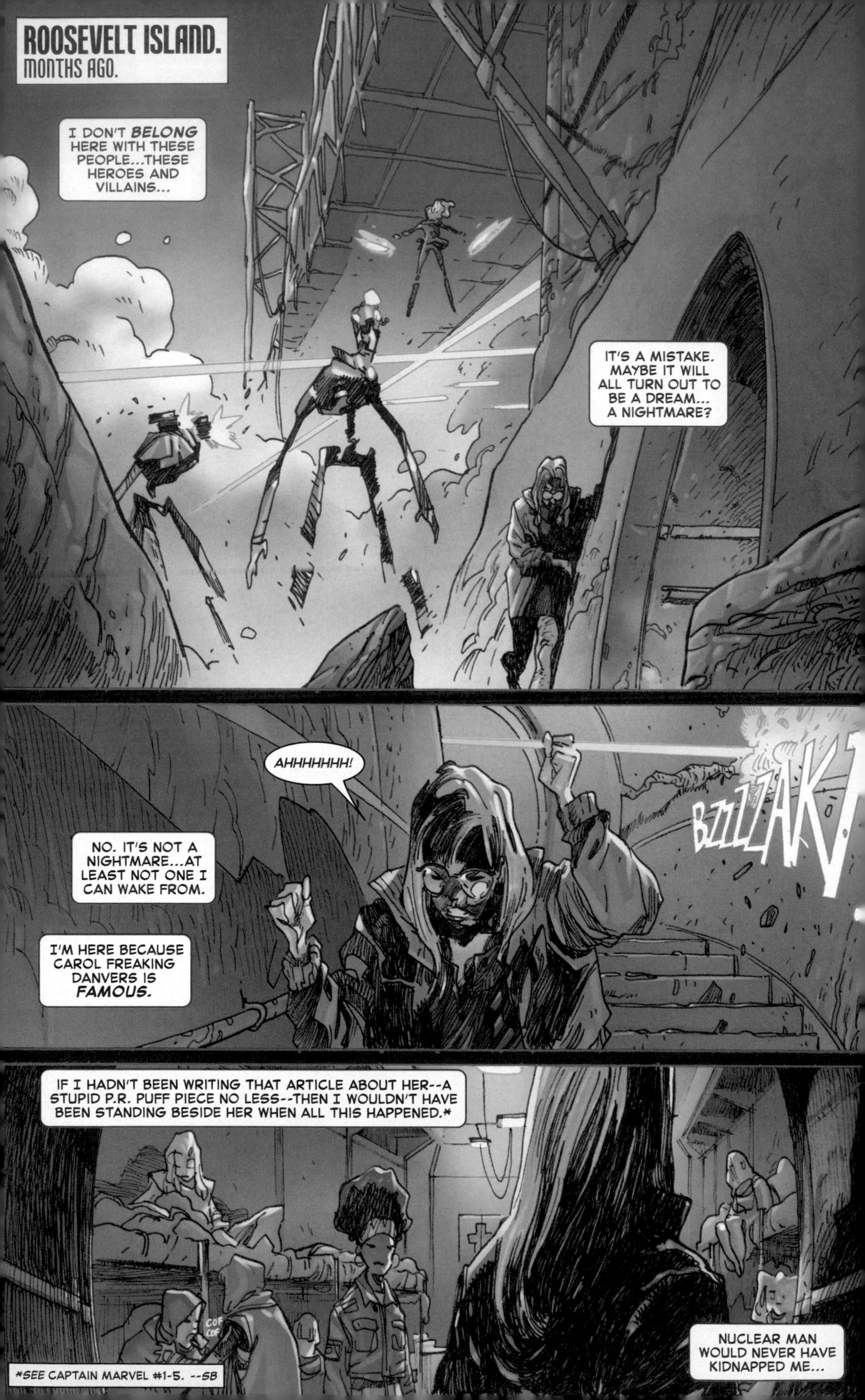
ROOSEVELT ISLAND.
MONTHS AGO.
I DON'T BELONG HERE WITH THESE PEOPLE...THESE HEROES AND VILLAINS...
IT'S A MISTAKE. MAYBE IT WILL ALL TURN OUT TO BE A DREAM... A NIGHTMARE?
AHHHHHHH!
BZZZZAK!
NO. IT'S NOT A NIGHTMARE...AT LEAST NOT ONE I CAN WAKE FROM.
I'M HERE BECAUSE CAROL FREAKING DANVERS IS FAMOUS.
IF I HADN'T BEEN WRITING THAT ARTICLE ABOUT HER--A STUPID P.R. PUFF PIECE NO LESS--THEN I WOULDN'T HAVE BEEN STANDING BESIDE HER WHEN ALL THIS HAPPENED.*
COF COF
NUCLEAR MAN WOULD NEVER HAVE KIDNAPPED ME...
*SEE CAPTAIN MARVEL #1-5. --SB

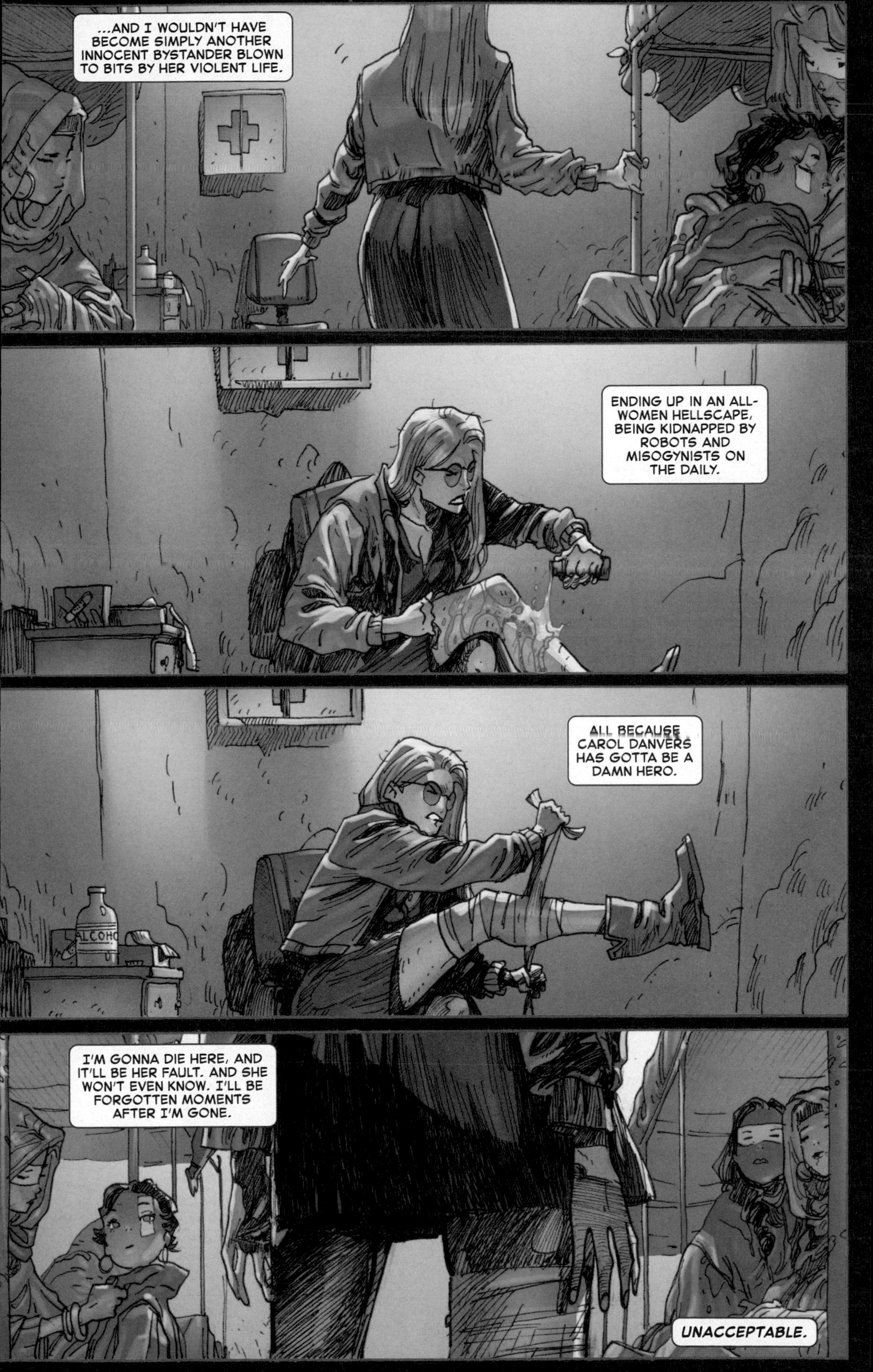
...AND I WOULDN'T HAVE BECOME SIMPLY ANOTHER INNOCENT BYSTANDER BLOWN TO BITS BY HER VIOLENT LIFE.
ENDING UP IN AN ALL-WOMEN HELLSCAPE, BEING KIDNAPPED BY ROBOTS AND MISOGYNISTS ON THE DAILY.
ALL BECAUSE CAROL DANVERS HAS GOTTA BE A DAMN HERO.
ALCOHO
I'M GONNA DIE HERE, AND IT'LL BE HER FAULT. AND SHE WON'T EVEN KNOW. I'LL BE FORGOTTEN MOMENTS AFTER I'M GONE.
UNACCEPTABLE.

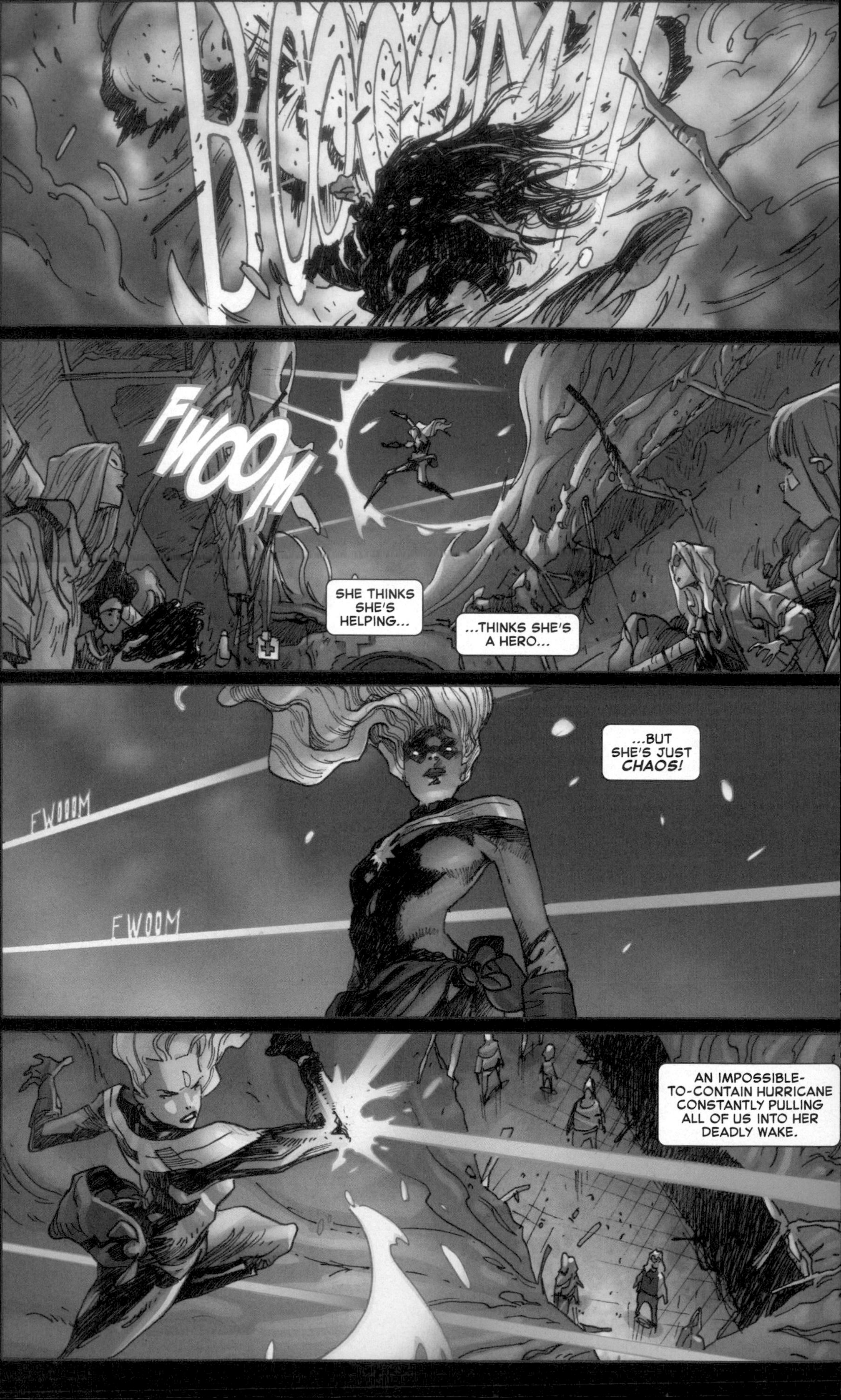

BOOOM!!
FWOOM
SHE THINKS SHE'S HELPING...
...THINKS SHE'S A HERO...
...BUT SHE'S JUST *CHAOS!*
FWOOOM
FWOOM
AN IMPOSSIBLE-TO-CONTAIN HURRICANE CONSTANTLY PULLING ALL OF US INTO HER DEADLY WAKE.

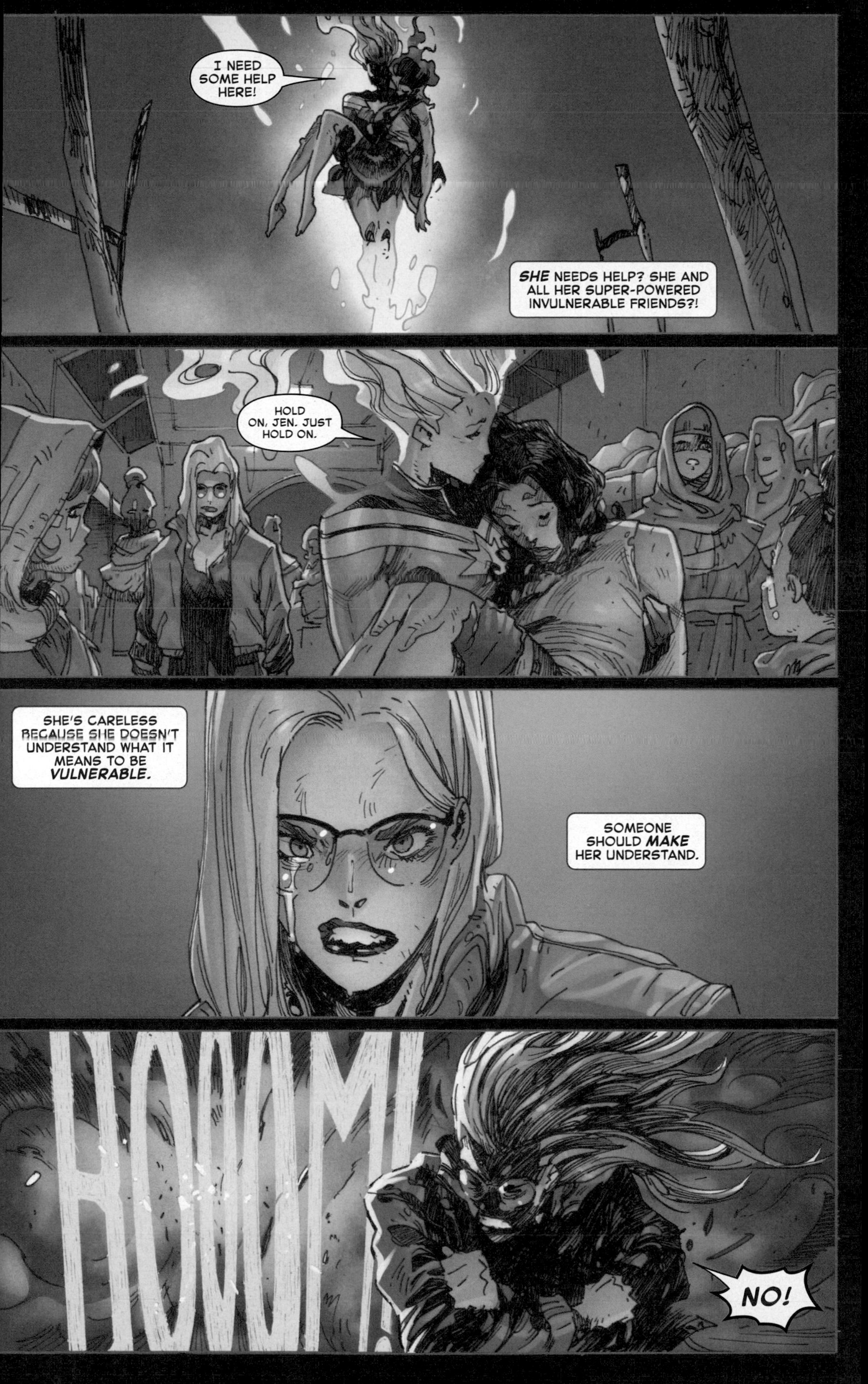
I NEED SOME HELP HERE!
SHE NEEDS HELP? SHE AND ALL HER SUPER-POWERED INVULNERABLE FRIENDS?!
HOLD ON, JEN. JUST HOLD ON.
SHE'S CARELESS BECAUSE SHE DOESN'T UNDERSTAND WHAT IT MEANS TO BE VULNERABLE.
SOMEONE SHOULD MAKE HER UNDERSTAND.
HOOOM!
NO!

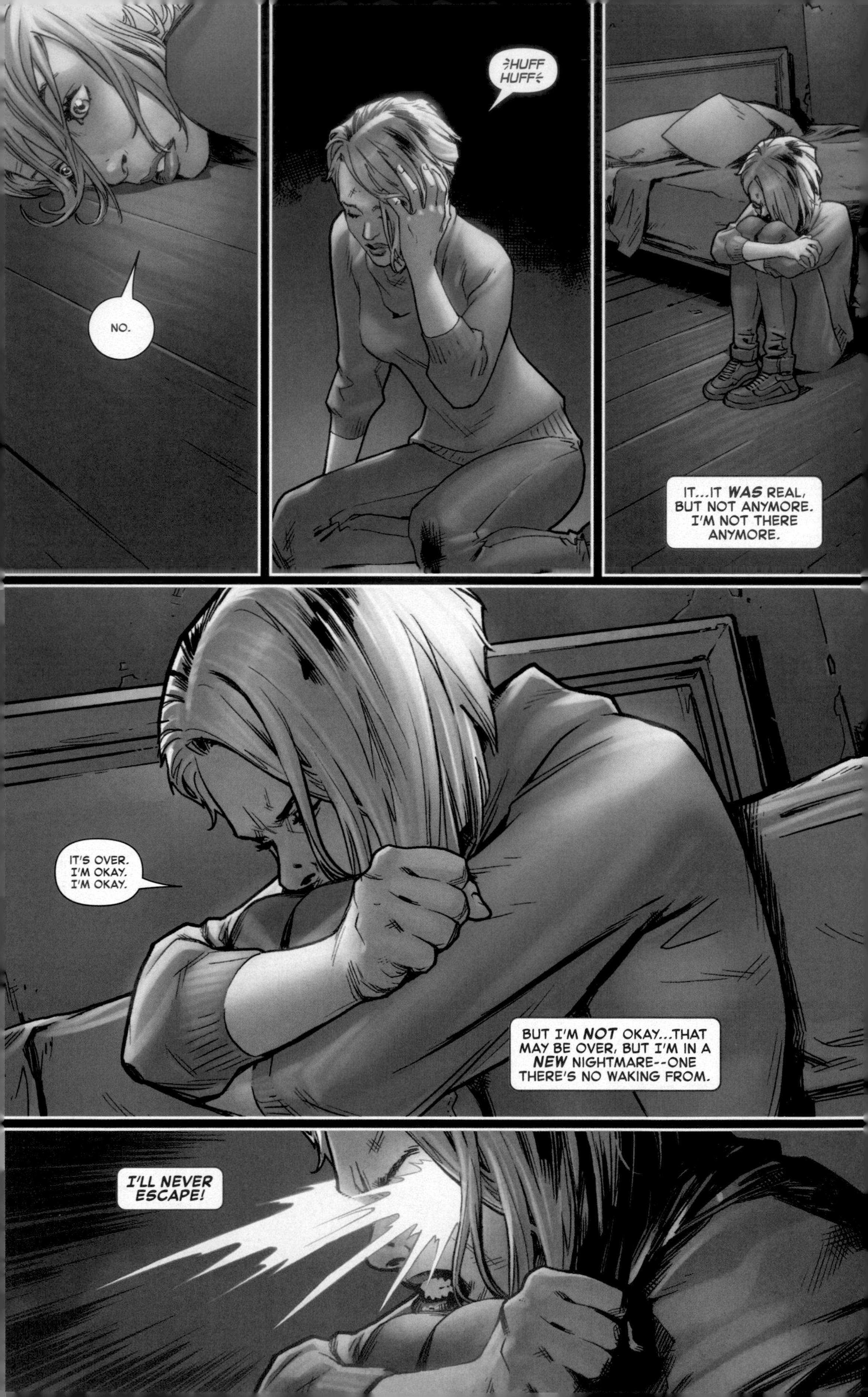
NO.
HUFF HUFF
IT...IT WAS REAL, BUT NOT ANYMORE. I'M NOT THERE ANYMORE.
IT'S OVER. I'M OKAY. I'M OKAY.
BUT I'M NOT OKAY...THAT MAY BE OVER, BUT I'M IN A NEW NIGHTMARE--ONE THERE'S NO WAKING FROM.
I'LL NEVER ESCAPE!

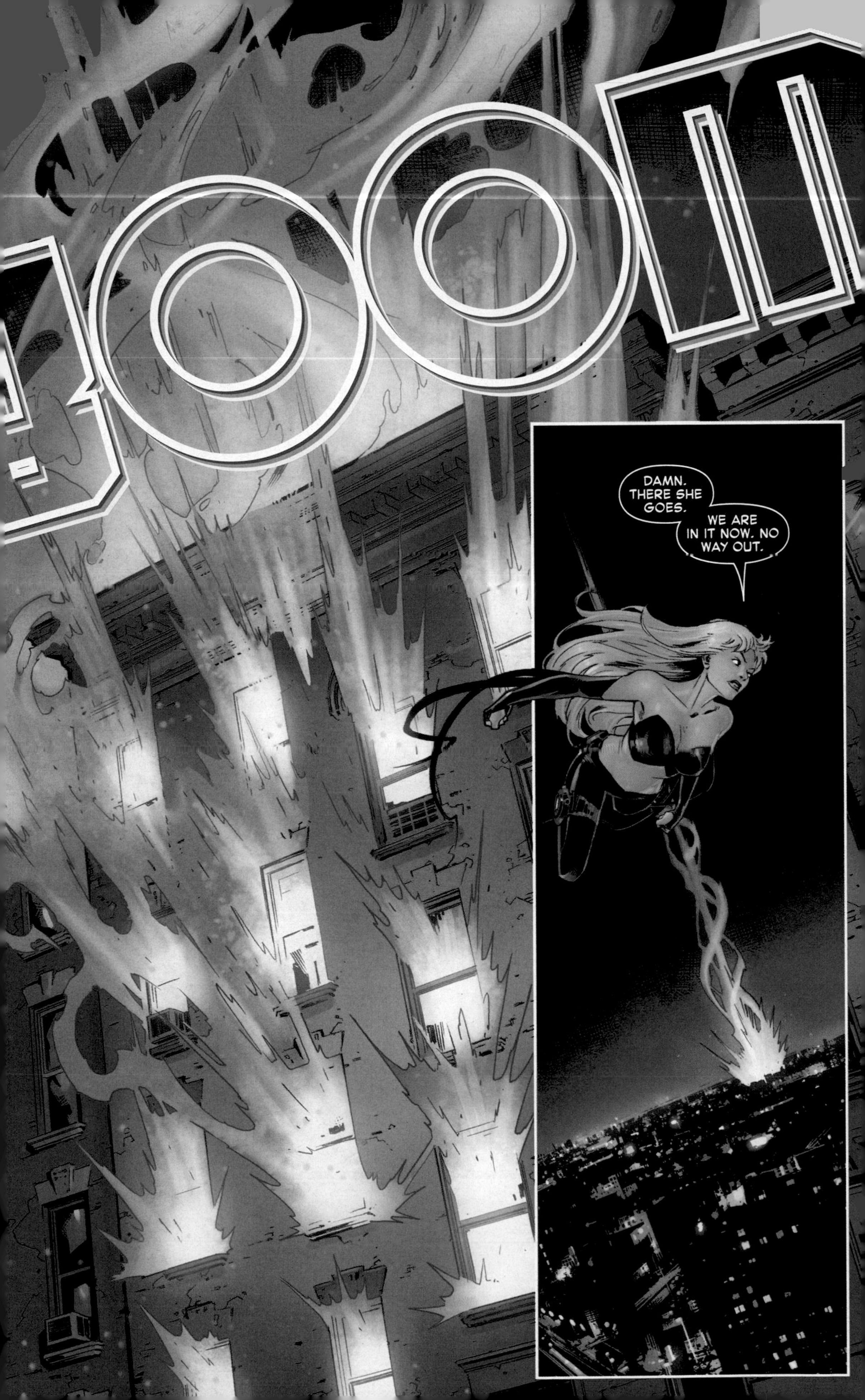
DAMN. THERE SHE GOES.
WE ARE IN IT NOW. NO WAY OUT.

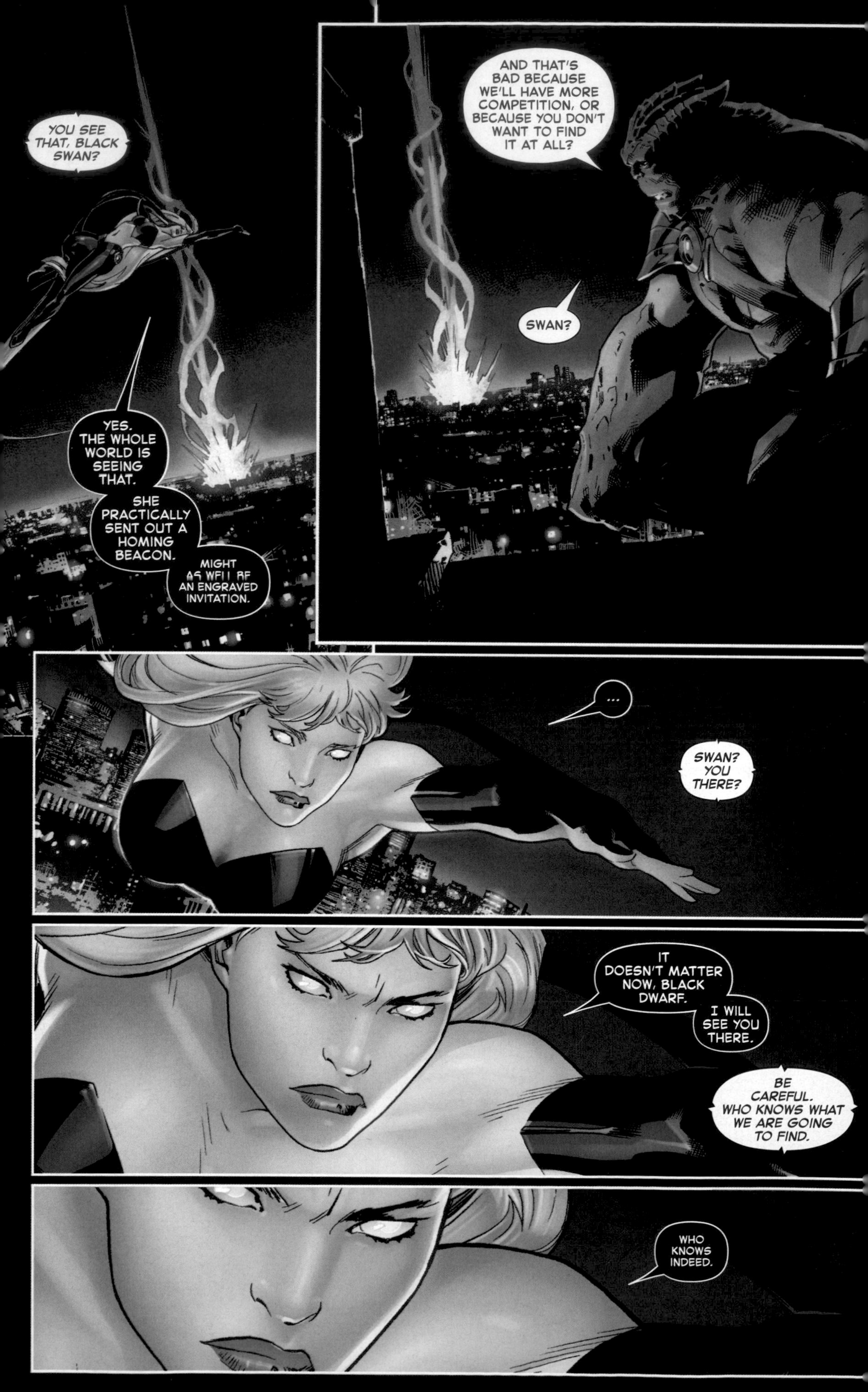
YOU SEE THAT, BLACK SWAN?
YES. THE WHOLE WORLD IS SEEING THAT.
SHE PRACTICALLY SENT OUT A HOMING BEACON.
MIGHT AS WELL BE AN ENGRAVED INVITATION.
AND THAT'S BAD BECAUSE WE'LL HAVE MORE COMPETITION, OR BECAUSE YOU DON'T WANT TO FIND IT AT ALL?
SWAN?
...
SWAN? YOU THERE?
IT DOESN'T MATTER NOW, BLACK DWARF.
I WILL SEE YOU THERE.
BE CAREFUL. WHO KNOWS WHAT WE ARE GOING TO FIND.
WHO KNOWS INDEED.

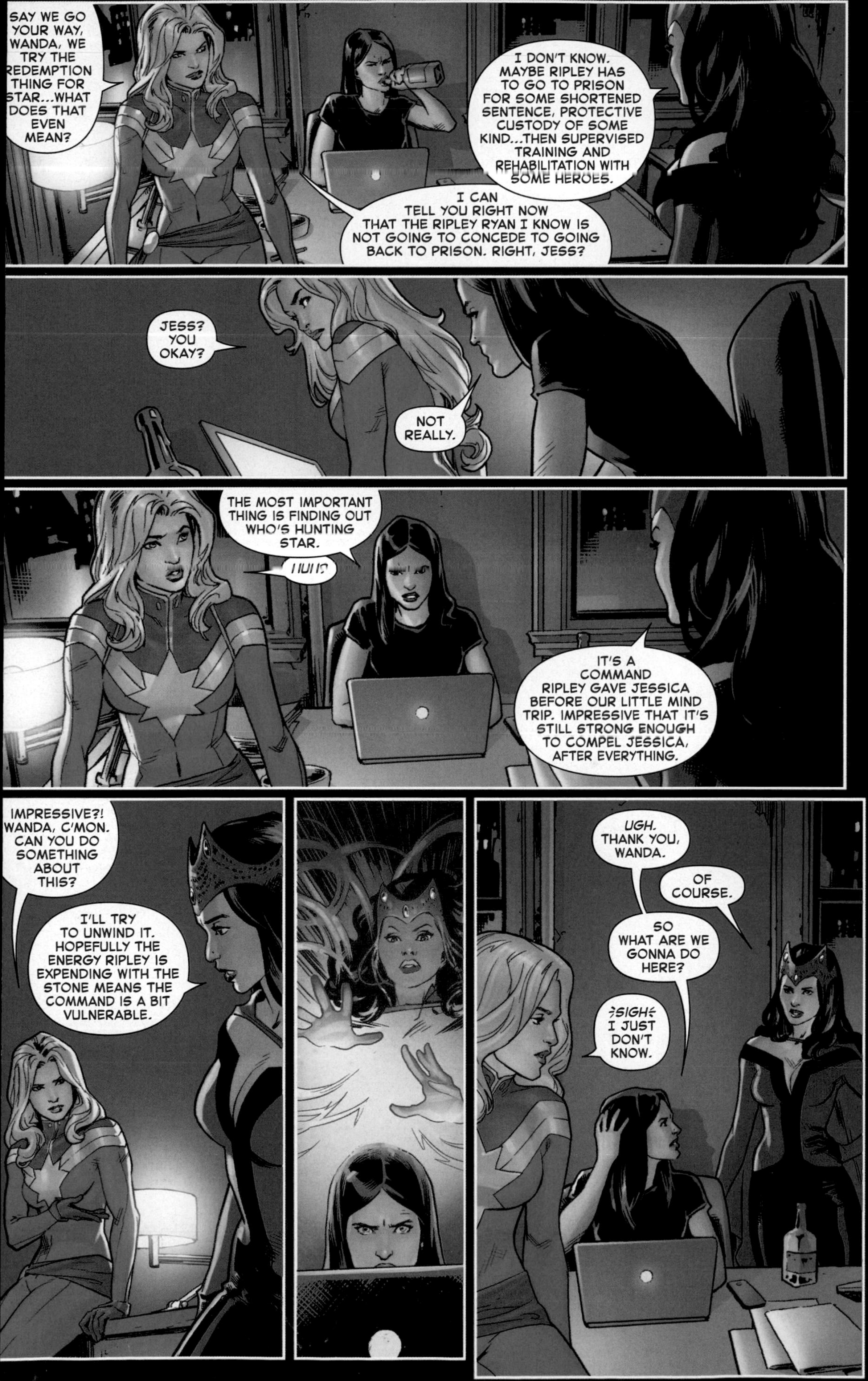
SAY WE GO YOUR WAY, WANDA, WE TRY THE REDEMPTION THING FOR STAR...WHAT DOES THAT EVEN MEAN?
I DON'T KNOW. MAYBE RIPLEY HAS TO GO TO PRISON FOR SOME SHORTENED SENTENCE, PROTECTIVE CUSTODY OF SOME KIND...THEN SUPERVISED TRAINING AND REHABILITATION WITH SOME HEROES.
I CAN TELL YOU RIGHT NOW THAT THE RIPLEY RYAN I KNOW IS NOT GOING TO CONCEDE TO GOING BACK TO PRISON. RIGHT, JESS?
JESS? YOU OKAY?
NOT REALLY.
THE MOST IMPORTANT THING IS FINDING OUT WHO'S HUNTING STAR.
HUH?
IT'S A COMMAND RIPLEY GAVE JESSICA BEFORE OUR LITTLE MIND TRIP. IMPRESSIVE THAT IT'S STILL STRONG ENOUGH TO COMPEL JESSICA, AFTER EVERYTHING.
IMPRESSIVE?! WANDA, C'MON. CAN YOU DO SOMETHING ABOUT THIS?
I'LL TRY TO UNWIND IT. HOPEFULLY THE ENERGY RIPLEY IS EXPENDING WITH THE STONE MEANS THE COMMAND IS A BIT VULNERABLE.
UGH. THANK YOU, WANDA.
OF COURSE.
SO WHAT ARE WE GONNA DO HERE?
SIGH I JUST DON'T KNOW.

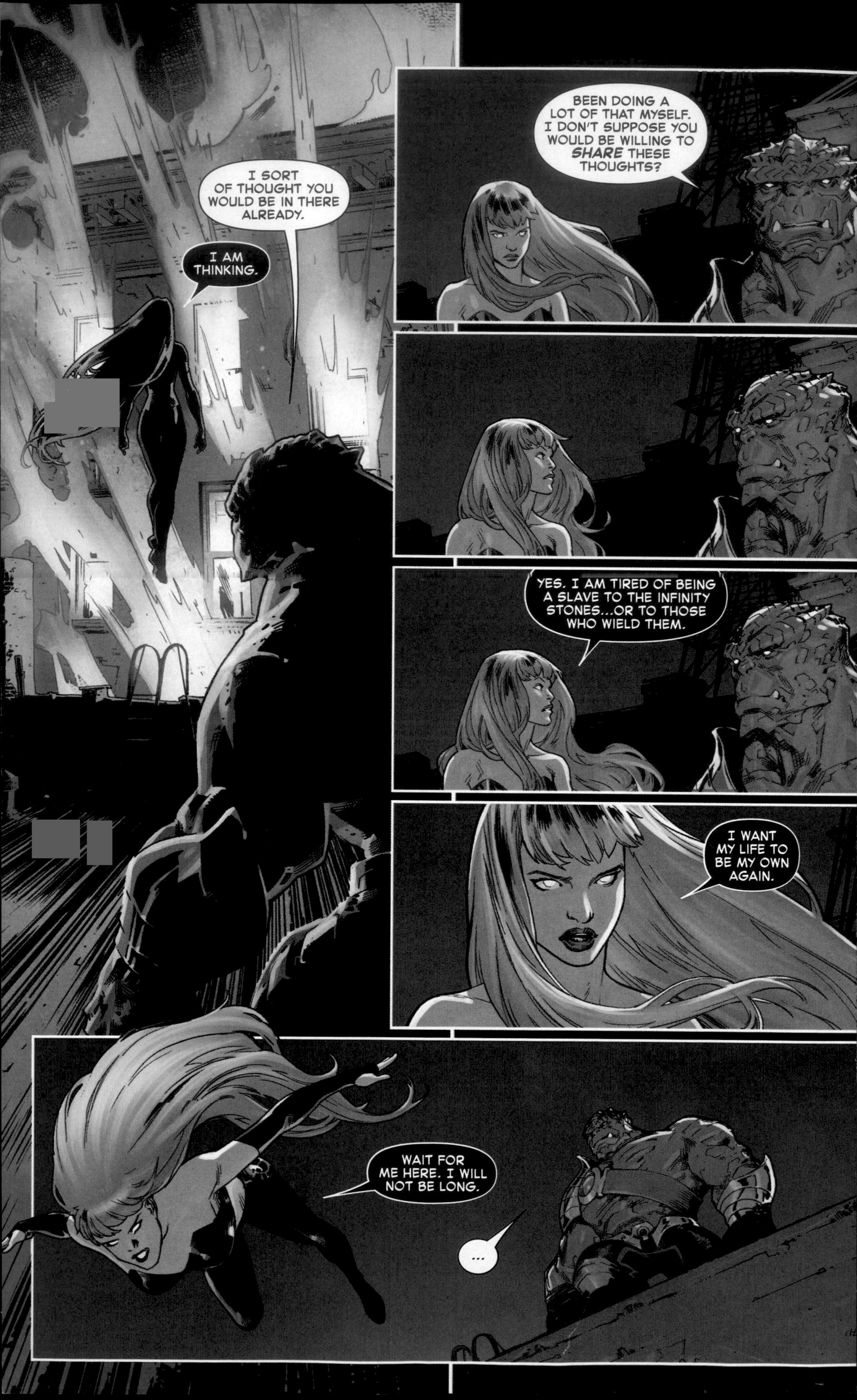

I SORT OF THOUGHT YOU WOULD BE IN THERE ALREADY.
I AM THINKING.
BEEN DOING A LOT OF THAT MYSELF. I DON'T SUPPOSE YOU WOULD BE WILLING TO *SHARE* THESE THOUGHTS?
YES. I AM TIRED OF BEING A SLAVE TO THE INFINITY STONES...OR TO THOSE WHO WIELD THEM.
I WANT MY LIFE TO BE MY OWN AGAIN.
WAIT FOR ME HERE. I WILL NOT BE LONG.
...

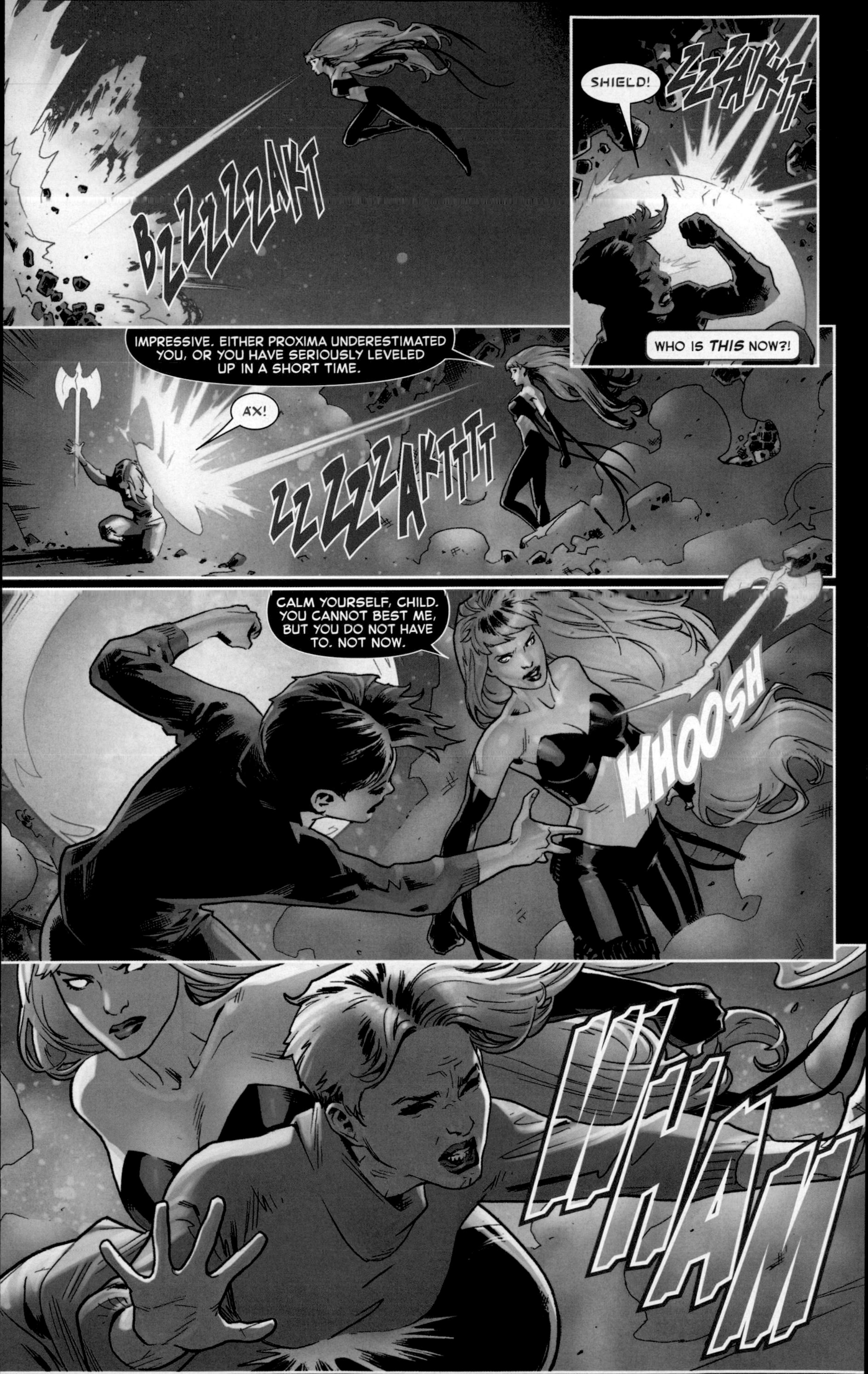
BZZZZZAKT
SHIELD!
ZZZAKTT
WHO IS THIS NOW?!
IMPRESSIVE. EITHER PROXIMA UNDERESTIMATED YOU, OR YOU HAVE SERIOUSLY LEVELED UP IN A SHORT TIME.
AX!
ZZZZZAKTTTT
CALM YOURSELF, CHILD. YOU CANNOT BEST ME, BUT YOU DO NOT HAVE TO. NOT NOW.
WHOOSH
WHAM

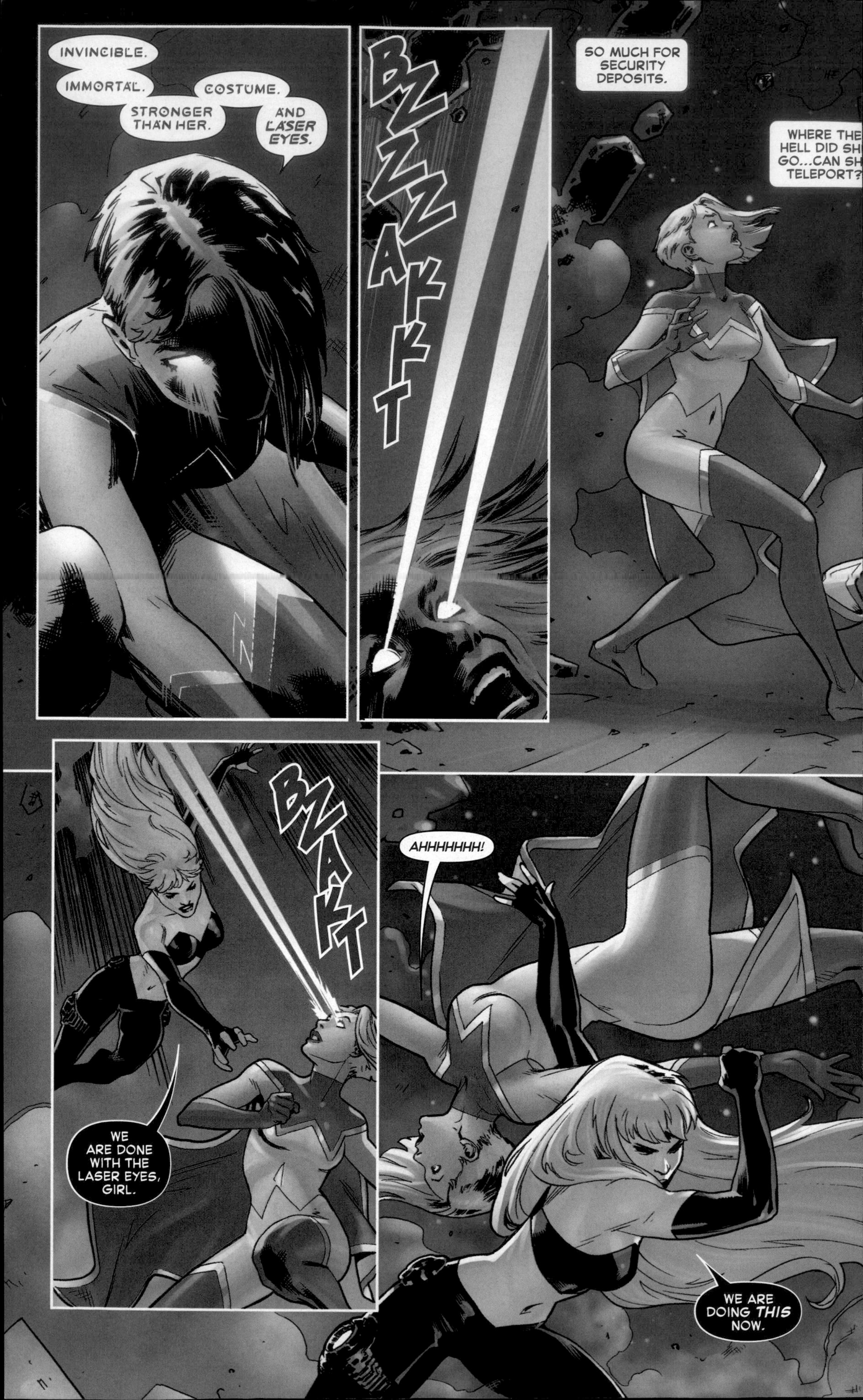
INVINCIBLE.
IMMORTAL.
STRONGER THAN HER.
COSTUME.
AND LASER EYES.
BZZZAKKT
SO MUCH FOR SECURITY DEPOSITS.
WHERE THE HELL DID SH GO...CAN SH TELEPORT?
BZAKT
WE ARE DONE WITH THE LASER EYES, GIRL.
AHHHHHHH!
WE ARE DOING THIS NOW.

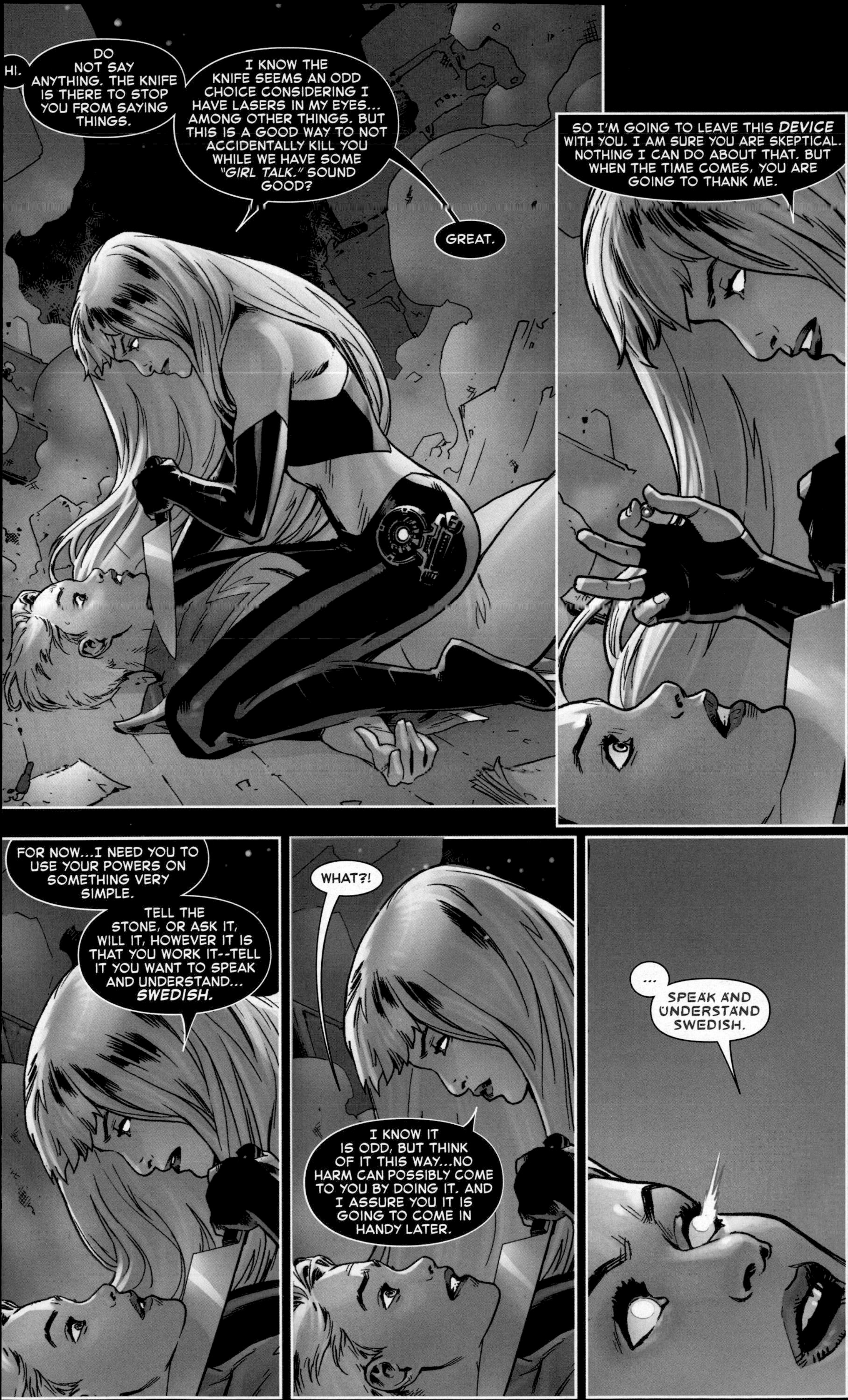

HI.
DO NOT SAY ANYTHING. THE KNIFE IS THERE TO STOP YOU FROM SAYING THINGS.
I KNOW THE KNIFE SEEMS AN ODD CHOICE CONSIDERING I HAVE LASERS IN MY EYES... AMONG OTHER THINGS. BUT THIS IS A GOOD WAY TO NOT ACCIDENTALLY KILL YOU WHILE WE HAVE SOME "GIRL TALK." SOUND GOOD?
GREAT.
SO I'M GOING TO LEAVE THIS DEVICE WITH YOU. I AM SURE YOU ARE SKEPTICAL. NOTHING I CAN DO ABOUT THAT. BUT WHEN THE TIME COMES, YOU ARE GOING TO THANK ME.
FOR NOW...I NEED YOU TO USE YOUR POWERS ON SOMETHING VERY SIMPLE.
TELL THE STONE, OR ASK IT, WILL IT, HOWEVER IT IS THAT YOU WORK IT--TELL IT YOU WANT TO SPEAK AND UNDERSTAND... SWEDISH.
WHAT?!
I KNOW IT IS ODD, BUT THINK OF IT THIS WAY...NO HARM CAN POSSIBLY COME TO YOU BY DOING IT. AND I ASSURE YOU IT IS GOING TO COME IN HANDY LATER.
...
SPEAK AND UNDERSTAND SWEDISH.

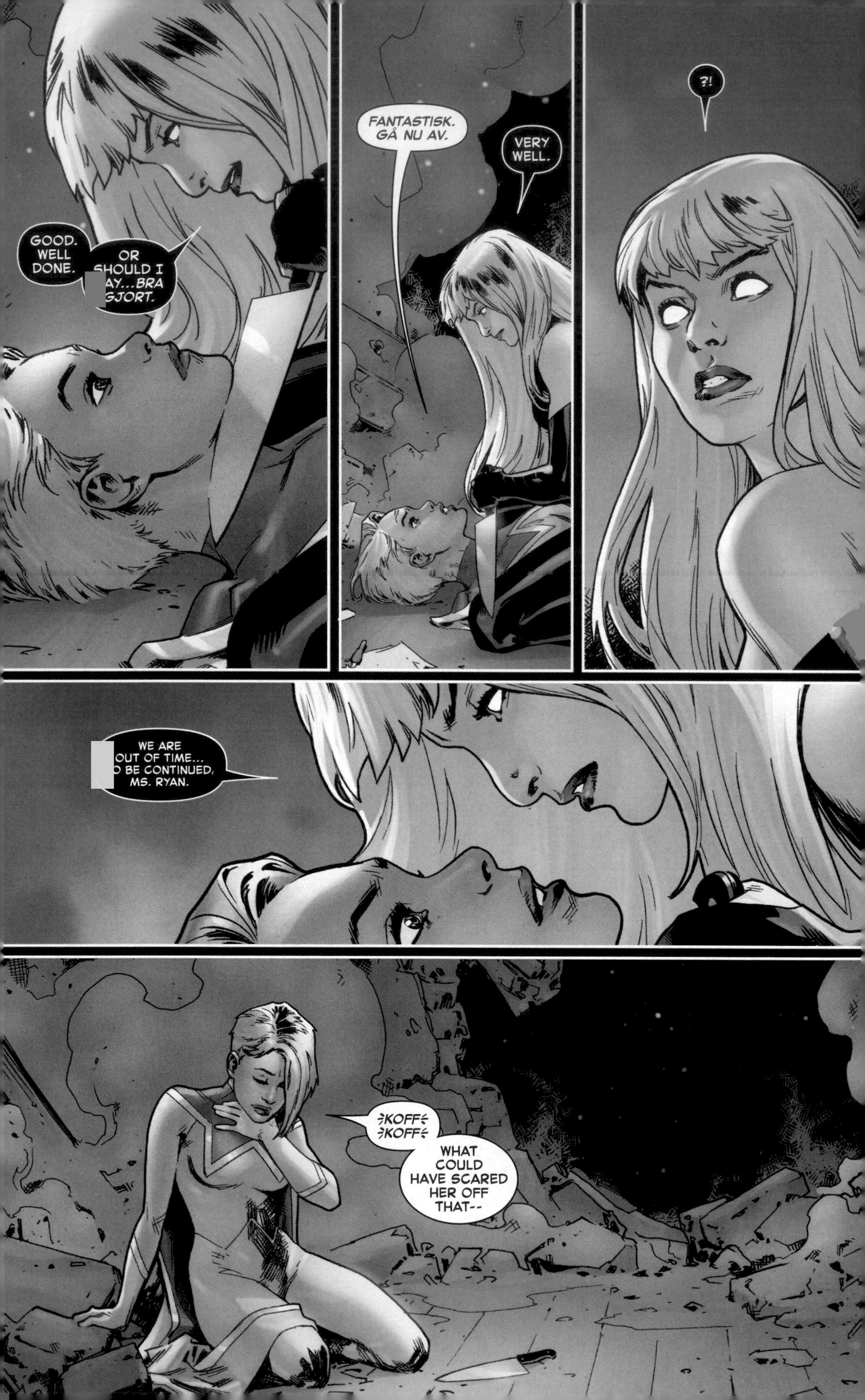
GOOD. WELL DONE.
OR SHOULD I AY...BRA GJORT.
FANTASTISK. GÅ NU AV.
VERY WELL.
?!
WE ARE OUT OF TIME... O BE CONTINUED, MS. RYAN.
⚡KOFF⚡ ⚡KOFF⚡
WHAT COULD HAVE SCARED HER OFF THAT--

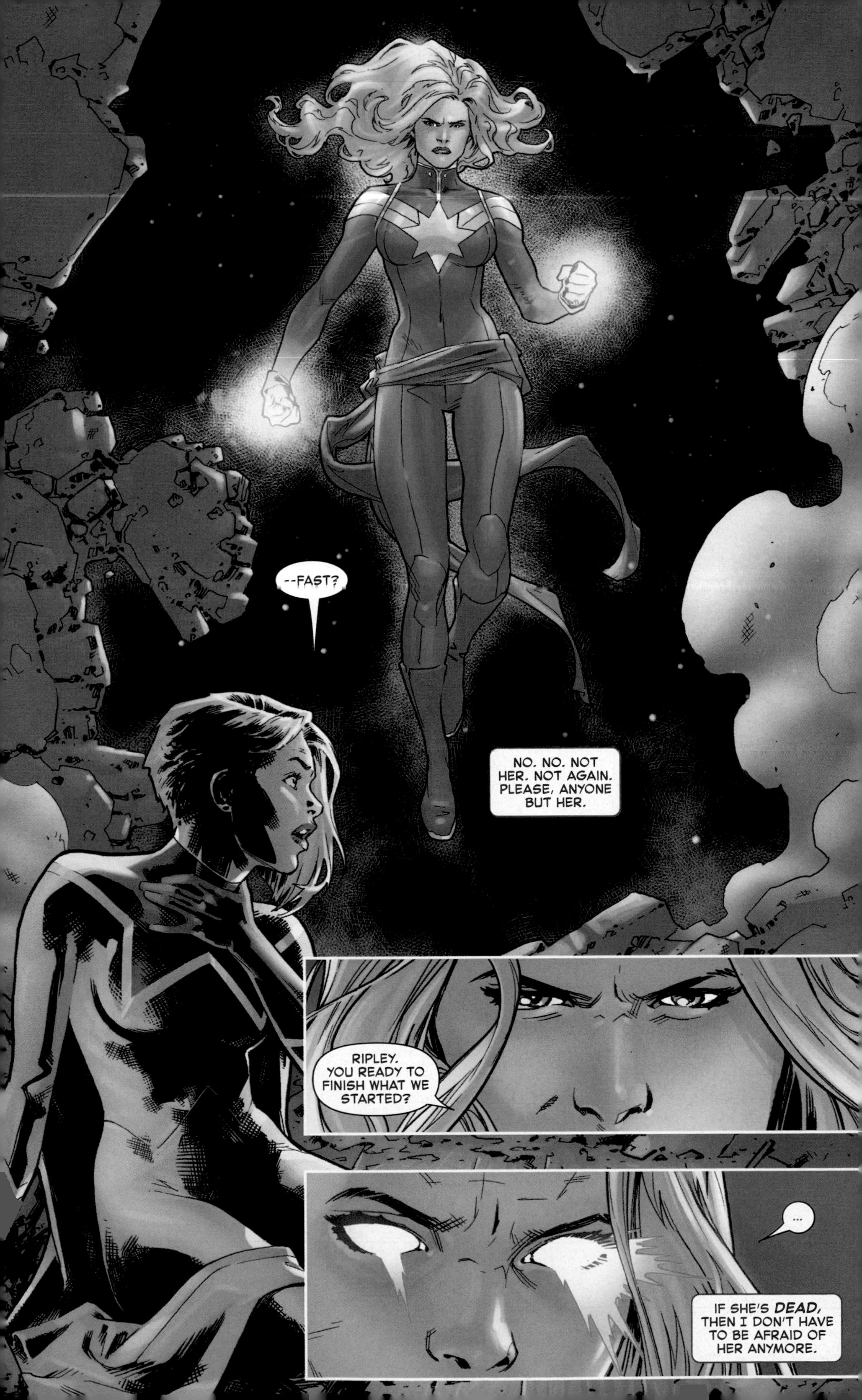
--FAST?
NO. NO. NOT HER. NOT AGAIN. PLEASE, ANYONE BUT HER.
RIPLEY. YOU READY TO FINISH WHAT WE STARTED?
...
IF SHE'S *DEAD,* THEN I DON'T HAVE TO BE AFRAID OF HER ANYMORE.

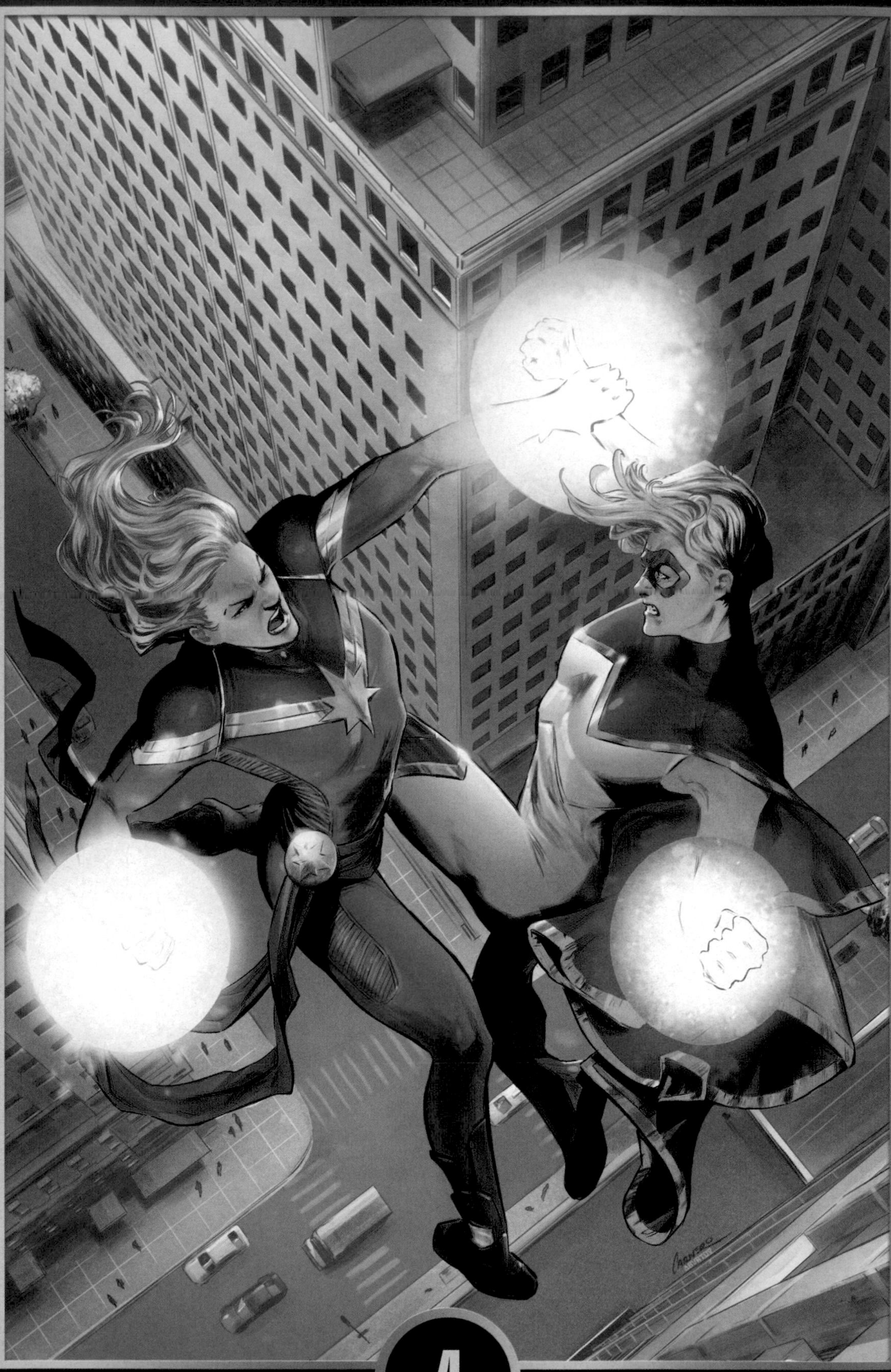

4

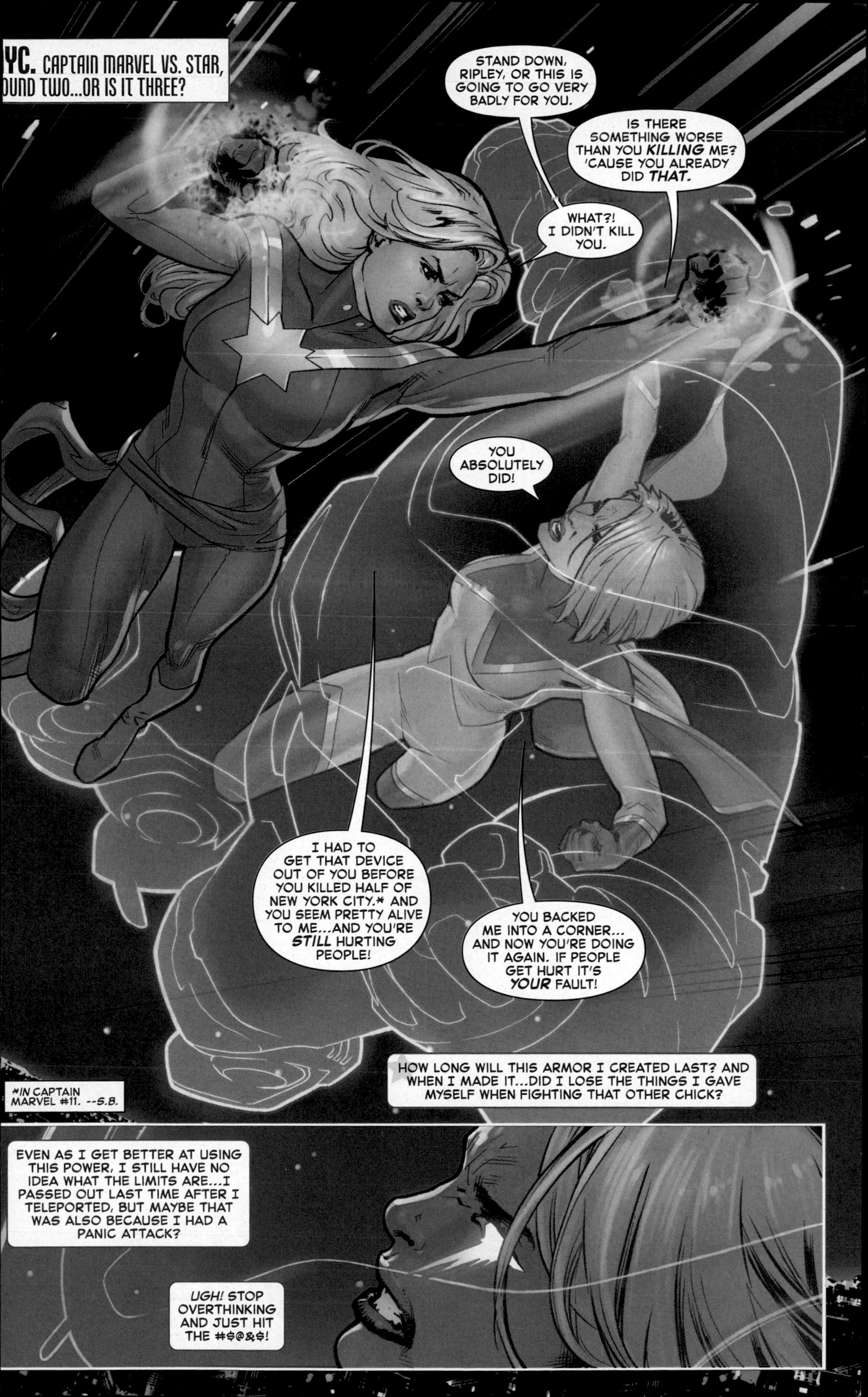

YC. CAPTAIN MARVEL VS. STAR, OUND TWO...OR IS IT THREE?
STAND DOWN, RIPLEY, OR THIS IS GOING TO GO VERY BADLY FOR YOU.
IS THERE SOMETHING WORSE THAN YOU KILLING ME? 'CAUSE YOU ALREADY DID THAT.
WHAT?! I DIDN'T KILL YOU.
YOU ABSOLUTELY DID!
I HAD TO GET THAT DEVICE OUT OF YOU BEFORE YOU KILLED HALF OF NEW YORK CITY.* AND YOU SEEM PRETTY ALIVE TO ME...AND YOU'RE STILL HURTING PEOPLE!
YOU BACKED ME INTO A CORNER... AND NOW YOU'RE DOING IT AGAIN. IF PEOPLE GET HURT IT'S YOUR FAULT!
*IN CAPTAIN MARVEL #11. --S.B.
HOW LONG WILL THIS ARMOR I CREATED LAST? AND WHEN I MADE IT...DID I LOSE THE THINGS I GAVE MYSELF WHEN FIGHTING THAT OTHER CHICK?
EVEN AS I GET BETTER AT USING THIS POWER, I STILL HAVE NO IDEA WHAT THE LIMITS ARE...I PASSED OUT LAST TIME AFTER I TELEPORTED, BUT MAYBE THAT WAS ALSO BECAUSE I HAD A PANIC ATTACK?
UGH! STOP OVERTHINKING AND JUST HIT THE #$@&$!

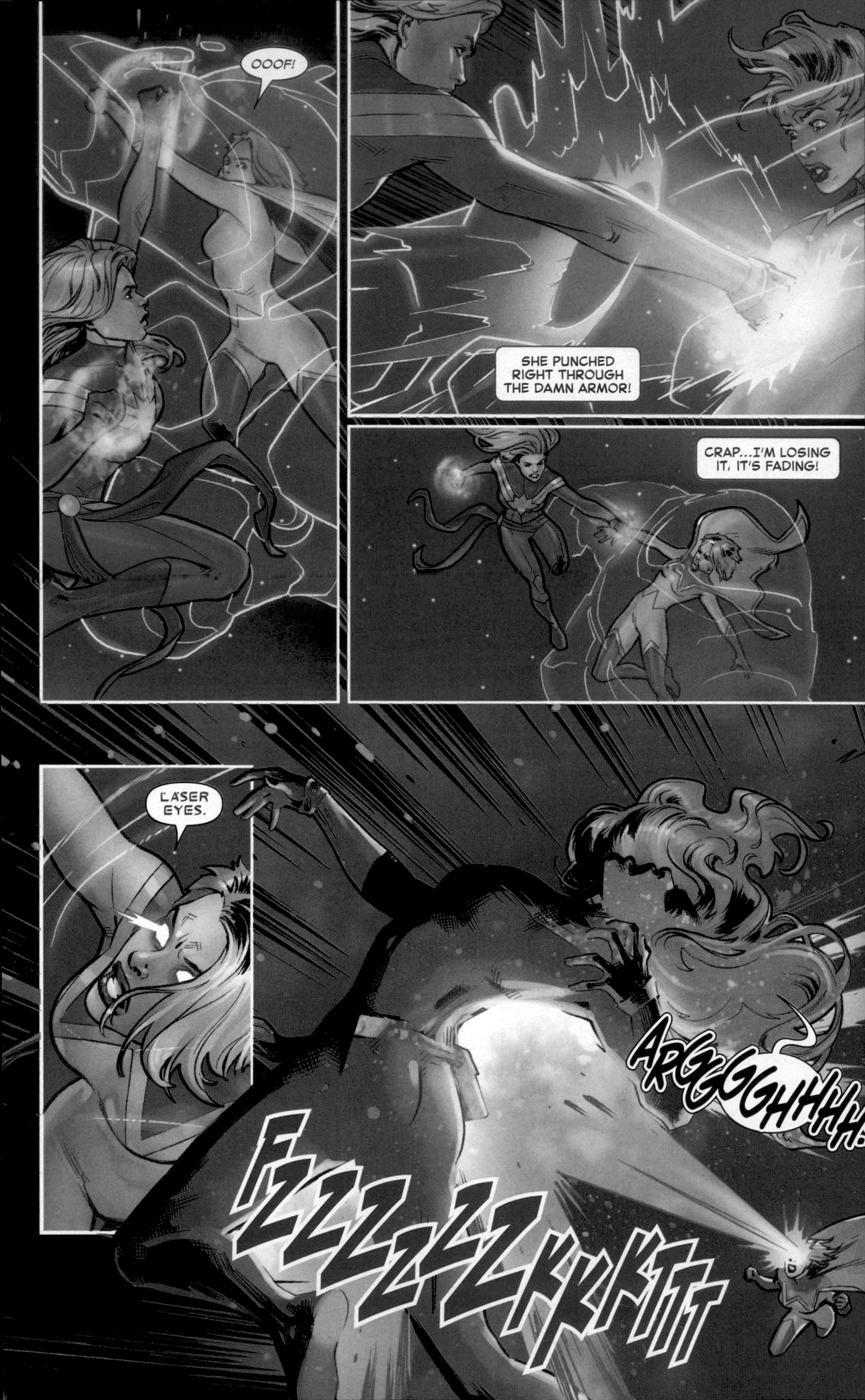

OOOF!
SHE PUNCHED RIGHT THROUGH THE DAMN ARMOR!
CRAP...I'M LOSING IT, IT'S FADING!
LASER EYES.
ARGGGGHHHHH!
FZZZZZZKKKTTT

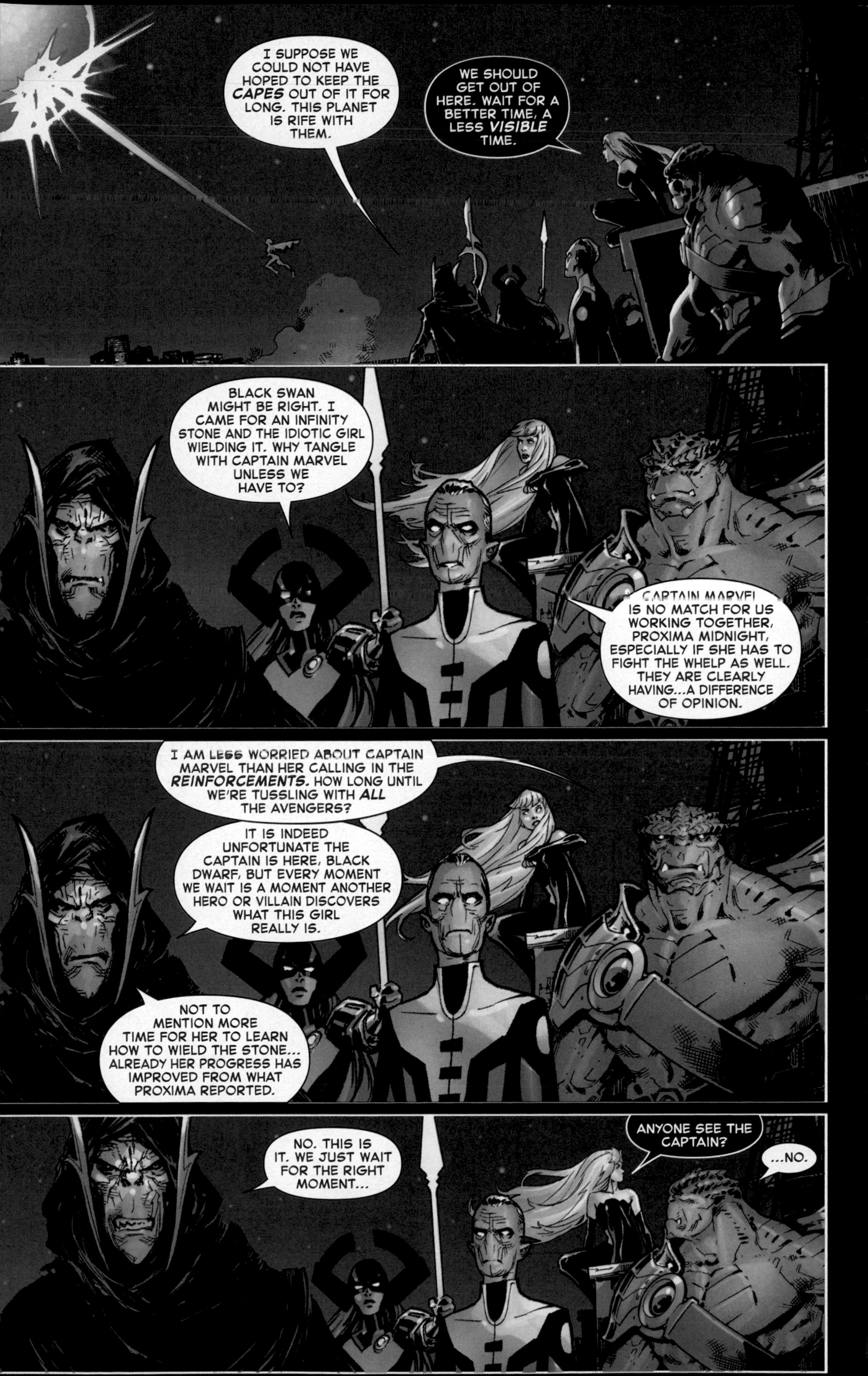
I SUPPOSE WE COULD NOT HAVE HOPED TO KEEP THE CAPES OUT OF IT FOR LONG. THIS PLANET IS RIFE WITH THEM.
WE SHOULD GET OUT OF HERE. WAIT FOR A BETTER TIME, A LESS VISIBLE TIME.
BLACK SWAN MIGHT BE RIGHT. I CAME FOR AN INFINITY STONE AND THE IDIOTIC GIRL WIELDING IT. WHY TANGLE WITH CAPTAIN MARVEL UNLESS WE HAVE TO?
CAPTAIN MARVEL IS NO MATCH FOR US WORKING TOGETHER, PROXIMA MIDNIGHT, ESPECIALLY IF SHE HAS TO FIGHT THE WHELP AS WELL. THEY ARE CLEARLY HAVING...A DIFFERENCE OF OPINION.
I AM LESS WORRIED ABOUT CAPTAIN MARVEL THAN HER CALLING IN THE REINFORCEMENTS. HOW LONG UNTIL WE'RE TUSSLING WITH ALL THE AVENGERS?
IT IS INDEED UNFORTUNATE THE CAPTAIN IS HERE, BLACK DWARF, BUT EVERY MOMENT WE WAIT IS A MOMENT ANOTHER HERO OR VILLAIN DISCOVERS WHAT THIS GIRL REALLY IS.
NOT TO MENTION MORE TIME FOR HER TO LEARN HOW TO WIELD THE STONE... ALREADY HER PROGRESS HAS IMPROVED FROM WHAT PROXIMA REPORTED.
NO. THIS IS IT. WE JUST WAIT FOR THE RIGHT MOMENT...
ANYONE SEE THE CAPTAIN?
...NO.

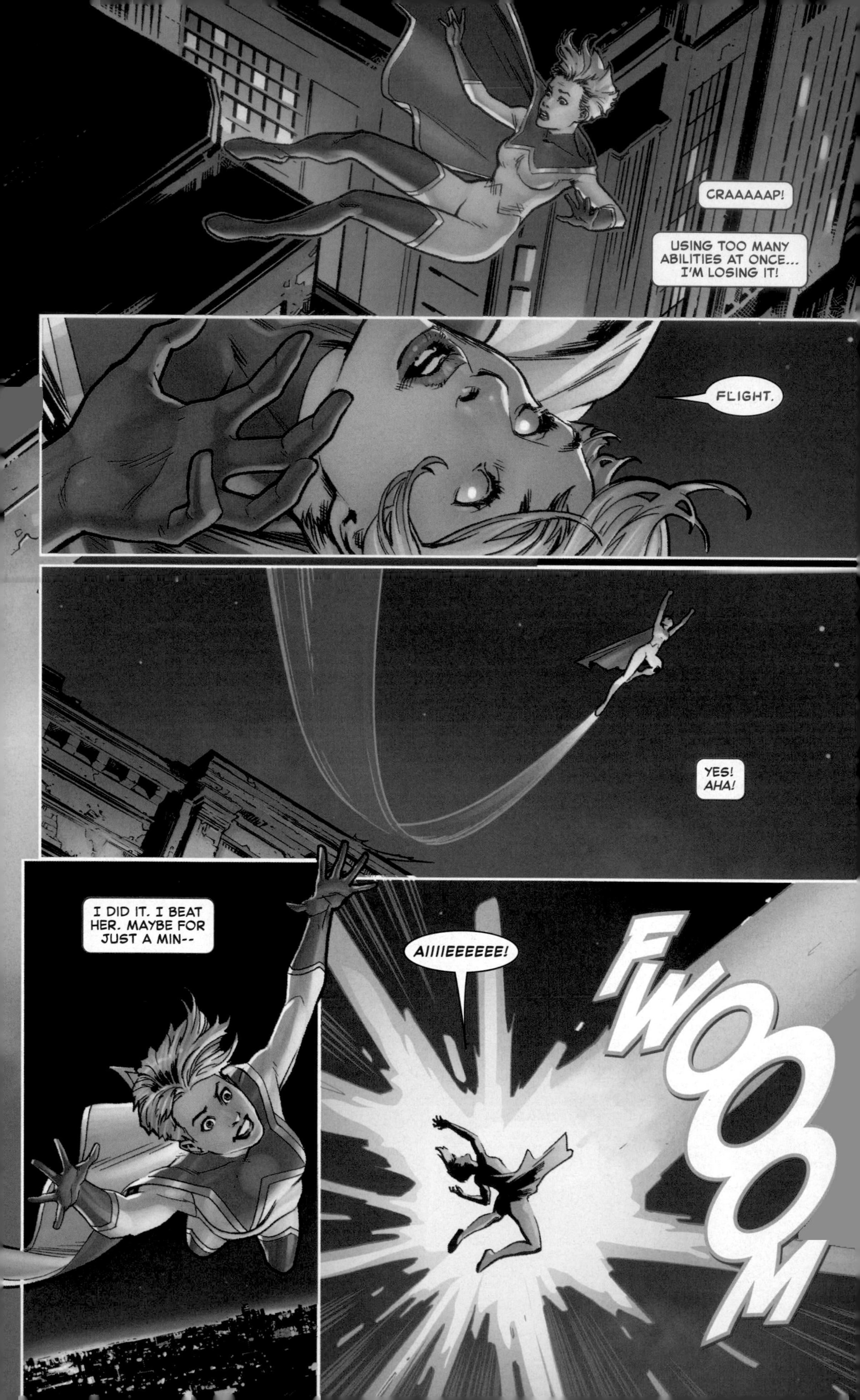
CRAAAAAP!
USING TOO MANY ABILITIES AT ONCE... I'M LOSING IT!
FLIGHT.
YES! AHA!
I DID IT. I BEAT HER. MAYBE FOR JUST A MIN--
AIIIIEEEEEE!
FWOOOM

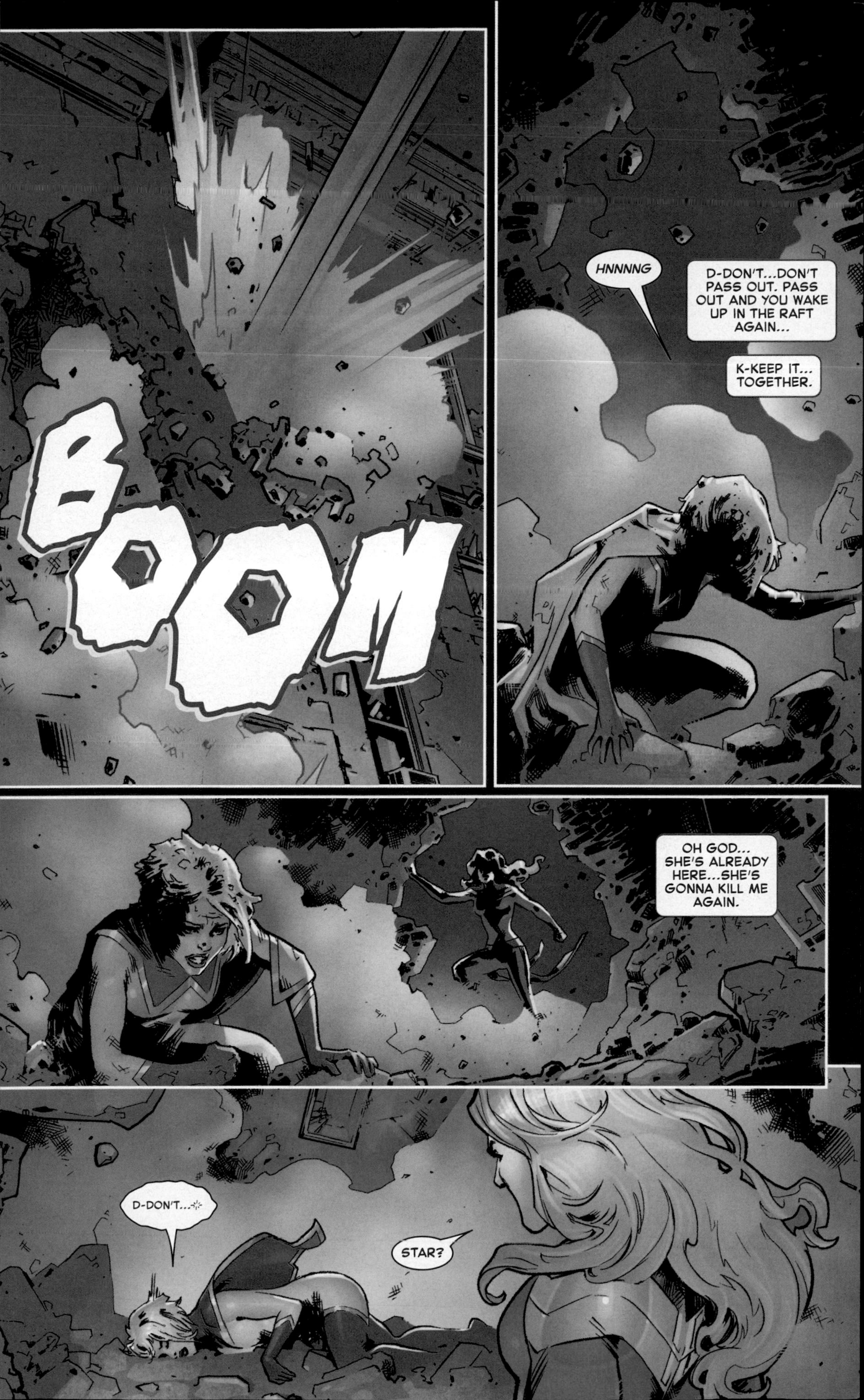
BOOM
HNNNNG
D-DON'T...DON'T PASS OUT. PASS OUT AND YOU WAKE UP IN THE RAFT AGAIN...
K-KEEP IT... TOGETHER.
OH GOD... SHE'S ALREADY HERE...SHE'S GONNA KILL ME AGAIN.
D-DON'T...
STAR?

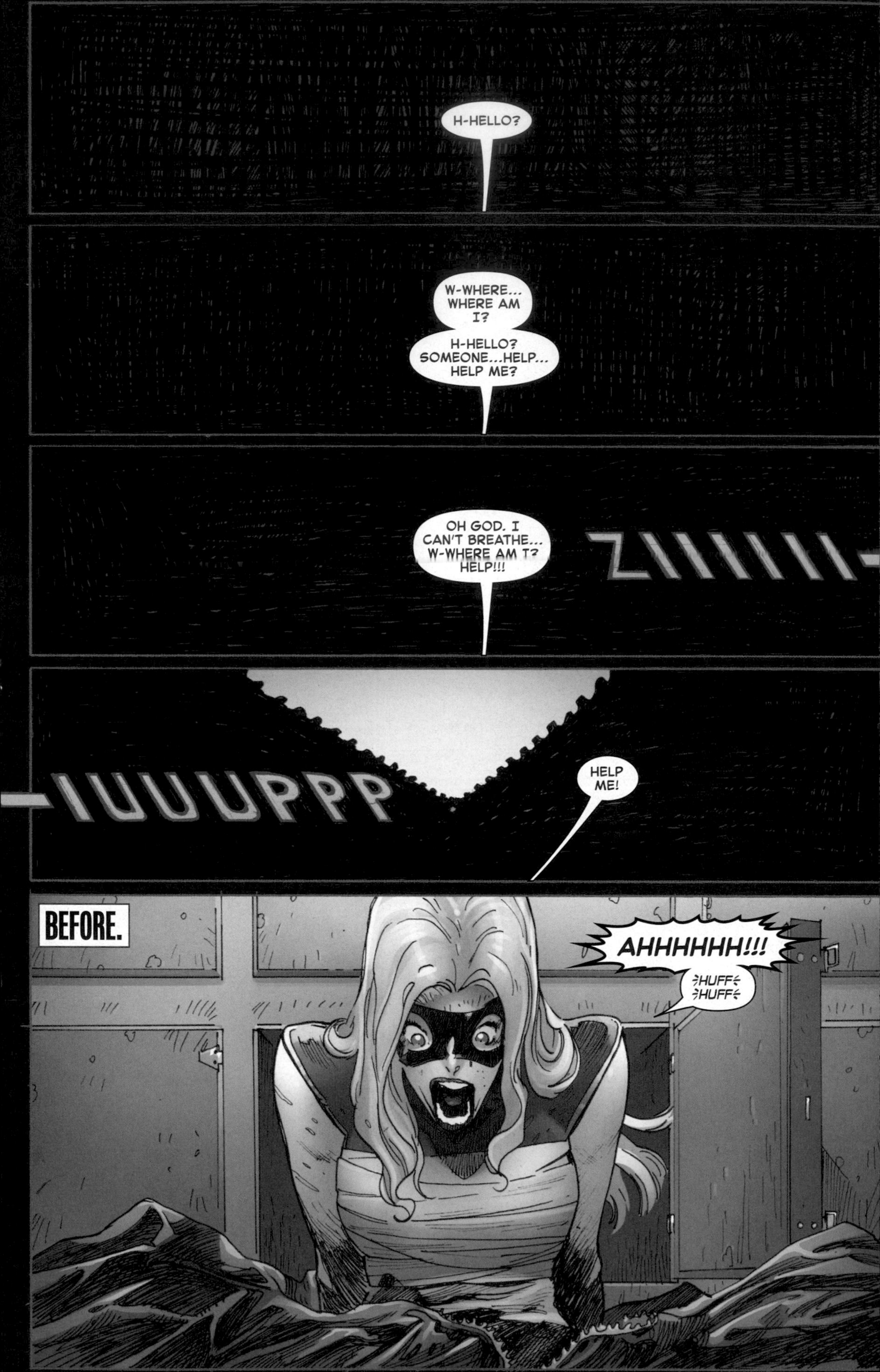

H-HELLO?
W-WHERE... WHERE AM I?
H-HELLO? SOMEONE...HELP... HELP ME?
OH GOD. I CAN'T BREATHE... W-WHERE AM I? HELP!!!
ZIIIIII-
-IUUUPPP
HELP ME!
BEFORE.
AHHHHHH!!!
HUFF HUFF

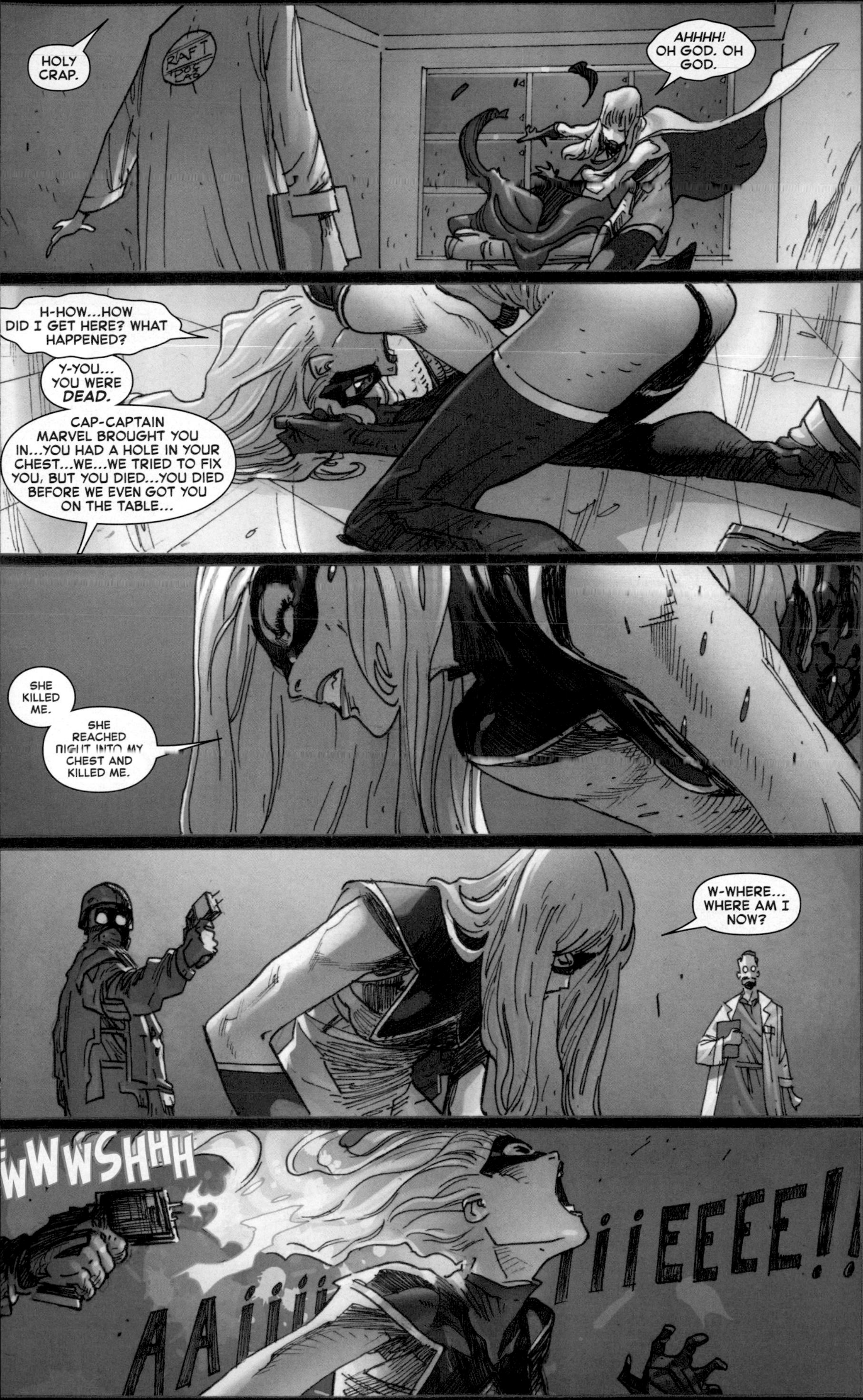
HOLY CRAP.
RAFT
AHHHH! OH GOD. OH GOD.
H-HOW...HOW DID I GET HERE? WHAT HAPPENED?
Y-YOU... YOU WERE DEAD.
CAP-CAPTAIN MARVEL BROUGHT YOU IN...YOU HAD A HOLE IN YOUR CHEST...WE...WE TRIED TO FIX YOU, BUT YOU DIED...YOU DIED BEFORE WE EVEN GOT YOU ON THE TABLE...
SHE KILLED ME.
SHE REACHED INTO MY CHEST AND KILLED ME.
W-WHERE... WHERE AM I NOW?
WWWSHHH
AAiiiiEEEE!!

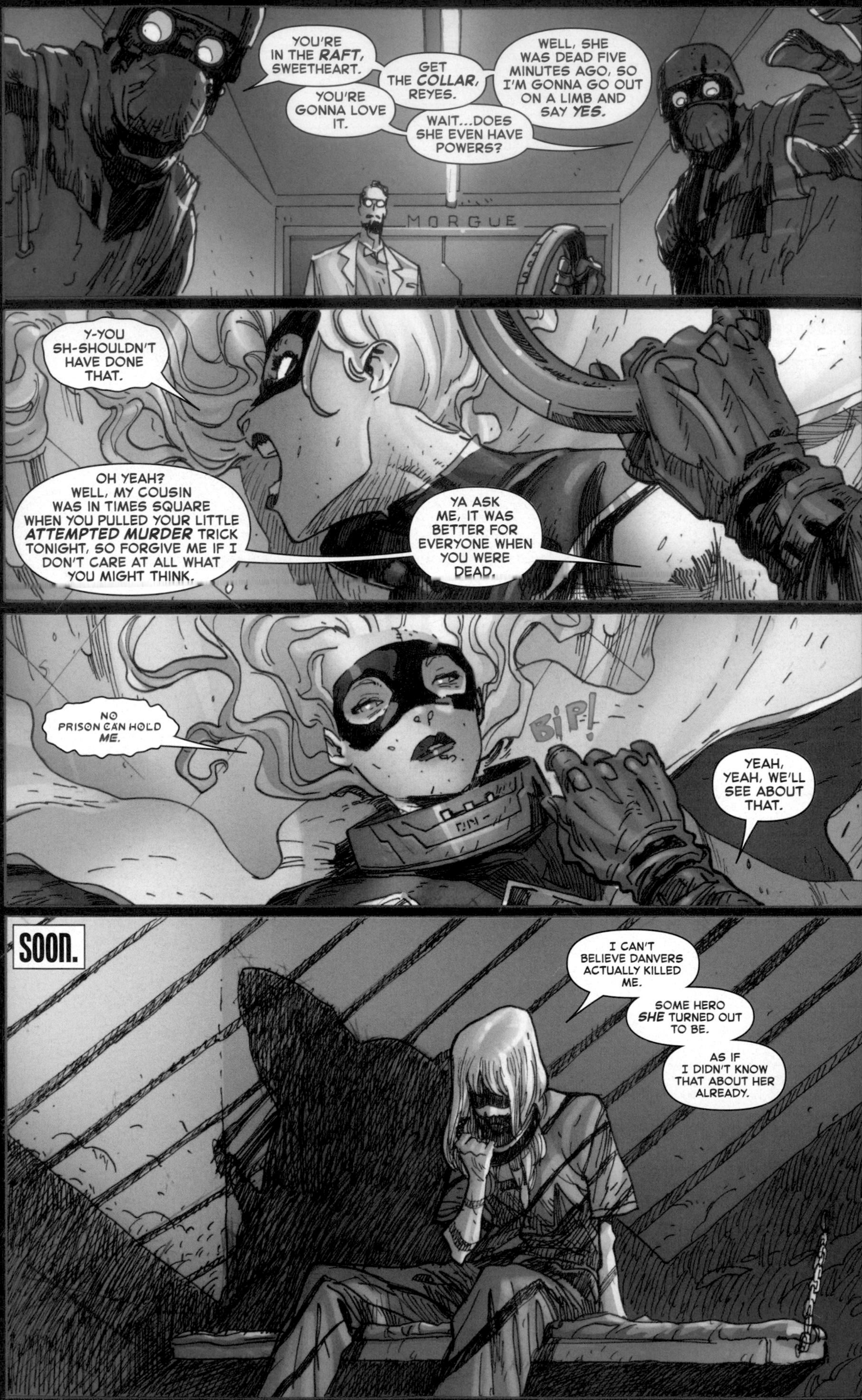
YOU'RE IN THE RAFT, SWEETHEART.
YOU'RE GONNA LOVE IT.
GET THE COLLAR, REYES.
WAIT...DOES SHE EVEN HAVE POWERS?
WELL, SHE WAS DEAD FIVE MINUTES AGO, SO I'M GONNA GO OUT ON A LIMB AND SAY YES.
MORGUE
Y-YOU SH-SHOULDN'T HAVE DONE THAT.
OH YEAH? WELL, MY COUSIN WAS IN TIMES SQUARE WHEN YOU PULLED YOUR LITTLE ATTEMPTED MURDER TRICK TONIGHT, SO FORGIVE ME IF I DON'T CARE AT ALL WHAT YOU MIGHT THINK.
YA ASK ME, IT WAS BETTER FOR EVERYONE WHEN YOU WERE DEAD.
NO PRISON CAN HOLD ME.
BIP!
YEAH, YEAH, WE'LL SEE ABOUT THAT.
SOON.
I CAN'T BELIEVE DANVERS ACTUALLY KILLED ME.
SOME HERO SHE TURNED OUT TO BE.
AS IF I DIDN'T KNOW THAT ABOUT HER ALREADY.

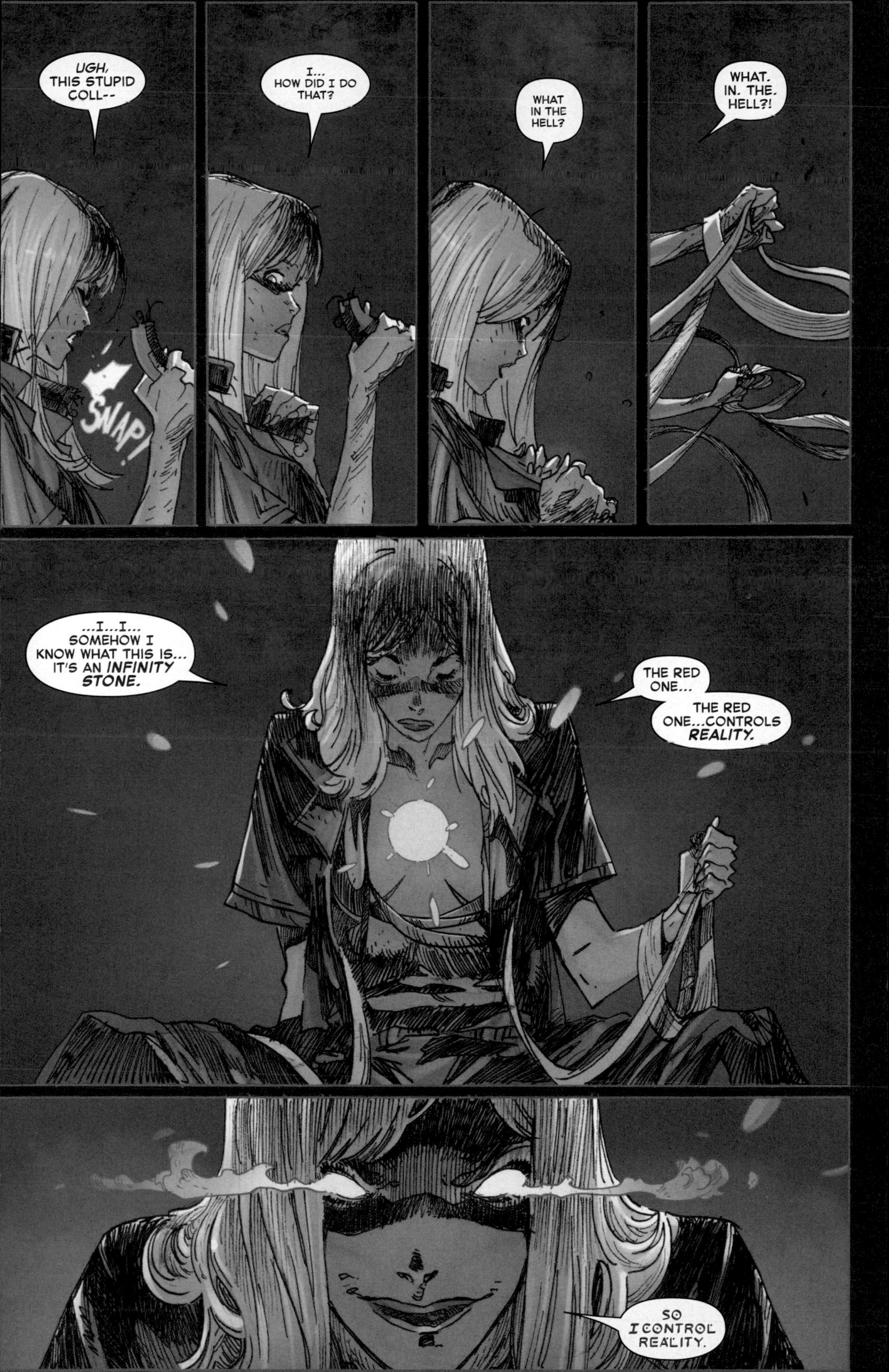
UGH, THIS STUPID COLL--
SNAP!
I... HOW DID I DO THAT?
WHAT IN THE HELL?
WHAT. IN. THE. HELL?!
...I...I... SOMEHOW I KNOW WHAT THIS IS... IT'S AN *INFINITY STONE.*
THE RED ONE...
THE RED ONE...CONTROLS *REALITY.*
SO *I* CONTROL REALITY.

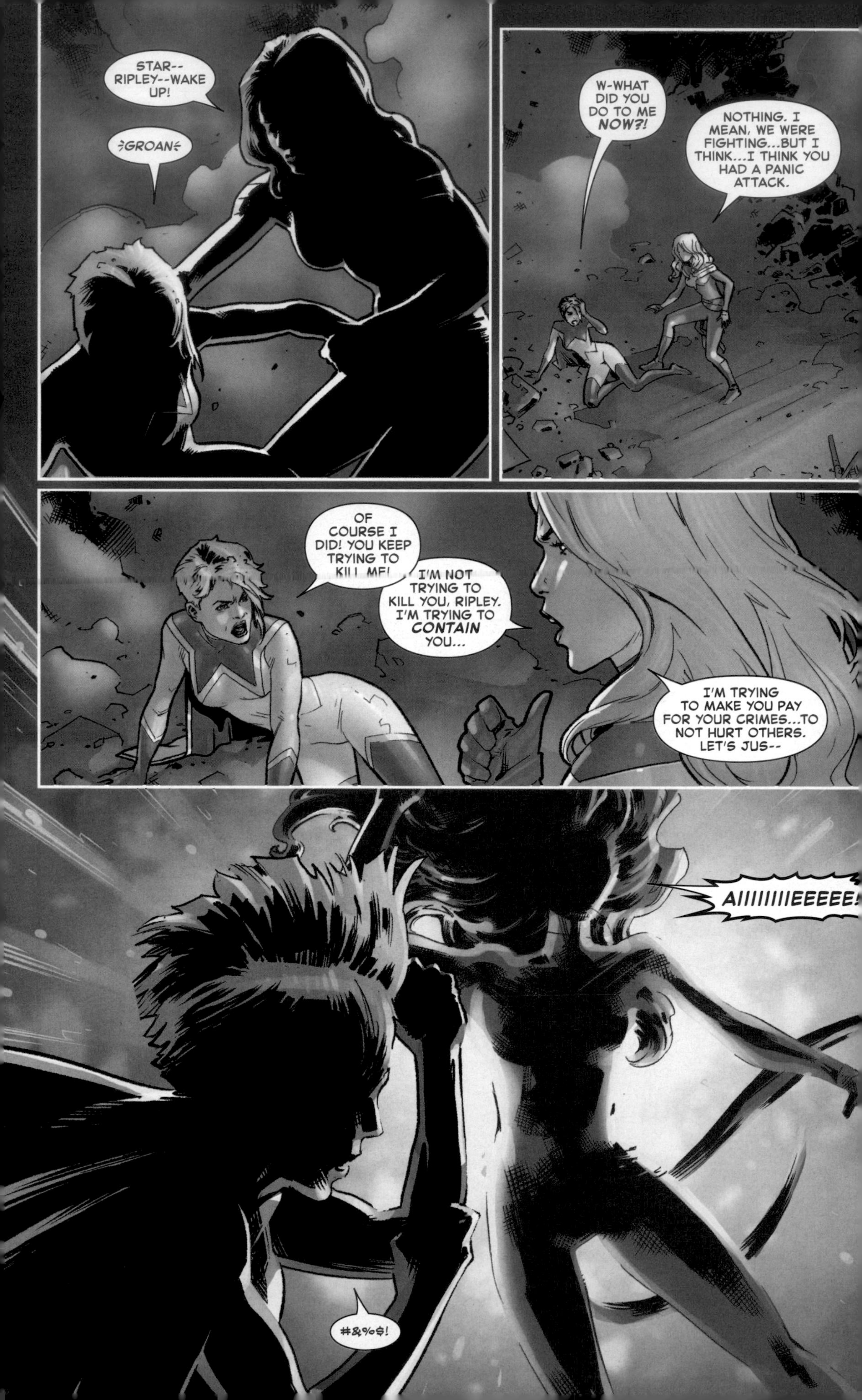
STAR--
RIPLEY--WAKE UP!
GROAN
W-WHAT DID YOU DO TO ME NOW?!
NOTHING. I MEAN, WE WERE FIGHTING...BUT I THINK...I THINK YOU HAD A PANIC ATTACK.
OF COURSE I DID! YOU KEEP TRYING TO KILL ME!
I'M NOT TRYING TO KILL YOU, RIPLEY. I'M TRYING TO CONTAIN YOU...
I'M TRYING TO MAKE YOU PAY FOR YOUR CRIMES...TO NOT HURT OTHERS. LET'S JUS--
AIIIIIIIIEEEEE!
#&%$!

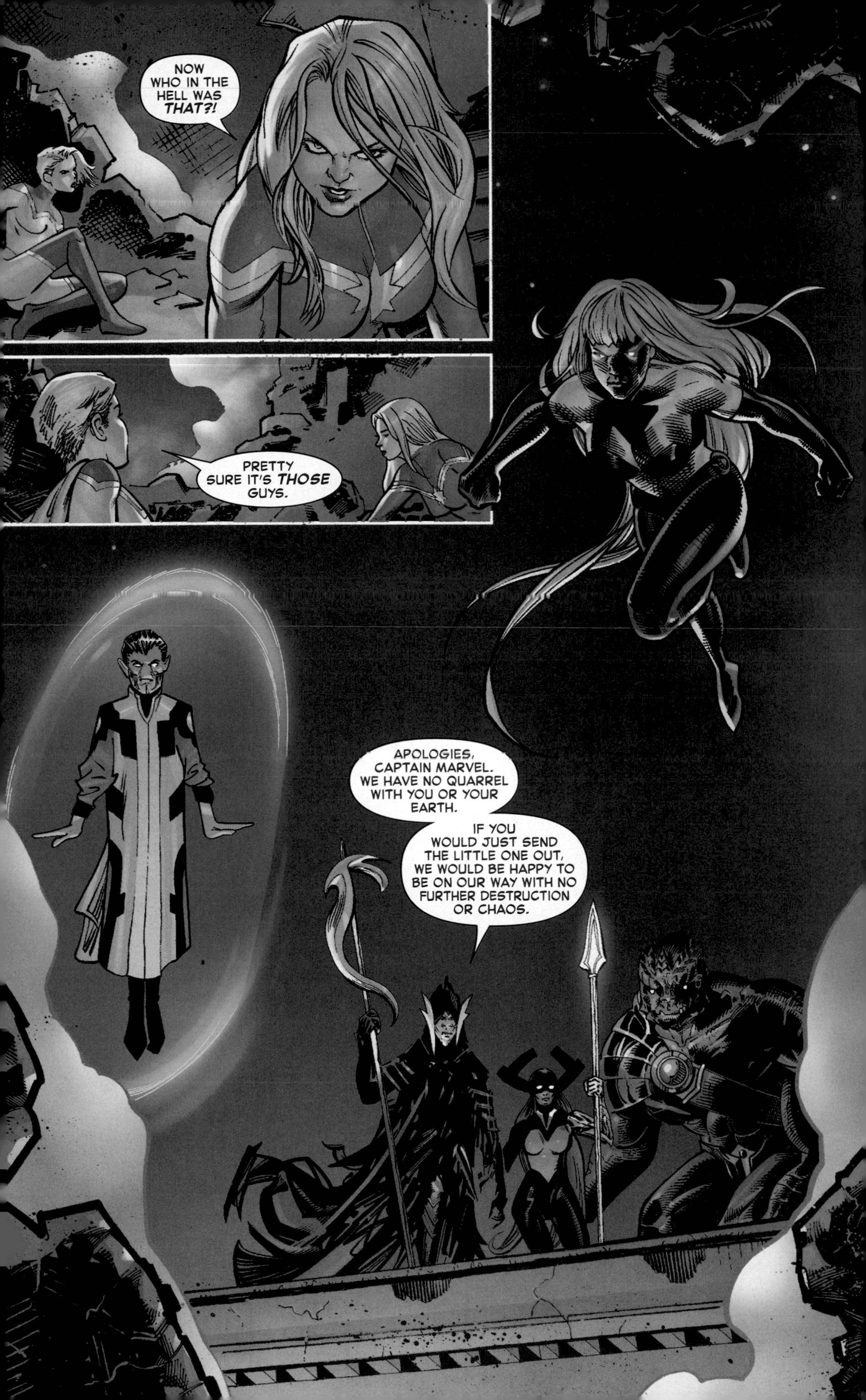
NOW WHO IN THE HELL WAS THAT?!
PRETTY SURE IT'S THOSE GUYS.
APOLOGIES, CAPTAIN MARVEL. WE HAVE NO QUARREL WITH YOU OR YOUR EARTH.
IF YOU WOULD JUST SEND THE LITTLE ONE OUT, WE WOULD BE HAPPY TO BE ON OUR WAY WITH NO FURTHER DESTRUCTION OR CHAOS.

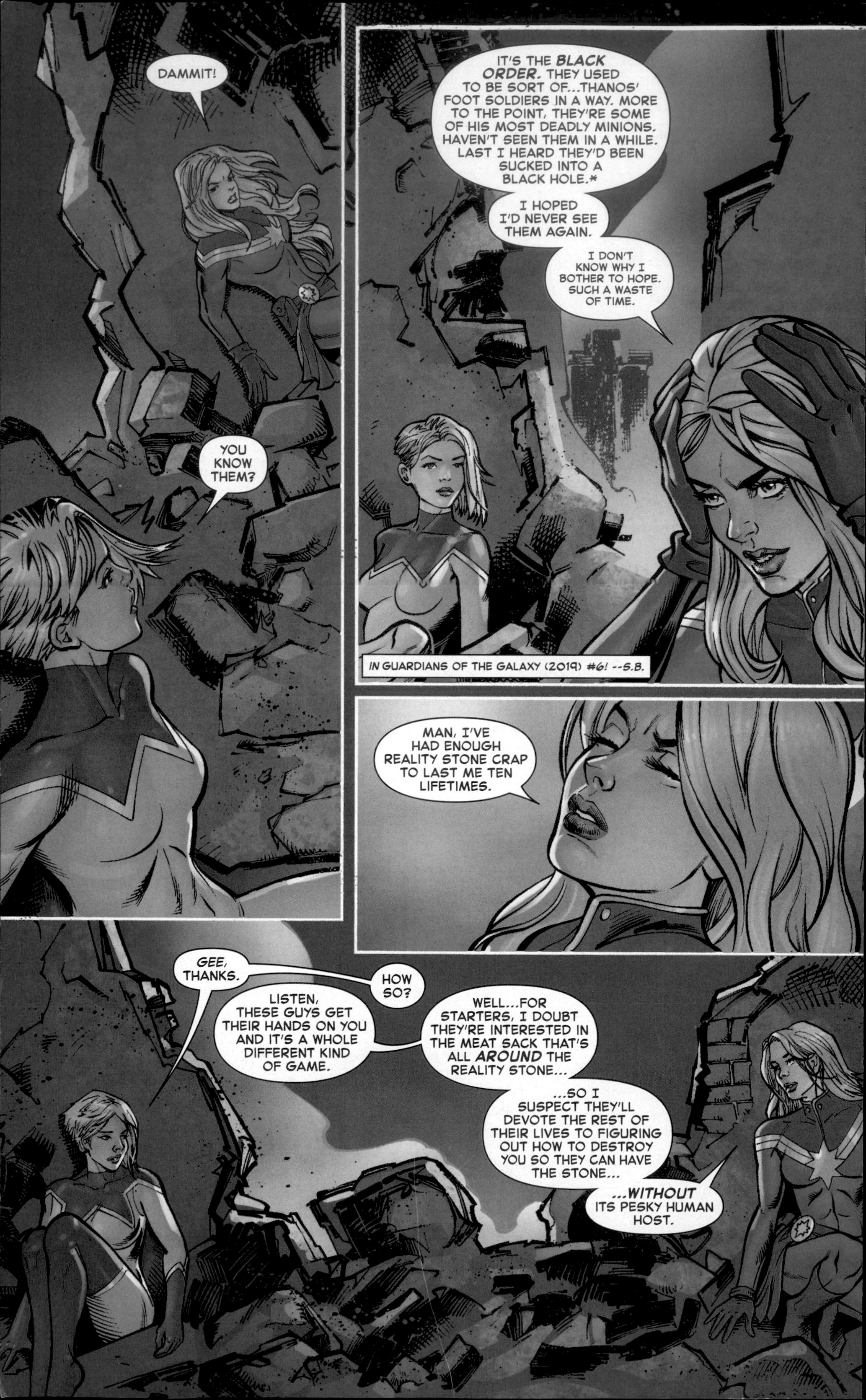
DAMMIT!
YOU KNOW THEM?
IT'S THE BLACK ORDER. THEY USED TO BE SORT OF...THANOS' FOOT SOLDIERS IN A WAY. MORE TO THE POINT, THEY'RE SOME OF HIS MOST DEADLY MINIONS. HAVEN'T SEEN THEM IN A WHILE. LAST I HEARD THEY'D BEEN SUCKED INTO A BLACK HOLE.*
I HOPED I'D NEVER SEE THEM AGAIN.
I DON'T KNOW WHY I BOTHER TO HOPE. SUCH A WASTE OF TIME.
*IN GUARDIANS OF THE GALAXY (2019) #6! --S.B.
MAN, I'VE HAD ENOUGH REALITY STONE CRAP TO LAST ME TEN LIFETIMES.
GEE, THANKS.
HOW SO?
LISTEN, THESE GUYS GET THEIR HANDS ON YOU AND IT'S A WHOLE DIFFERENT KIND OF GAME.
WELL...FOR STARTERS, I DOUBT THEY'RE INTERESTED IN THE MEAT SACK THAT'S ALL AROUND THE REALITY STONE...
...SO I SUSPECT THEY'LL DEVOTE THE REST OF THEIR LIVES TO FIGURING OUT HOW TO DESTROY YOU SO THEY CAN HAVE THE STONE...
...WITHOUT ITS PESKY HUMAN HOST.

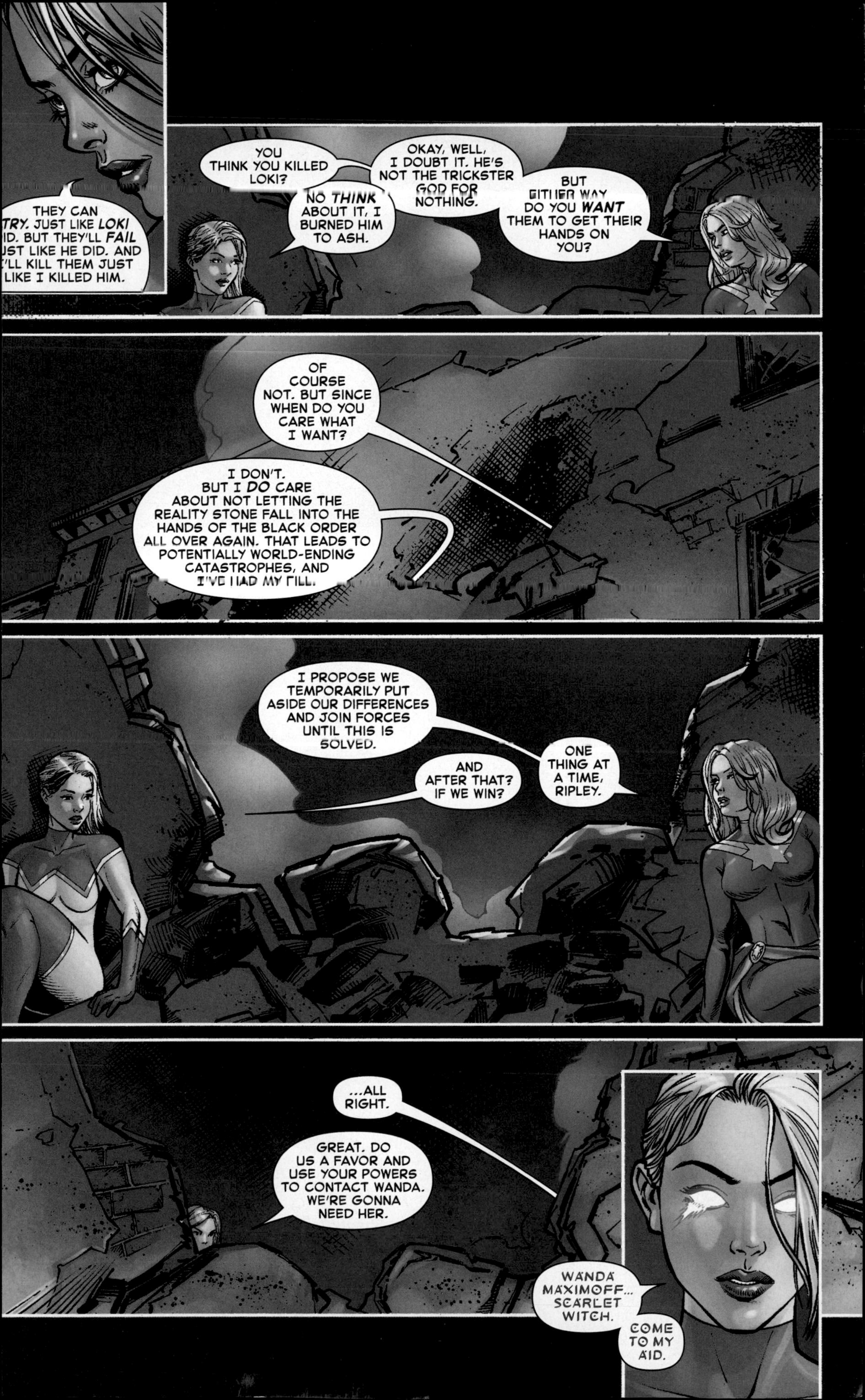

THEY CAN TRY. JUST LIKE LOKI ID. BUT THEY'LL FAIL UST LIKE HE DID. AND 'LL KILL THEM JUST LIKE I KILLED HIM.
YOU THINK YOU KILLED LOKI?
NO THINK ABOUT IT, I BURNED HIM TO ASH.
OKAY, WELL, I DOUBT IT. HE'S NOT THE TRICKSTER GOD FOR NOTHING.
BUT EITHER WAY DO YOU WANT THEM TO GET THEIR HANDS ON YOU?
OF COURSE NOT. BUT SINCE WHEN DO YOU CARE WHAT I WANT?
I DON'T. BUT I DO CARE ABOUT NOT LETTING THE REALITY STONE FALL INTO THE HANDS OF THE BLACK ORDER ALL OVER AGAIN. THAT LEADS TO POTENTIALLY WORLD-ENDING CATASTROPHES, AND I'VE HAD MY FILL.
I PROPOSE WE TEMPORARILY PUT ASIDE OUR DIFFERENCES AND JOIN FORCES UNTIL THIS IS SOLVED.
AND AFTER THAT? IF WE WIN?
ONE THING AT A TIME, RIPLEY.
...ALL RIGHT.
GREAT. DO US A FAVOR AND USE YOUR POWERS TO CONTACT WANDA. WE'RE GONNA NEED HER.
WANDA MAXIMOFF... SCARLET WITCH.
COME TO MY AID.

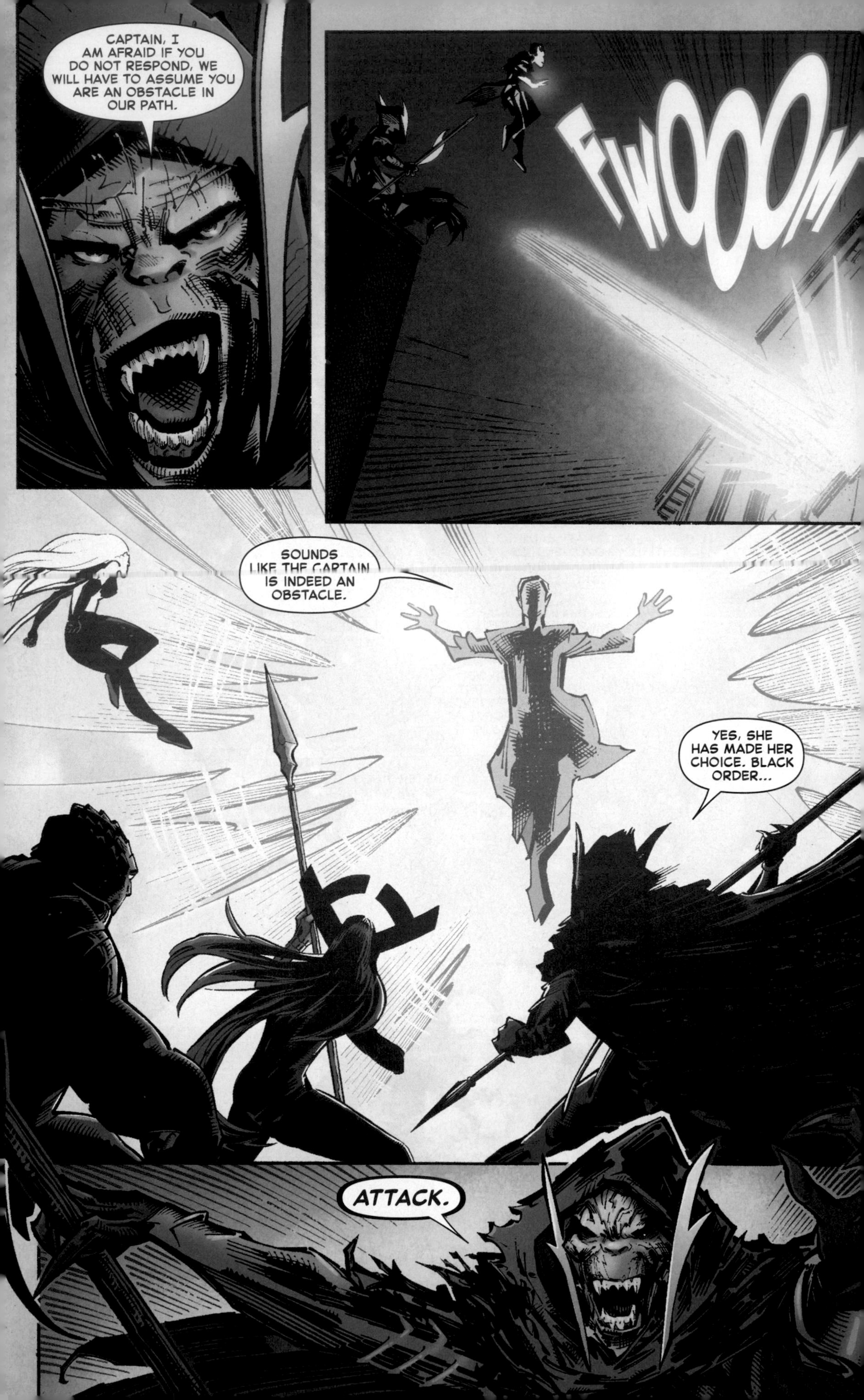
CAPTAIN, I AM AFRAID IF YOU DO NOT RESPOND, WE WILL HAVE TO ASSUME YOU ARE AN OBSTACLE IN OUR PATH.
FWOOOM
SOUNDS LIKE THE CAPTAIN IS INDEED AN OBSTACLE.
YES, SHE HAS MADE HER CHOICE. BLACK ORDER...
ATTACK.

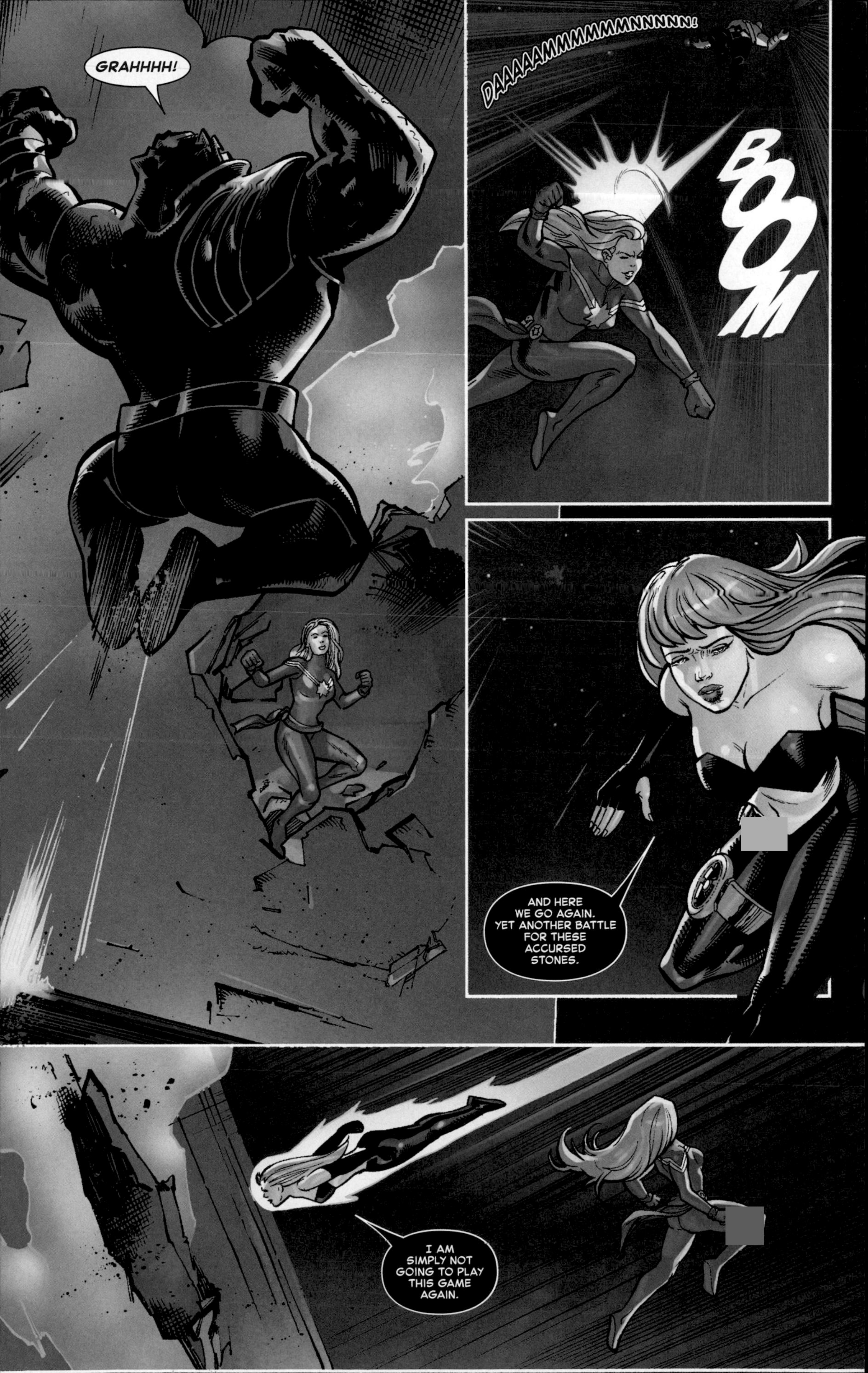
GRAHHHH!
DAAAAAMMMMMMMNNNNNN!
BOOM
AND HERE WE GO AGAIN. YET ANOTHER BATTLE FOR THESE ACCURSED STONES.
I AM SIMPLY NOT GOING TO PLAY THIS GAME AGAIN.

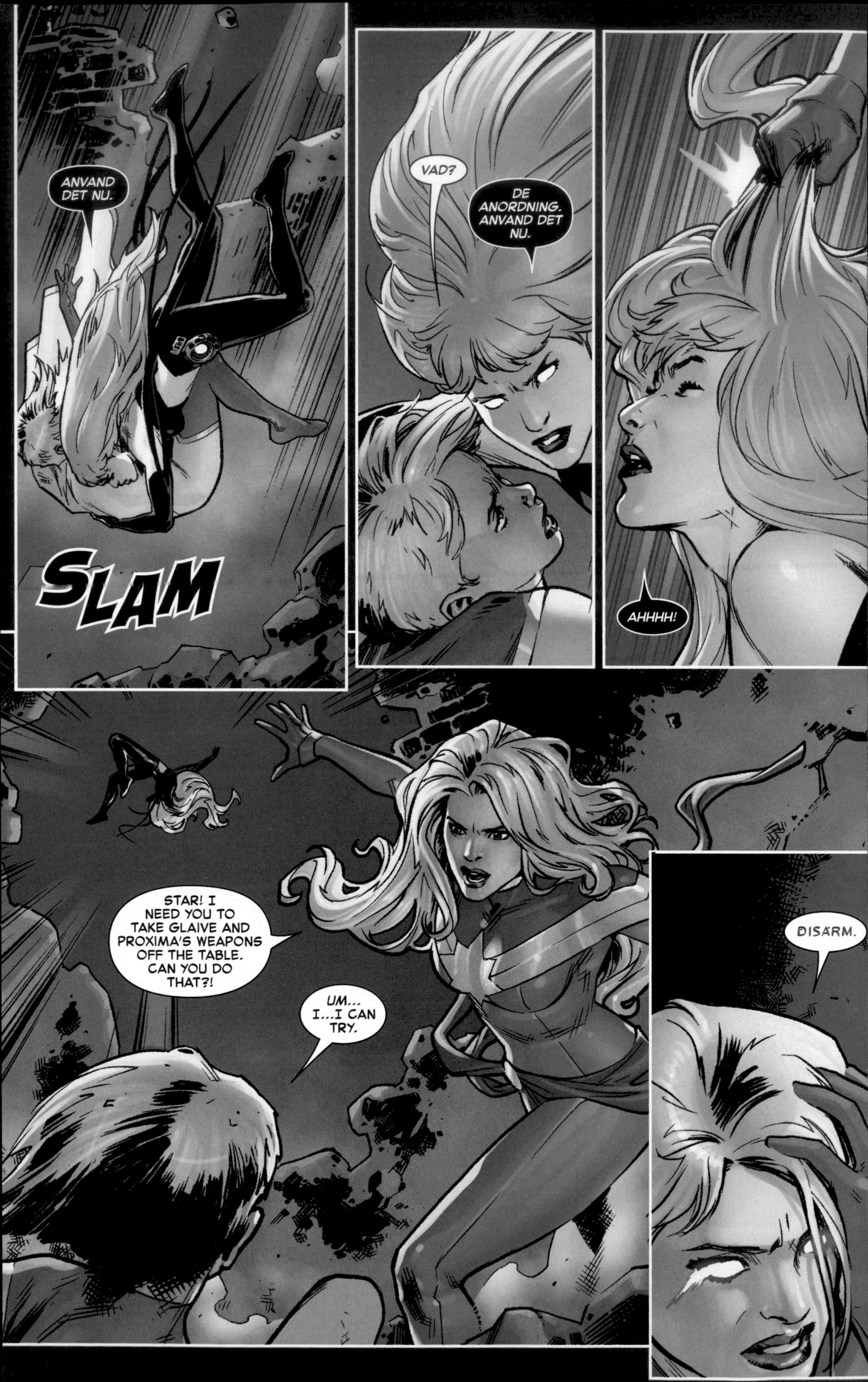
ANVAND DET NU.
SLAM
VAD?
DE ANORDNING. ANVAND DET NU.
AHHHH!
STAR! I NEED YOU TO TAKE GLAIVE AND PROXIMA'S WEAPONS OFF THE TABLE. CAN YOU DO THAT?!
UM... I...I CAN TRY.
DISARM.

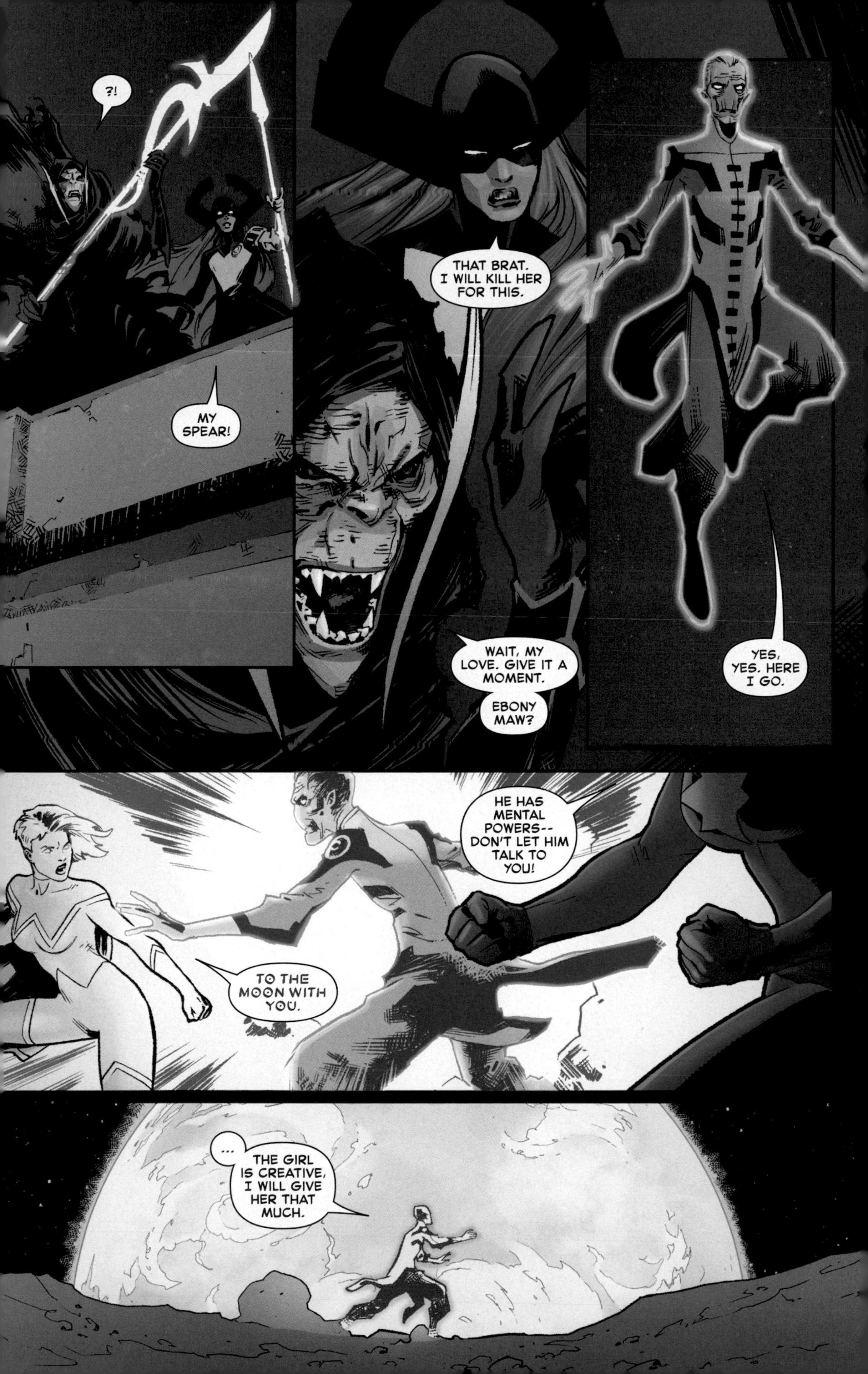
?!
MY SPEAR!
THAT BRAT. I WILL KILL HER FOR THIS.
WAIT, MY LOVE. GIVE IT A MOMENT.
EBONY MAW?
YES, YES. HERE I GO.
HE HAS MENTAL POWERS-- DON'T LET HIM TALK TO YOU!
TO THE MOON WITH YOU.
...
THE GIRL IS CREATIVE, I WILL GIVE HER THAT MUCH.

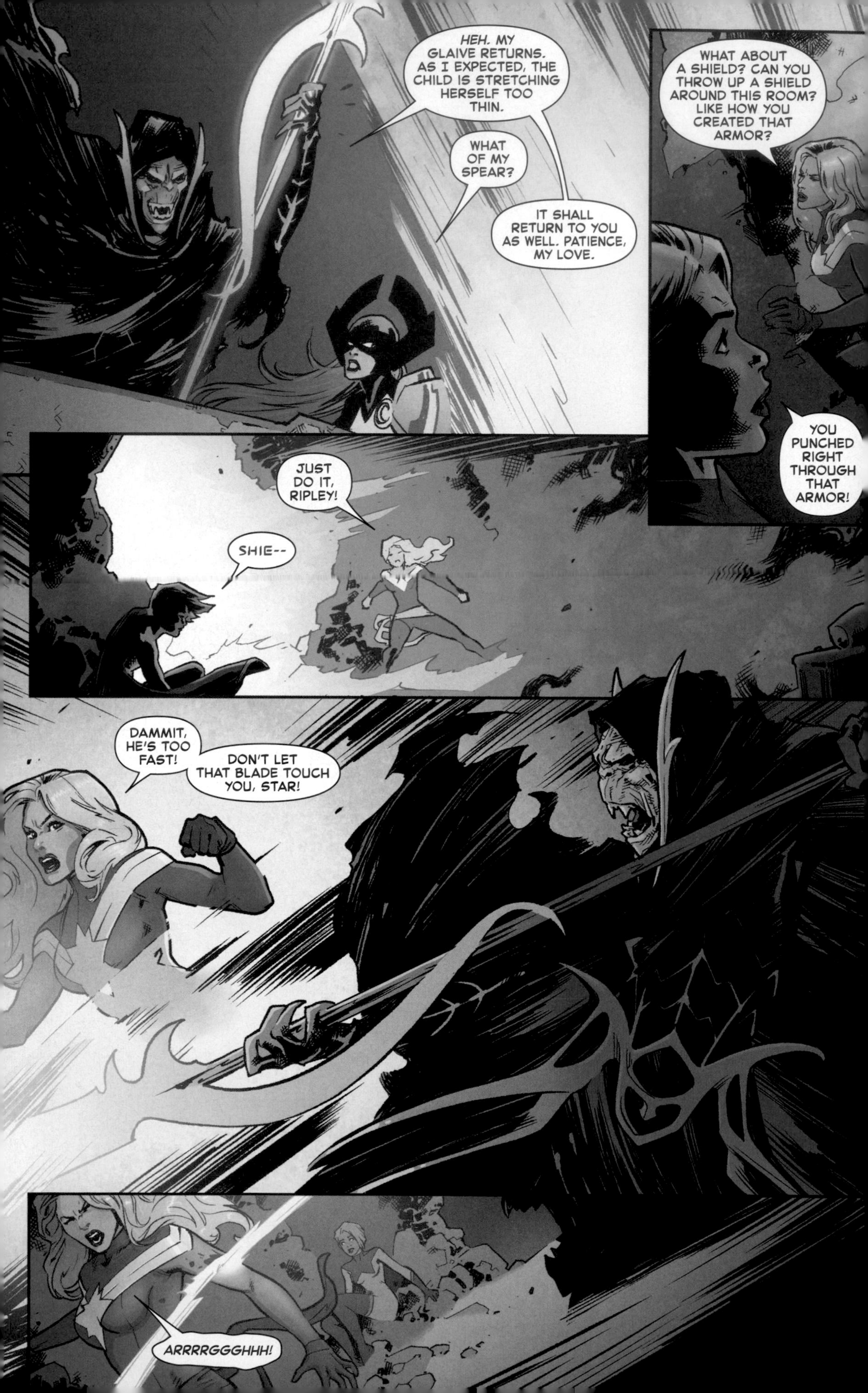
HEH. MY GLAIVE RETURNS. AS I EXPECTED, THE CHILD IS STRETCHING HERSELF TOO THIN.
WHAT OF MY SPEAR?
IT SHALL RETURN TO YOU AS WELL. PATIENCE, MY LOVE.
WHAT ABOUT A SHIELD? CAN YOU THROW UP A SHIELD AROUND THIS ROOM? LIKE HOW YOU CREATED THAT ARMOR?
YOU PUNCHED RIGHT THROUGH THAT ARMOR!
JUST DO IT, RIPLEY!
SHIE--
DAMMIT, HE'S TOO FAST!
DON'T LET THAT BLADE TOUCH YOU, STAR!
ARRRRGGGHHH!

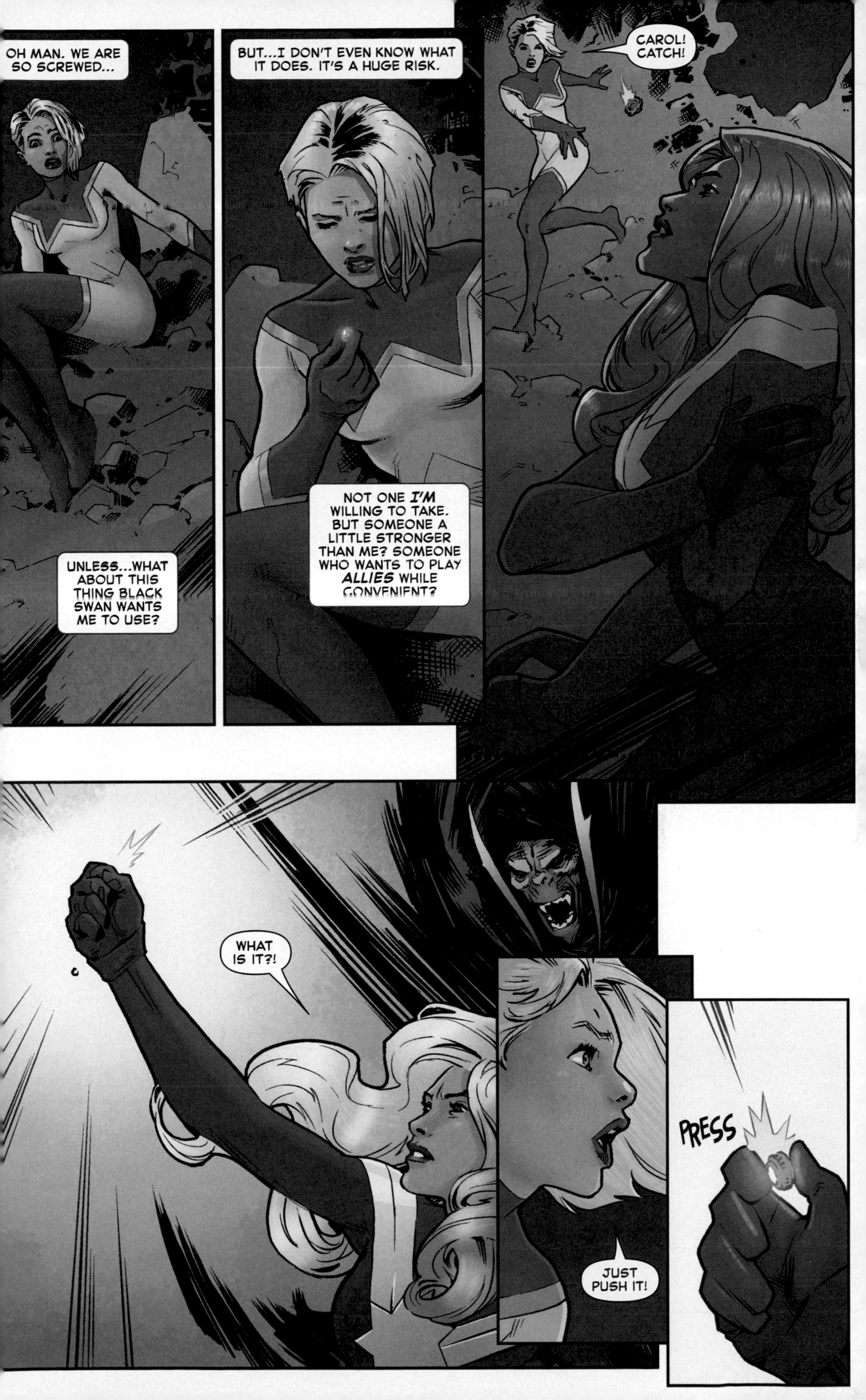
OH MAN. WE ARE SO SCREWED...
UNLESS...WHAT ABOUT THIS THING BLACK SWAN WANTS ME TO USE?
BUT...I DON'T EVEN KNOW WHAT IT DOES. IT'S A HUGE RISK.
NOT ONE I'M WILLING TO TAKE. BUT SOMEONE A LITTLE STRONGER THAN ME? SOMEONE WHO WANTS TO PLAY ALLIES WHILE CONVENIENT?
CAROL! CATCH!
WHAT IS IT?!
JUST PUSH IT!
PRESS

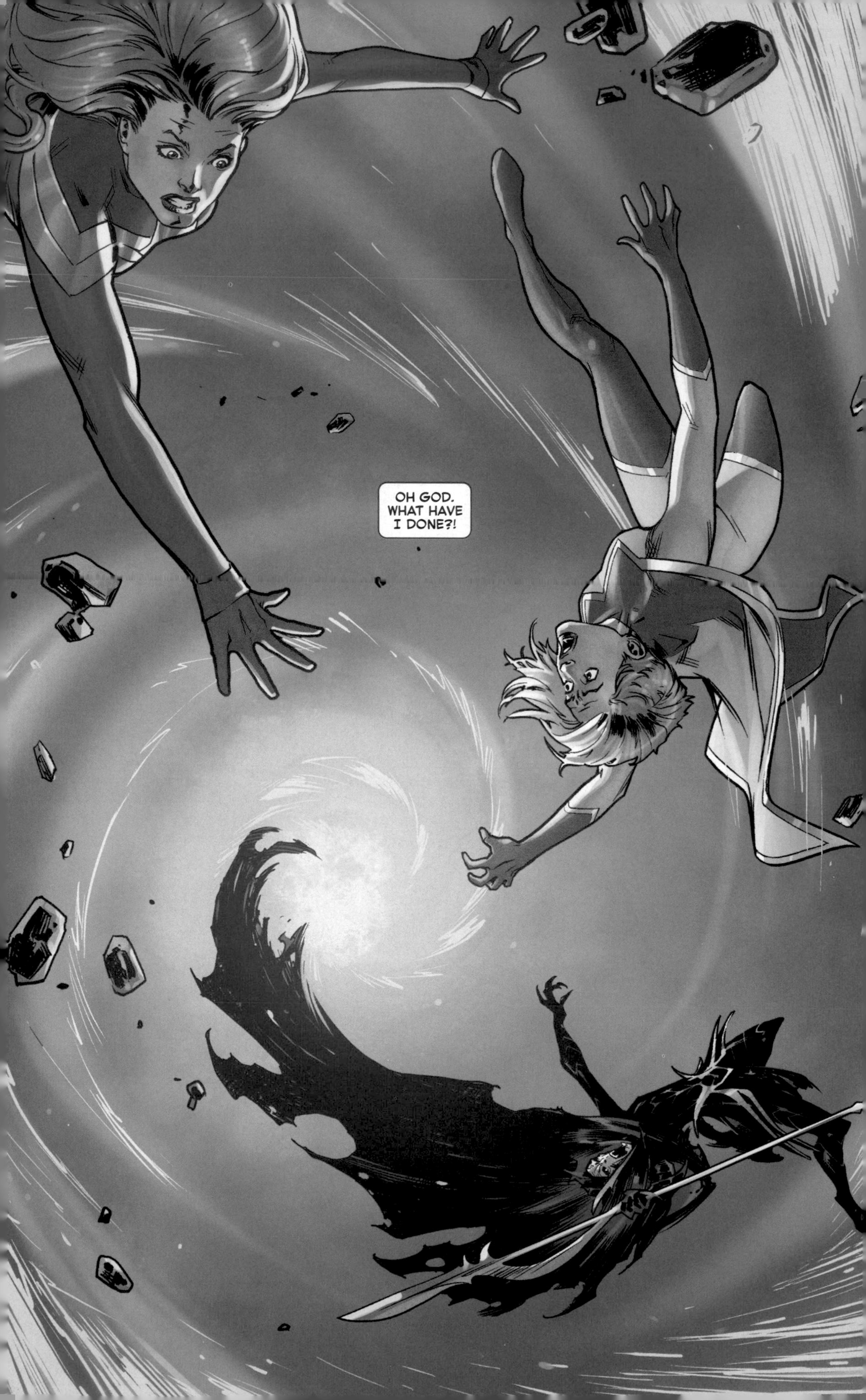
OH GOD. WHAT HAVE I DONE?!

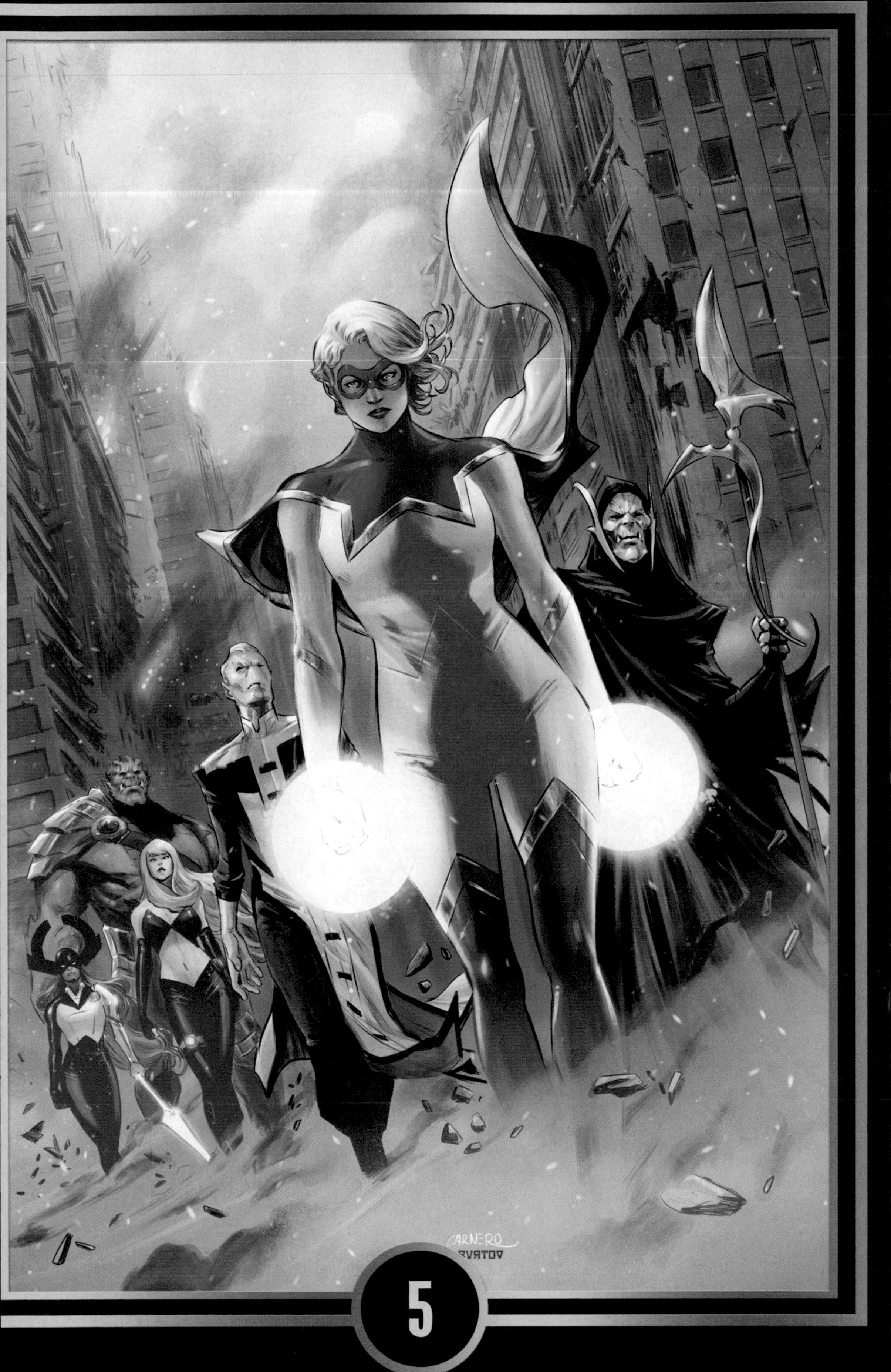

5

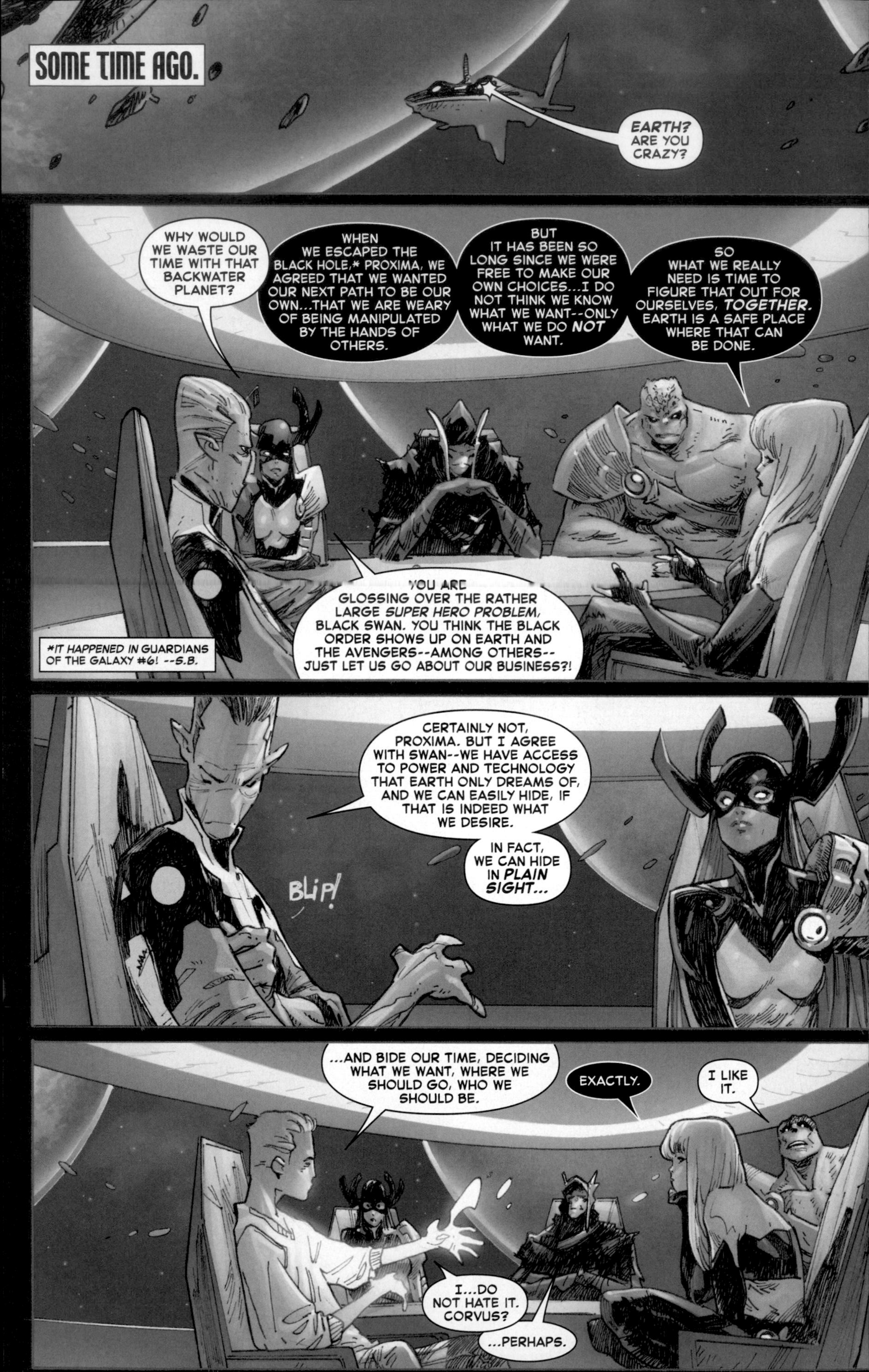
SOME TIME AGO.
EARTH? ARE YOU CRAZY?
WHY WOULD WE WASTE OUR TIME WITH THAT BACKWATER PLANET?
WHEN WE ESCAPED THE BLACK HOLE,* PROXIMA, WE AGREED THAT WE WANTED OUR NEXT PATH TO BE OUR OWN...THAT WE ARE WEARY OF BEING MANIPULATED BY THE HANDS OF OTHERS.
BUT IT HAS BEEN SO LONG SINCE WE WERE FREE TO MAKE OUR OWN CHOICES...I DO NOT THINK WE KNOW WHAT WE WANT--ONLY WHAT WE DO NOT WANT.
SO WHAT WE REALLY NEED IS TIME TO FIGURE THAT OUT FOR OURSELVES, TOGETHER. EARTH IS A SAFE PLACE WHERE THAT CAN BE DONE.
YOU ARE GLOSSING OVER THE RATHER LARGE SUPER HERO PROBLEM, BLACK SWAN. YOU THINK THE BLACK ORDER SHOWS UP ON EARTH AND THE AVENGERS--AMONG OTHERS--JUST LET US GO ABOUT OUR BUSINESS?!
*IT HAPPENED IN GUARDIANS OF THE GALAXY #6! --S.B.
CERTAINLY NOT, PROXIMA. BUT I AGREE WITH SWAN--WE HAVE ACCESS TO POWER AND TECHNOLOGY THAT EARTH ONLY DREAMS OF, AND WE CAN EASILY HIDE, IF THAT IS INDEED WHAT WE DESIRE.
IN FACT, WE CAN HIDE IN PLAIN SIGHT...
BLIP!
...AND BIDE OUR TIME, DECIDING WHAT WE WANT, WHERE WE SHOULD GO, WHO WE SHOULD BE.
EXACTLY.
I LIKE IT.
I...DO NOT HATE IT. CORVUS?
...PERHAPS.

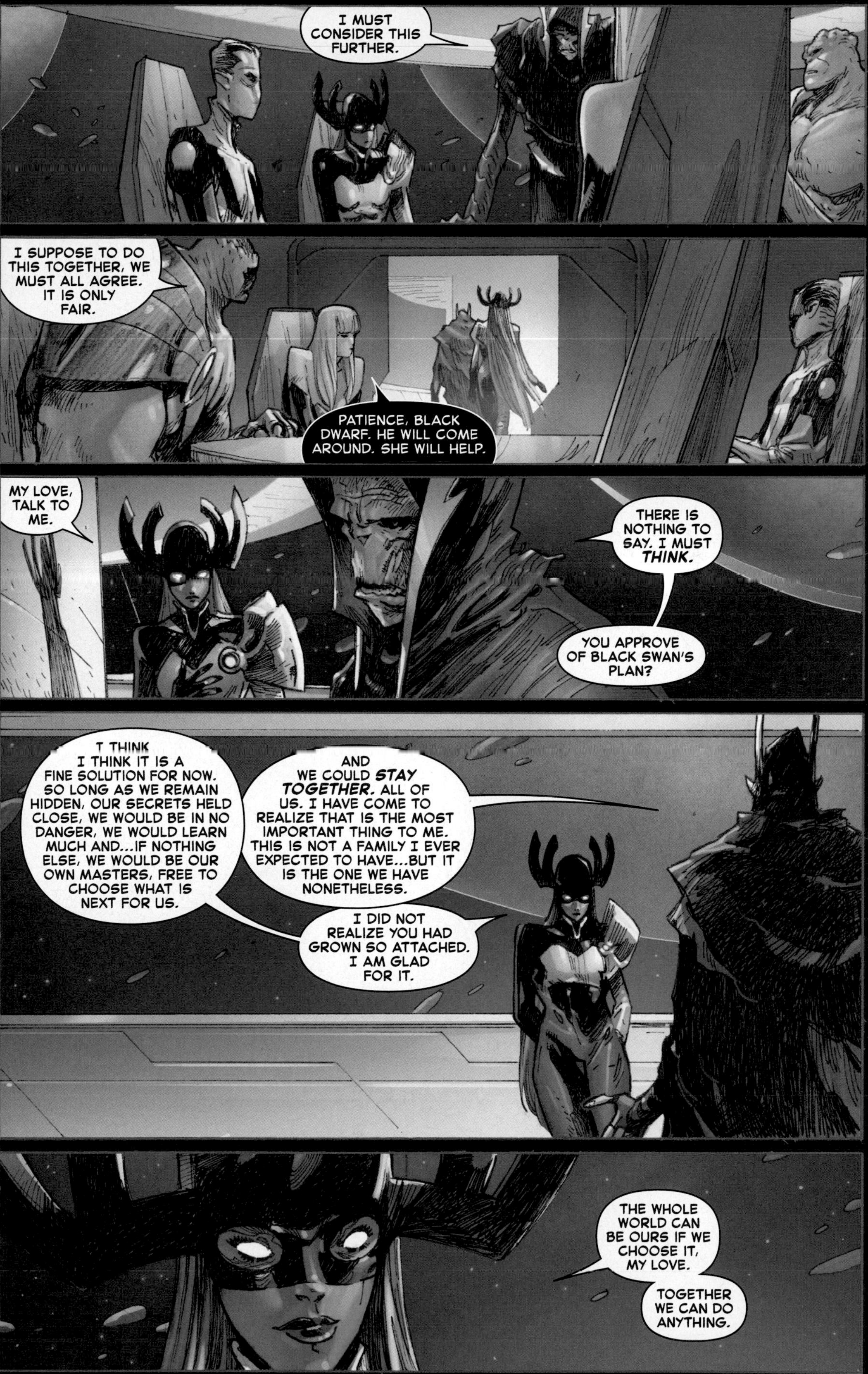
I MUST CONSIDER THIS FURTHER.
I SUPPOSE TO DO THIS TOGETHER, WE MUST ALL AGREE. IT IS ONLY FAIR.
PATIENCE, BLACK DWARF. HE WILL COME AROUND. SHE WILL HELP.
MY LOVE, TALK TO ME.
THERE IS NOTHING TO SAY. I MUST *THINK.*
YOU APPROVE OF BLACK SWAN'S PLAN?
T THINK
I THINK IT IS A FINE SOLUTION FOR NOW. SO LONG AS WE REMAIN HIDDEN, OUR SECRETS HELD CLOSE, WE WOULD BE IN NO DANGER, WE WOULD LEARN MUCH AND...IF NOTHING ELSE, WE WOULD BE OUR OWN MASTERS, FREE TO CHOOSE WHAT IS NEXT FOR US.
AND WE COULD *STAY TOGETHER.* ALL OF US. I HAVE COME TO REALIZE THAT IS THE MOST IMPORTANT THING TO ME. THIS IS NOT A FAMILY I EVER EXPECTED TO HAVE...BUT IT IS THE ONE WE HAVE NONETHELESS.
I DID NOT REALIZE YOU HAD GROWN SO ATTACHED. I AM GLAD FOR IT.
THE WHOLE WORLD CAN BE OURS IF WE CHOOSE IT, MY LOVE.
TOGETHER WE CAN DO ANYTHING.

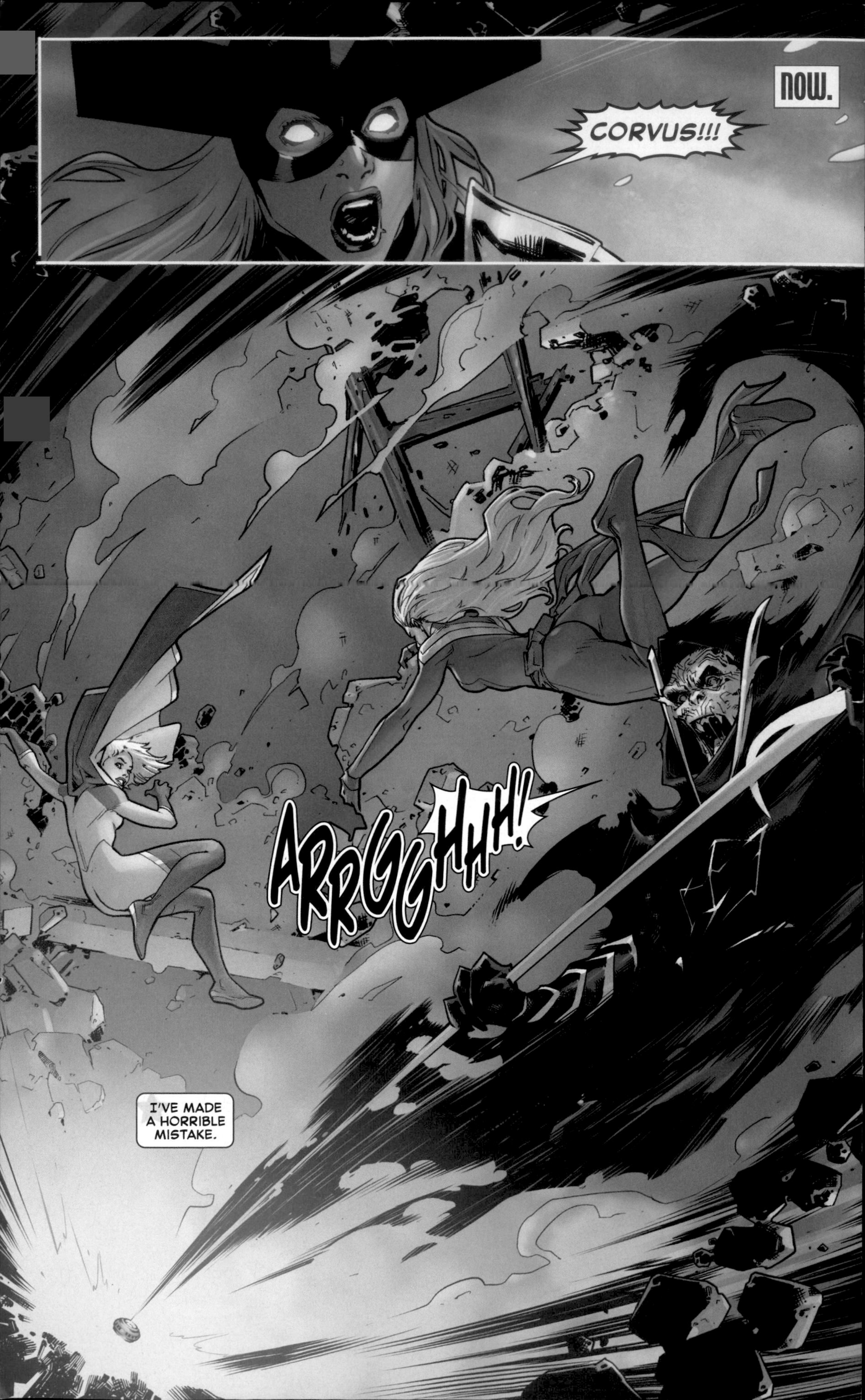
NOW.
CORVUS!!!
ARRGGHHH!
I'VE MADE A HORRIBLE MISTAKE.

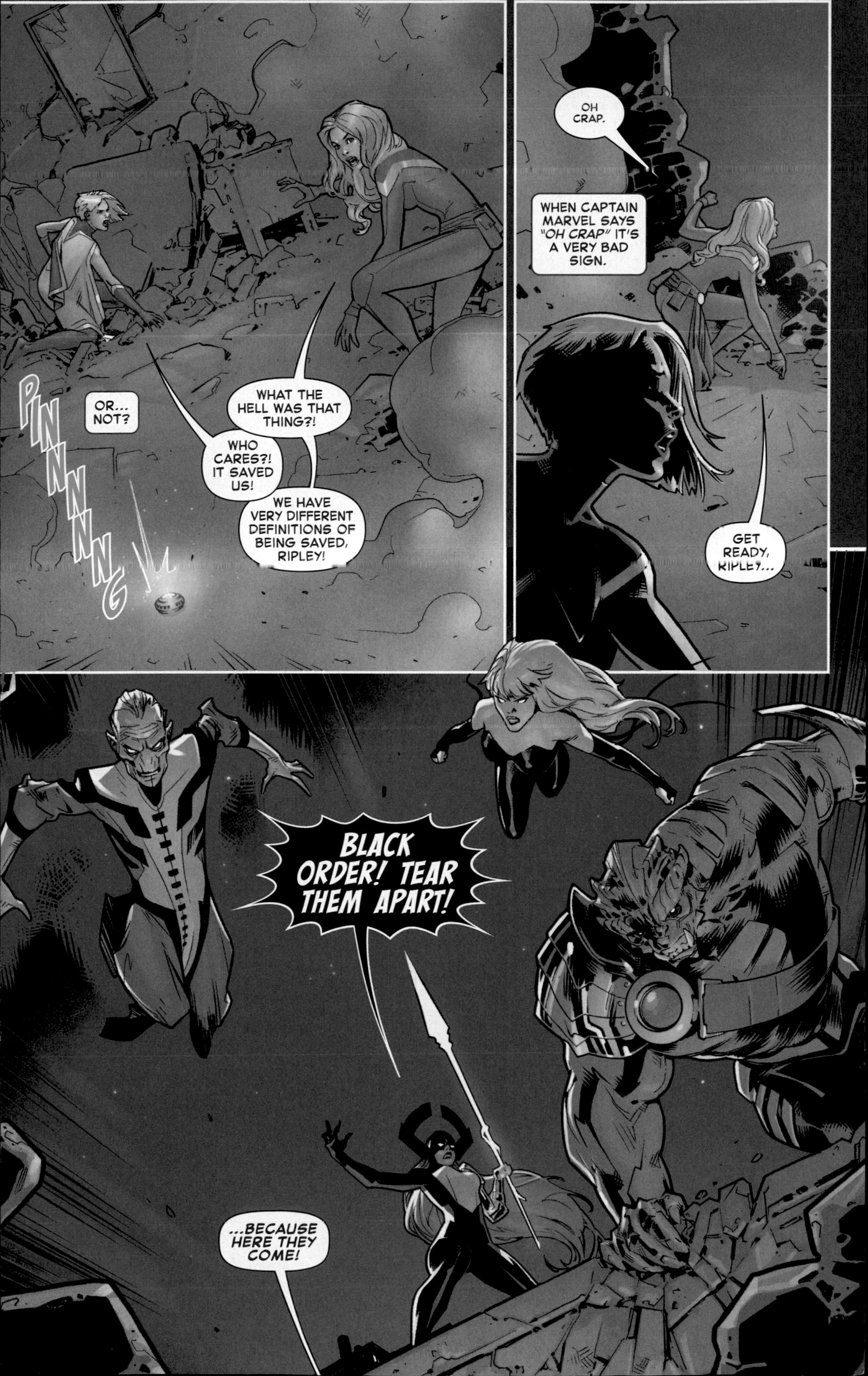
WHAT THE HELL WAS THAT THING?!
WHO CARES?! IT SAVED US!
WE HAVE VERY DIFFERENT DEFINITIONS OF BEING SAVED, RIPLEY!
PINNNNNG
OR... NOT?
OH CRAP.
WHEN CAPTAIN MARVEL SAYS "OH CRAP" IT'S A VERY BAD SIGN.
GET READY, RIPLEY...
BLACK ORDER! TEAR THEM APART!
...BECAUSE HERE THEY COME!

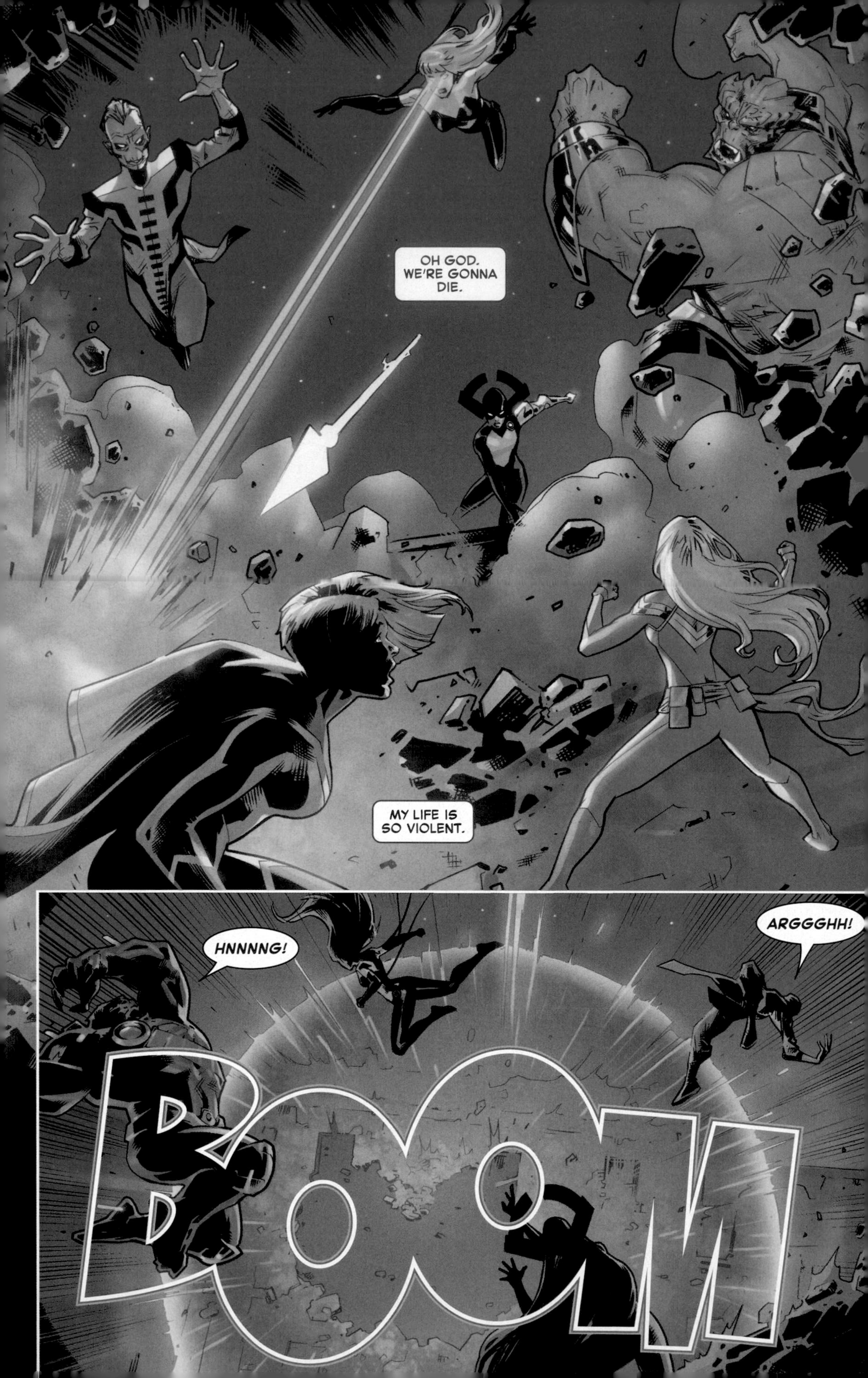
OH GOD. WE'RE GONNA DIE.
MY LIFE IS SO VIOLENT.
HNNNNG!
ARGGGHH!
BOOM

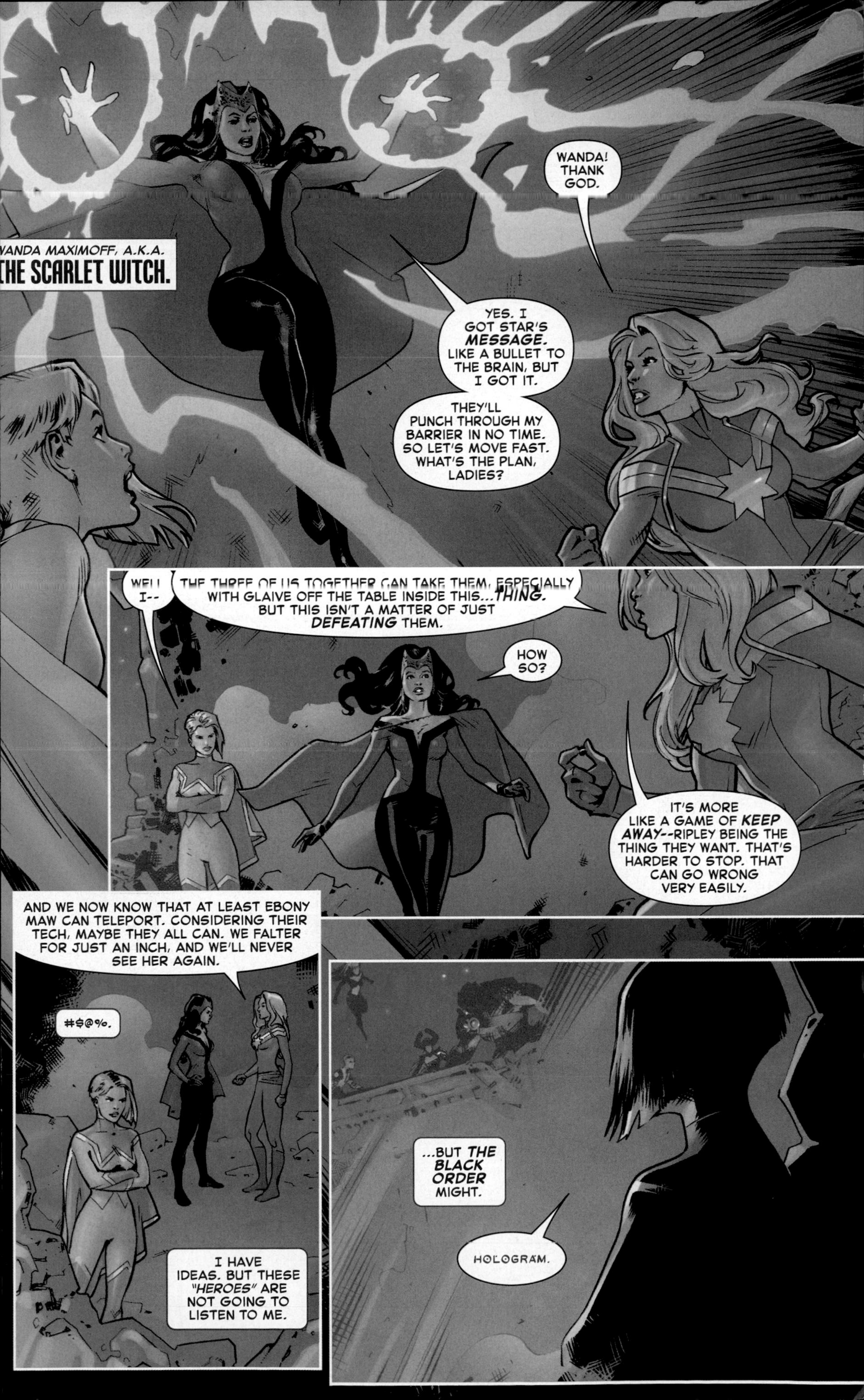
WANDA MAXIMOFF, A.K.A.
THE SCARLET WITCH.
WANDA! THANK GOD.
YES. I GOT STAR'S MESSAGE. LIKE A BULLET TO THE BRAIN, BUT I GOT IT.
THEY'LL PUNCH THROUGH MY BARRIER IN NO TIME. SO LET'S MOVE FAST. WHAT'S THE PLAN, LADIES?
WELL I--
THE THREE OF US TOGETHER CAN TAKE THEM, ESPECIALLY WITH GLAIVE OFF THE TABLE INSIDE THIS...THING. BUT THIS ISN'T A MATTER OF JUST DEFEATING THEM.
HOW SO?
IT'S MORE LIKE A GAME OF KEEP AWAY--RIPLEY BEING THE THING THEY WANT. THAT'S HARDER TO STOP. THAT CAN GO WRONG VERY EASILY.
AND WE NOW KNOW THAT AT LEAST EBONY MAW CAN TELEPORT. CONSIDERING THEIR TECH, MAYBE THEY ALL CAN. WE FALTER FOR JUST AN INCH, AND WE'LL NEVER SEE HER AGAIN.
#$@%.
I HAVE IDEAS. BUT THESE "HEROES" ARE NOT GOING TO LISTEN TO ME.
...BUT THE BLACK ORDER MIGHT.
HOLOGRAM.

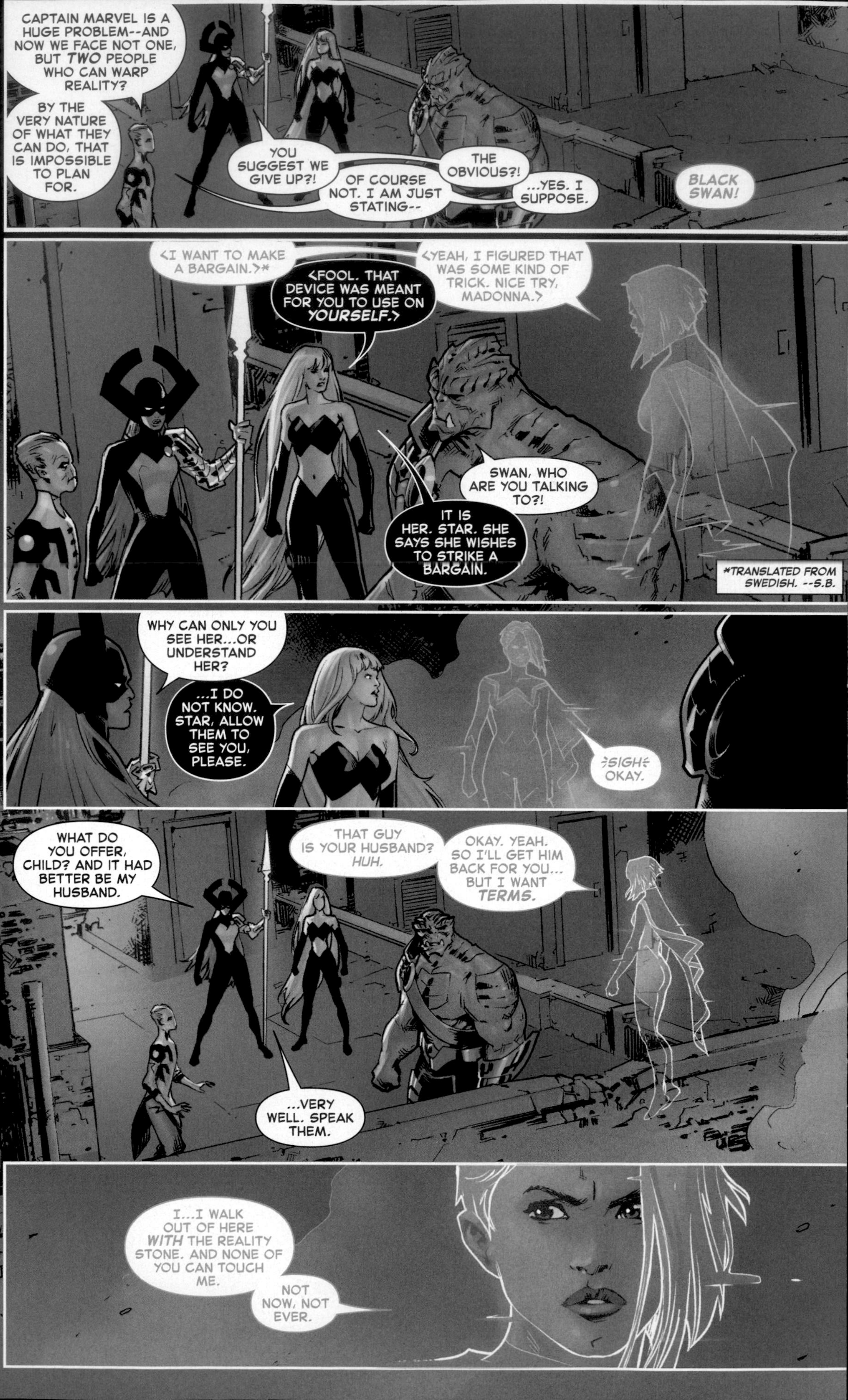
CAPTAIN MARVEL IS A HUGE PROBLEM--AND NOW WE FACE NOT ONE, BUT TWO PEOPLE WHO CAN WARP REALITY?
BY THE VERY NATURE OF WHAT THEY CAN DO, THAT IS IMPOSSIBLE TO PLAN FOR.
YOU SUGGEST WE GIVE UP?!
OF COURSE NOT. I AM JUST STATING--
THE OBVIOUS?!
...YES. I SUPPOSE.
BLACK SWAN!
<I WANT TO MAKE A BARGAIN.>*
<FOOL. THAT DEVICE WAS MEANT FOR YOU TO USE ON YOURSELF.>
<YEAH, I FIGURED THAT WAS SOME KIND OF TRICK. NICE TRY, MADONNA.>
SWAN, WHO ARE YOU TALKING TO?!
IT IS HER. STAR. SHE SAYS SHE WISHES TO STRIKE A BARGAIN.
*TRANSLATED FROM SWEDISH. --S.B.
WHY CAN ONLY YOU SEE HER...OR UNDERSTAND HER?
...I DO NOT KNOW. STAR, ALLOW THEM TO SEE YOU, PLEASE.
SIGH OKAY.
WHAT DO YOU OFFER, CHILD? AND IT HAD BETTER BE MY HUSBAND.
THAT GUY IS YOUR HUSBAND? HUH.
OKAY. YEAH. SO I'LL GET HIM BACK FOR YOU... BUT I WANT TERMS.
...VERY WELL. SPEAK THEM.
I...I WALK OUT OF HERE WITH THE REALITY STONE. AND NONE OF YOU CAN TOUCH ME.
NOT NOW, NOT EVER.

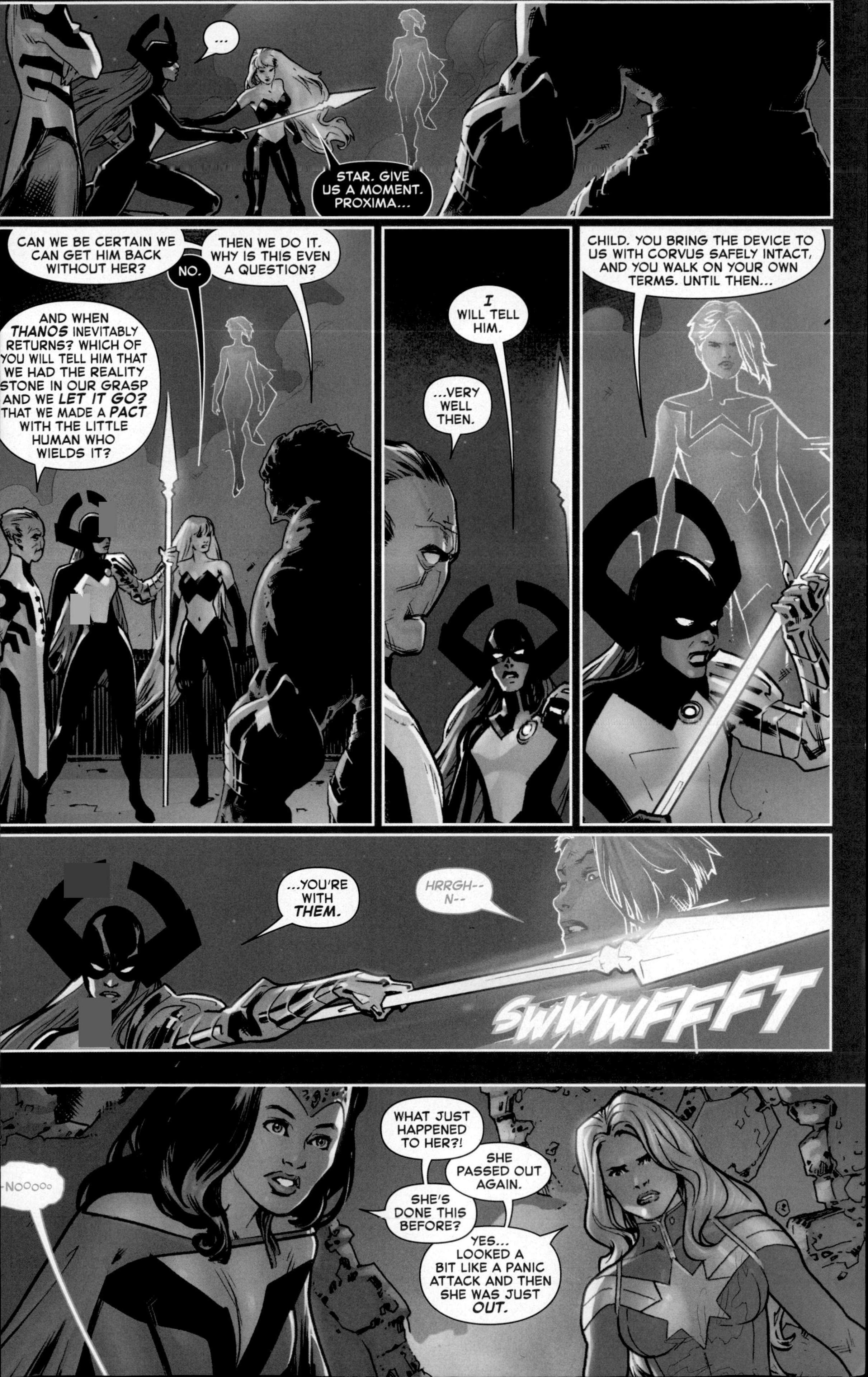
...
STAR. GIVE US A MOMENT. PROXIMA...
CAN WE BE CERTAIN WE CAN GET HIM BACK WITHOUT HER?
NO.
THEN WE DO IT. WHY IS THIS EVEN A QUESTION?
AND WHEN THANOS INEVITABLY RETURNS? WHICH OF YOU WILL TELL HIM THAT WE HAD THE REALITY STONE IN OUR GRASP AND WE LET IT GO? THAT WE MADE A PACT WITH THE LITTLE HUMAN WHO WIELDS IT?
I WILL TELL HIM.
...VERY WELL THEN.
CHILD. YOU BRING THE DEVICE TO US WITH CORVUS SAFELY INTACT, AND YOU WALK ON YOUR OWN TERMS. UNTIL THEN...
...YOU'RE WITH THEM.
HRRGH-- N--
SWWWFFFT
-NOOOOO
WHAT JUST HAPPENED TO HER?!
SHE PASSED OUT AGAIN.
SHE'S DONE THIS BEFORE?
YES... LOOKED A BIT LIKE A PANIC ATTACK AND THEN SHE WAS JUST OUT.

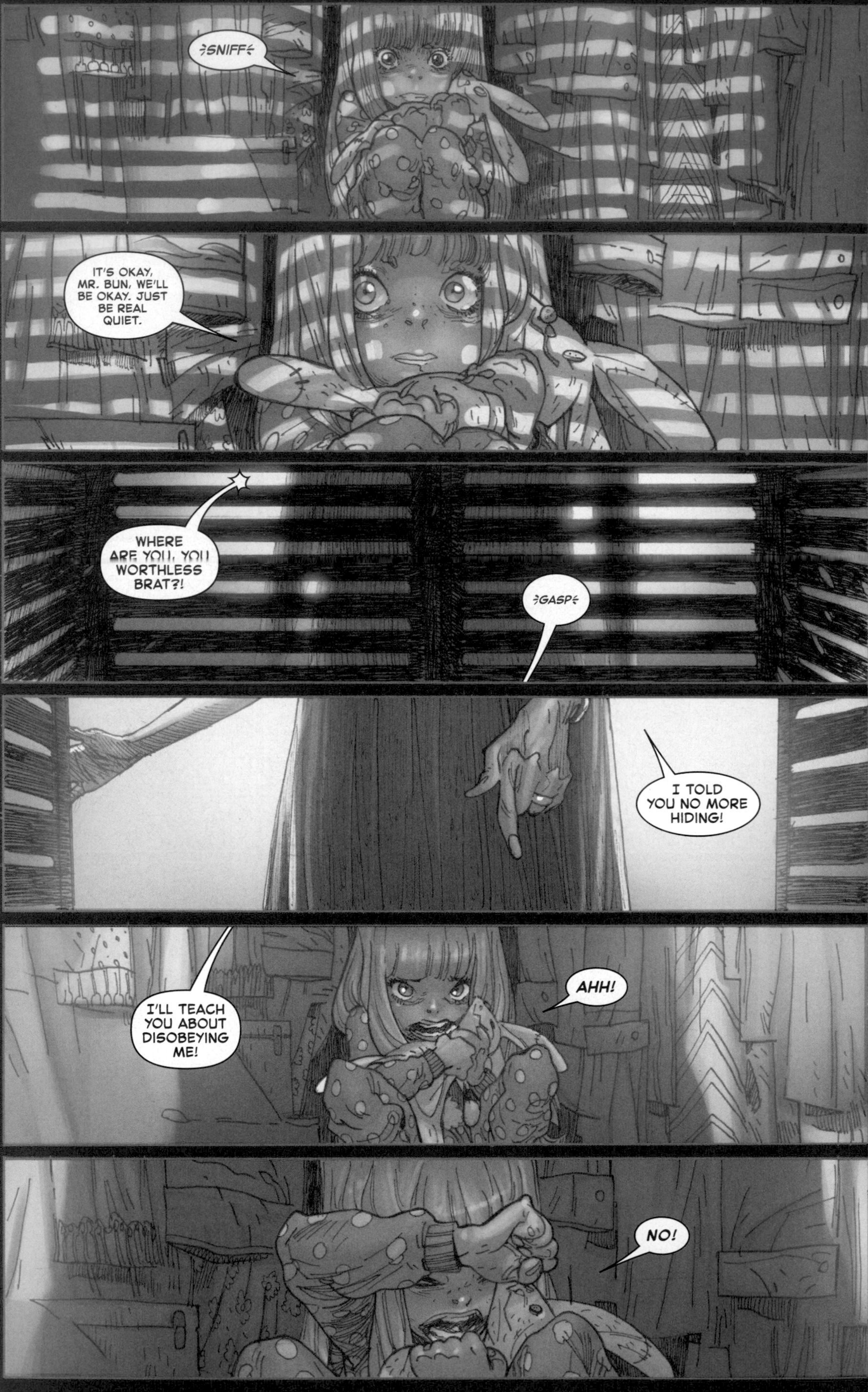

SNIFF
IT'S OKAY, MR. BUN, WE'LL BE OKAY. JUST BE REAL QUIET.
WHERE ARE YOU, YOU WORTHLESS BRAT?!
GASP
I TOLD YOU NO MORE HIDING!
I'LL TEACH YOU ABOUT DISOBEYING ME!
AHH!
NO!

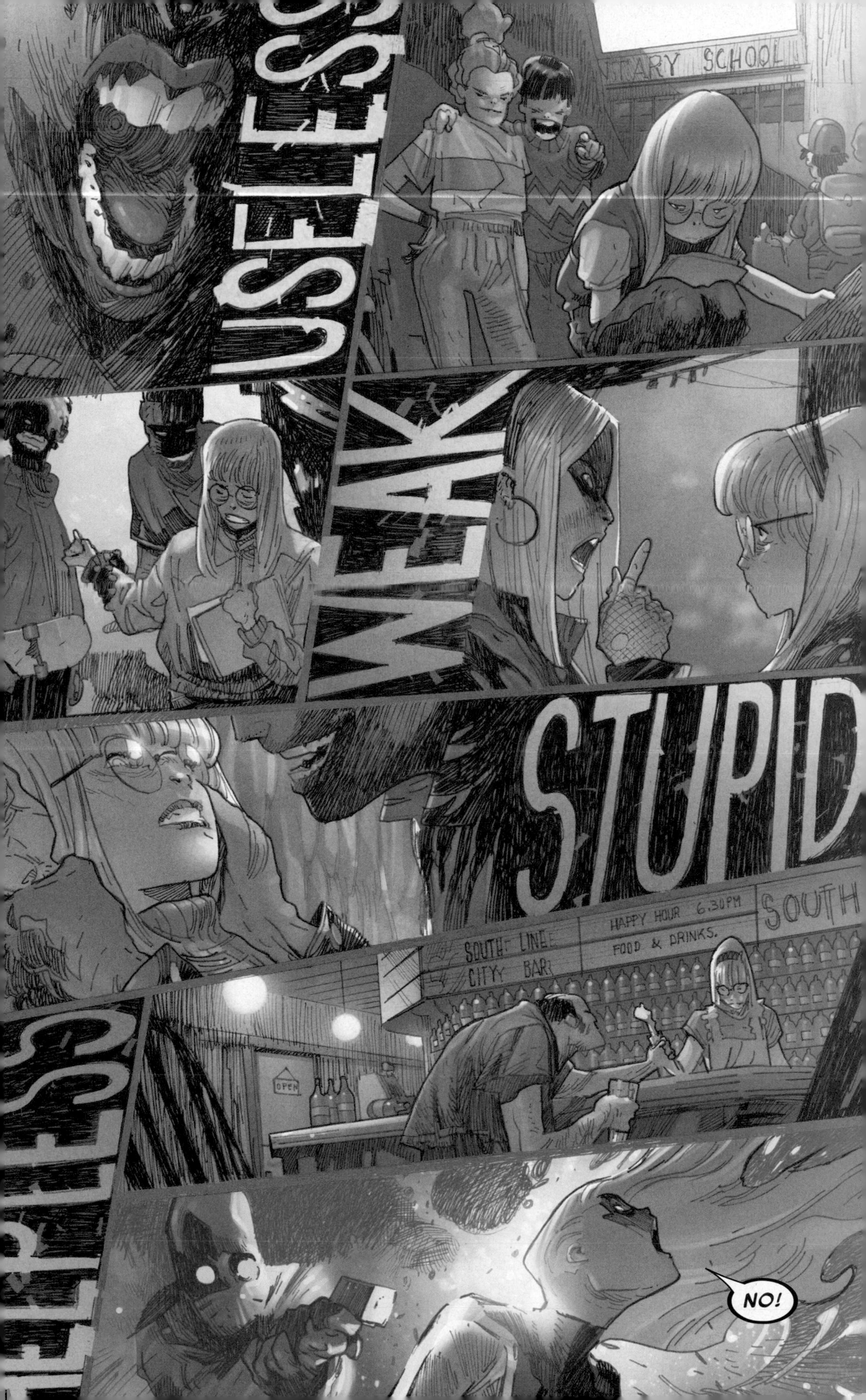
USELESS
TARY SCHOOL
WEAK
STUPID
HAPPY HOUR 6.30PM
FOOD & DRINKS.
SOUTH LINE
CITY BAR
SOUTH
OPEN
NO!

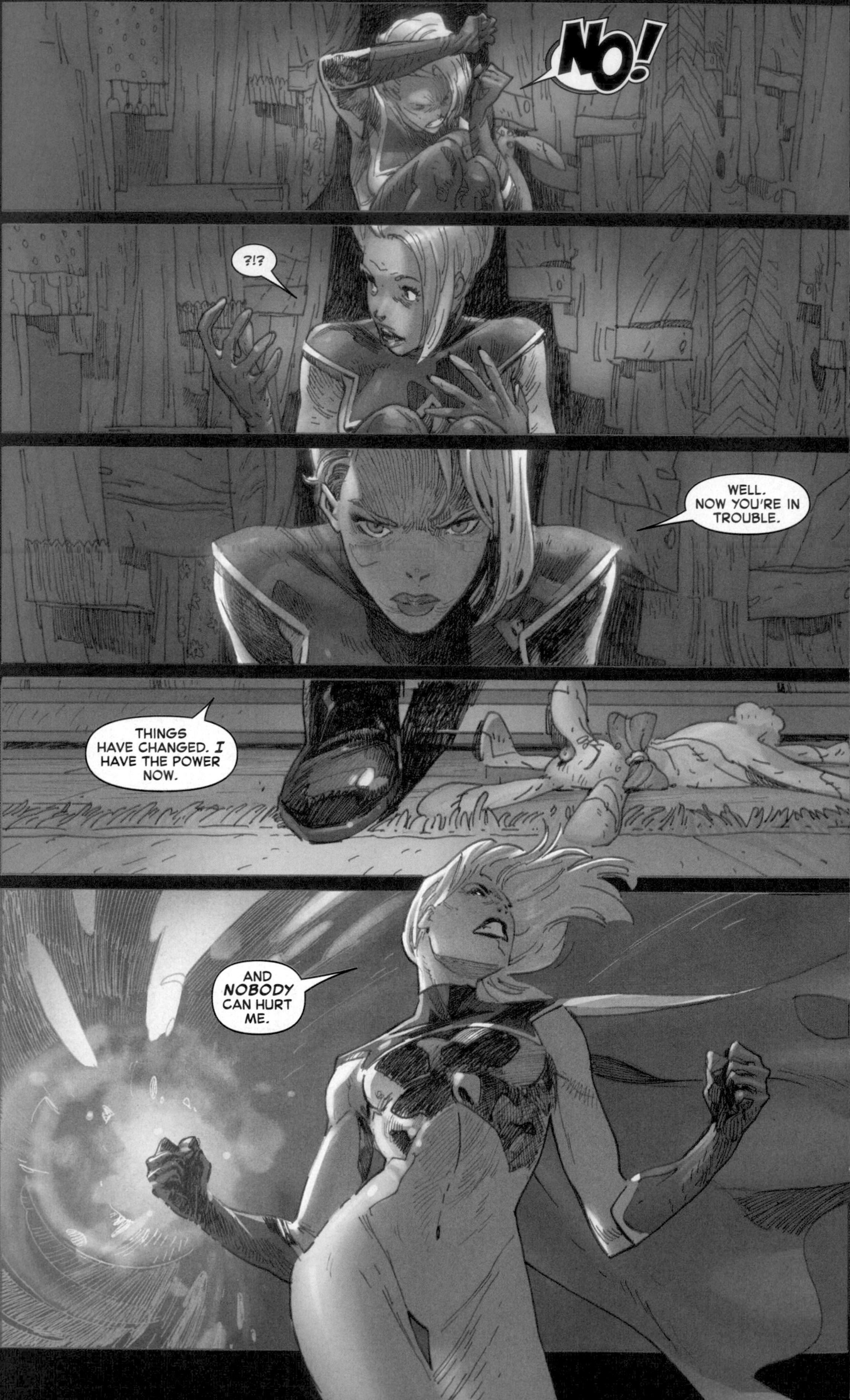
NO!
?!?
WELL. NOW YOU'RE IN TROUBLE.
THINGS HAVE CHANGED. I HAVE THE POWER NOW.
AND NOBODY CAN HURT ME.

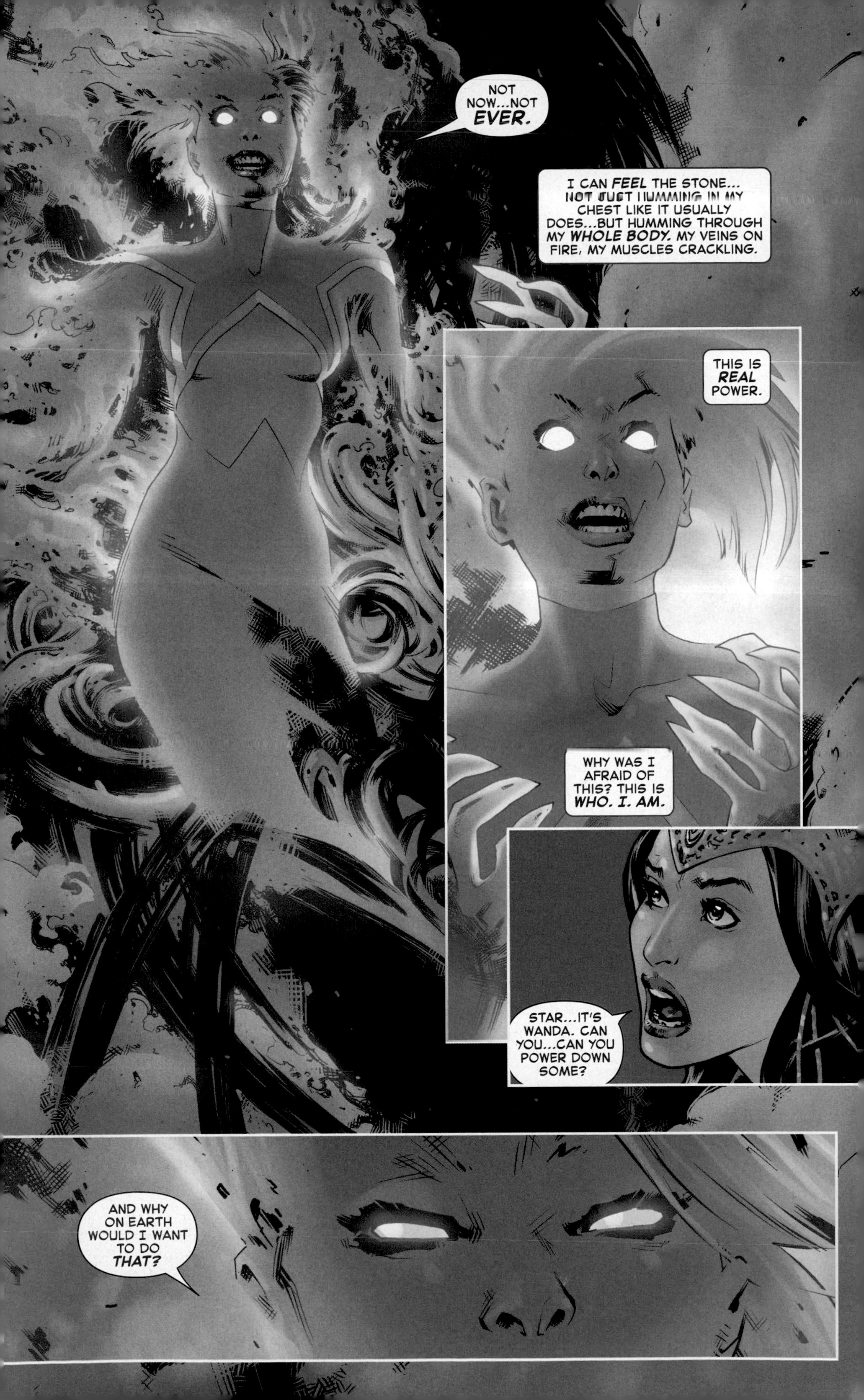

NOT NOW...NOT EVER.
I CAN FEEL THE STONE... NOT JUST HUMMING IN MY CHEST LIKE IT USUALLY DOES...BUT HUMMING THROUGH MY WHOLE BODY. MY VEINS ON FIRE, MY MUSCLES CRACKLING.
THIS IS REAL POWER.
WHY WAS I AFRAID OF THIS? THIS IS WHO. I. AM.
STAR...IT'S WANDA. CAN YOU...CAN YOU POWER DOWN SOME?
AND WHY ON EARTH WOULD I WANT TO DO THAT?

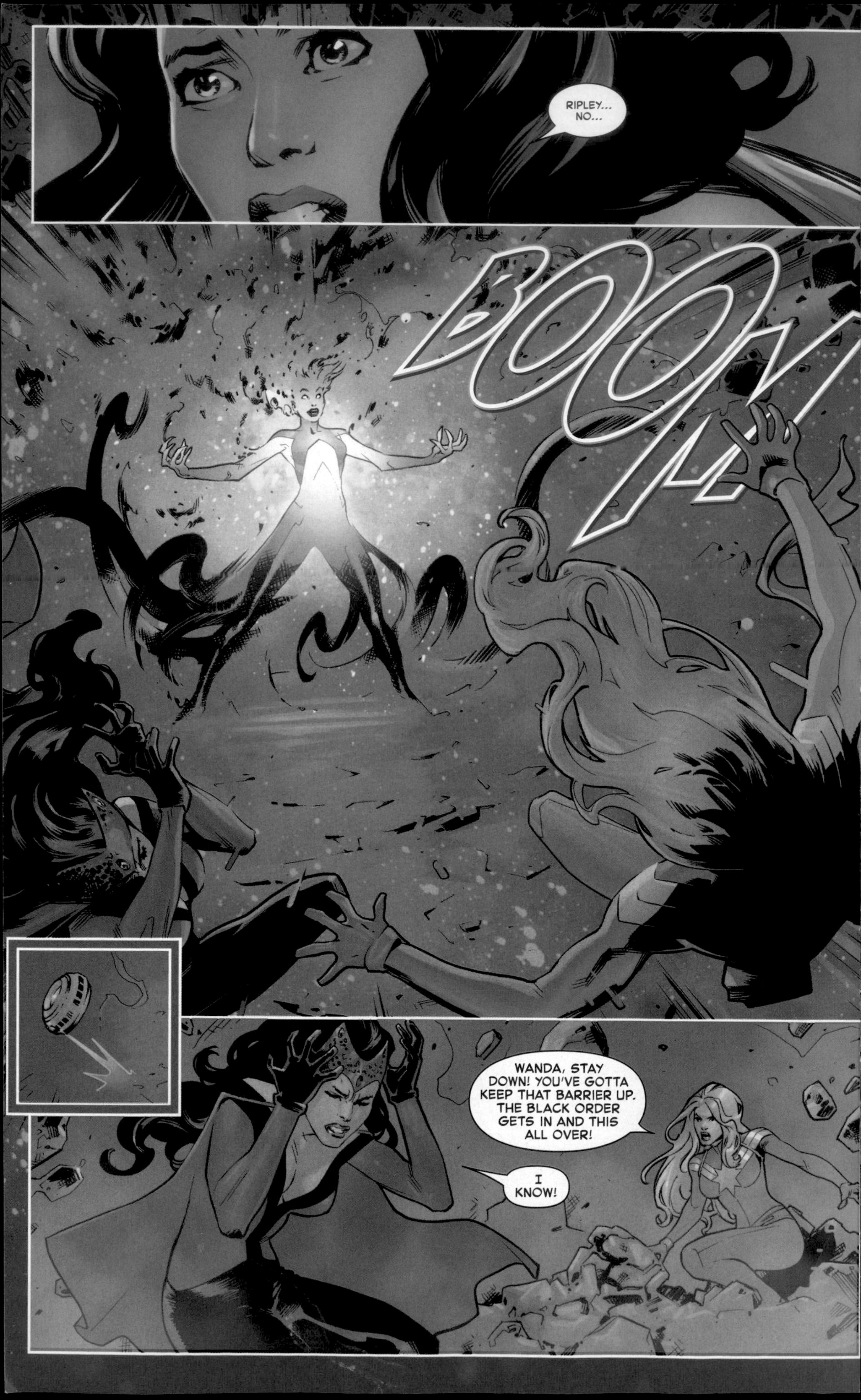
RIPLEY... NO...
BOOM!
WANDA, STAY DOWN! YOU'VE GOTTA KEEP THAT BARRIER UP. THE BLACK ORDER GETS IN AND THIS ALL OVER!
I KNOW!

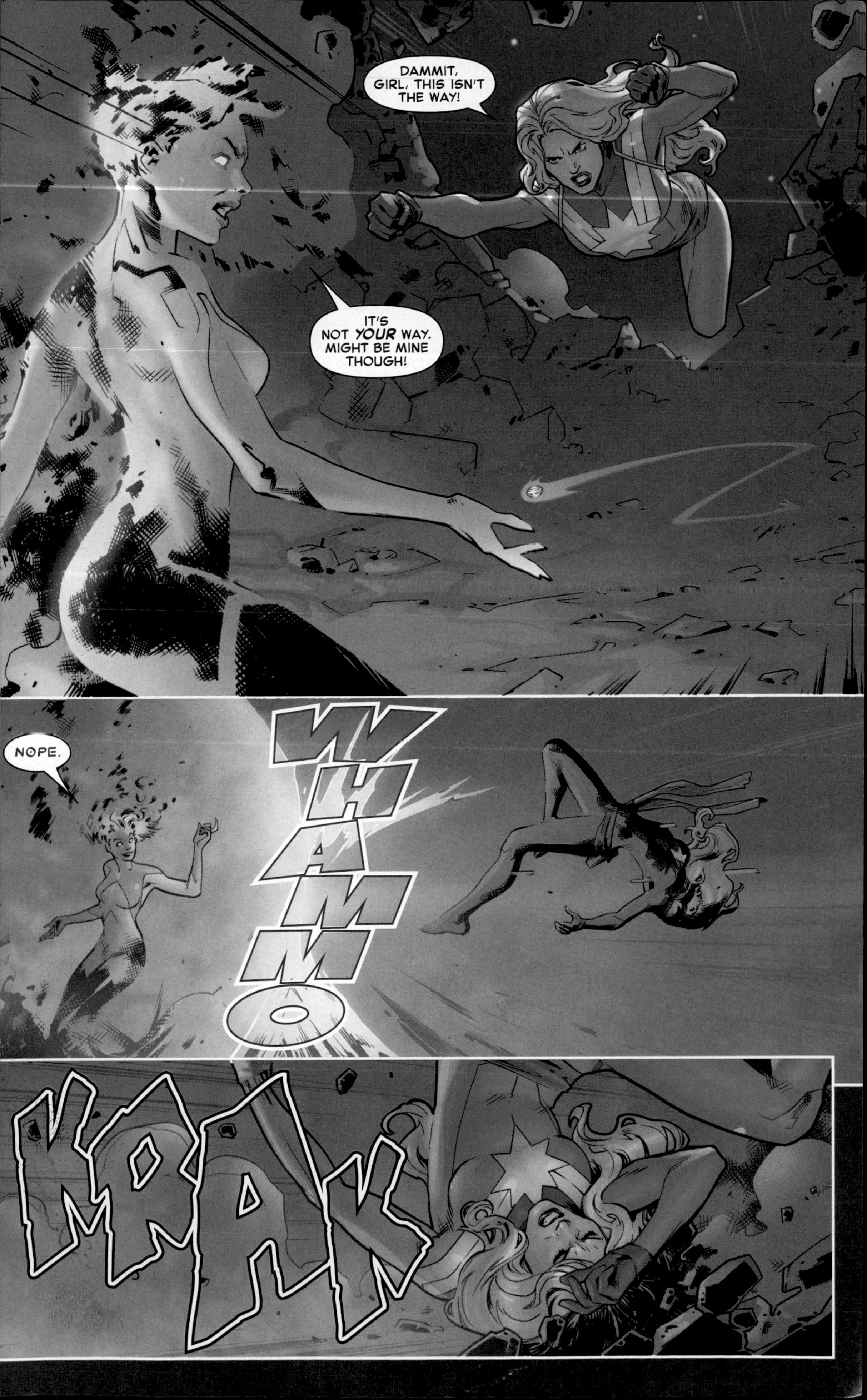
DAMMIT, GIRL, THIS ISN'T THE WAY!
IT'S NOT YOUR WAY. MIGHT BE MINE THOUGH!
NOPE.
WHAMMO
KRAK

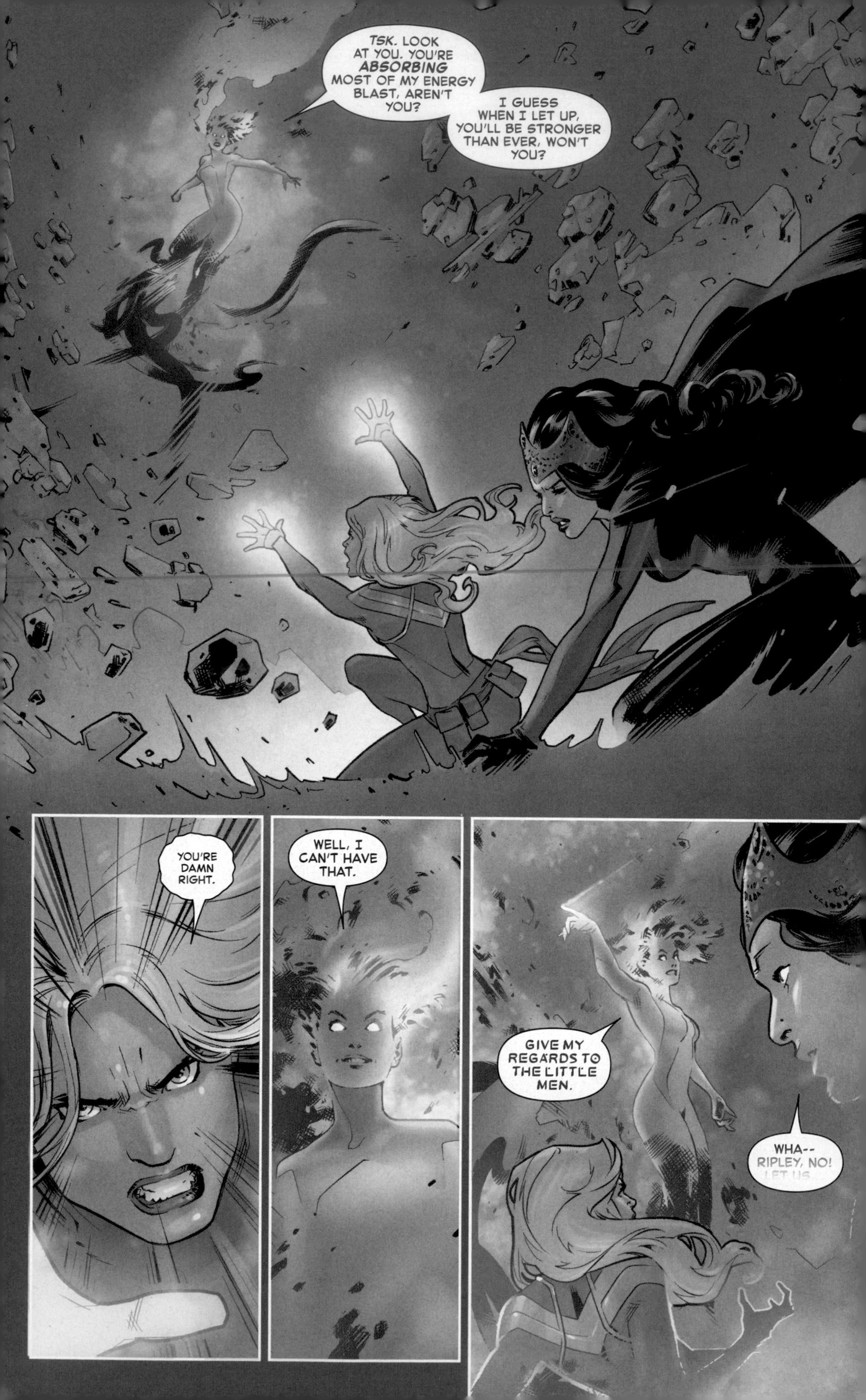
TSK. LOOK AT YOU. YOU'RE ABSORBING MOST OF MY ENERGY BLAST, AREN'T YOU?
I GUESS WHEN I LET UP, YOU'LL BE STRONGER THAN EVER, WON'T YOU?
YOU'RE DAMN RIGHT.
WELL, I CAN'T HAVE THAT.
GIVE MY REGARDS TO THE LITTLE MEN.
WHA-- RIPLEY, NO! LET US...

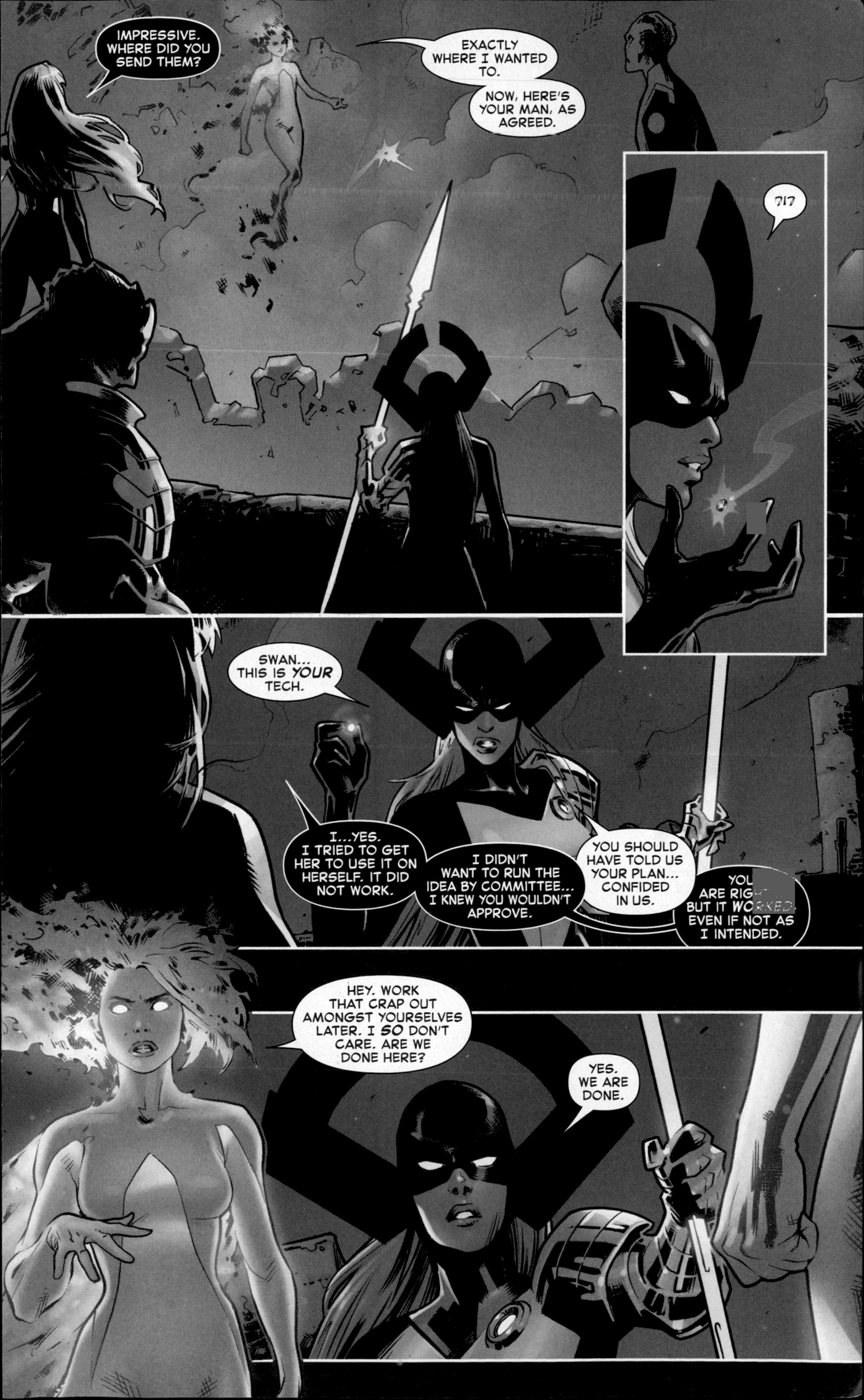
IMPRESSIVE. WHERE DID YOU SEND THEM?
EXACTLY WHERE I WANTED TO.
NOW, HERE'S YOUR MAN, AS AGREED.
?!?
SWAN... THIS IS *YOUR* TECH.
I...YES. I TRIED TO GET HER TO USE IT ON HERSELF. IT DID NOT WORK.
I DIDN'T WANT TO RUN THE IDEA BY COMMITTEE... I KNEW YOU WOULDN'T APPROVE.
YOU SHOULD HAVE TOLD US YOUR PLAN... CONFIDED IN US.
YOU ARE RIGHT. BUT IT *WORKED.* EVEN IF NOT AS I INTENDED.
HEY. WORK THAT CRAP OUT AMONGST YOURSELVES LATER. I *SO* DON'T CARE. ARE WE DONE HERE?
YES. WE ARE DONE.

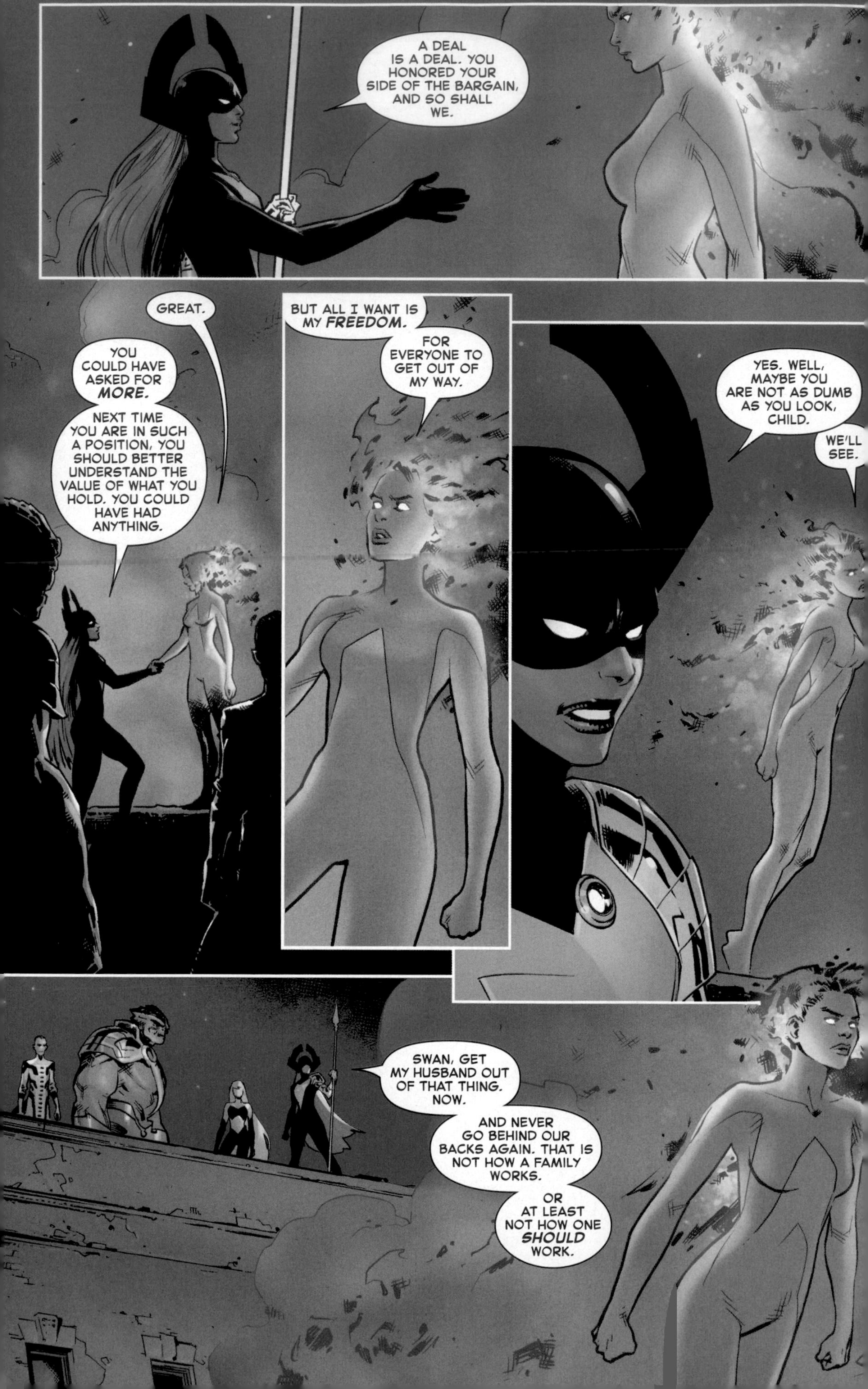
A DEAL IS A DEAL. YOU HONORED YOUR SIDE OF THE BARGAIN, AND SO SHALL WE.
GREAT.
YOU COULD HAVE ASKED FOR MORE.
NEXT TIME YOU ARE IN SUCH A POSITION, YOU SHOULD BETTER UNDERSTAND THE VALUE OF WHAT YOU HOLD. YOU COULD HAVE HAD ANYTHING.
BUT ALL I WANT IS MY FREEDOM.
FOR EVERYONE TO GET OUT OF MY WAY.
YES. WELL, MAYBE YOU ARE NOT AS DUMB AS YOU LOOK, CHILD.
WE'LL SEE.
SWAN, GET MY HUSBAND OUT OF THAT THING. NOW.
AND NEVER GO BEHIND OUR BACKS AGAIN. THAT IS NOT HOW A FAMILY WORKS.
OR AT LEAST NOT HOW ONE SHOULD WORK.

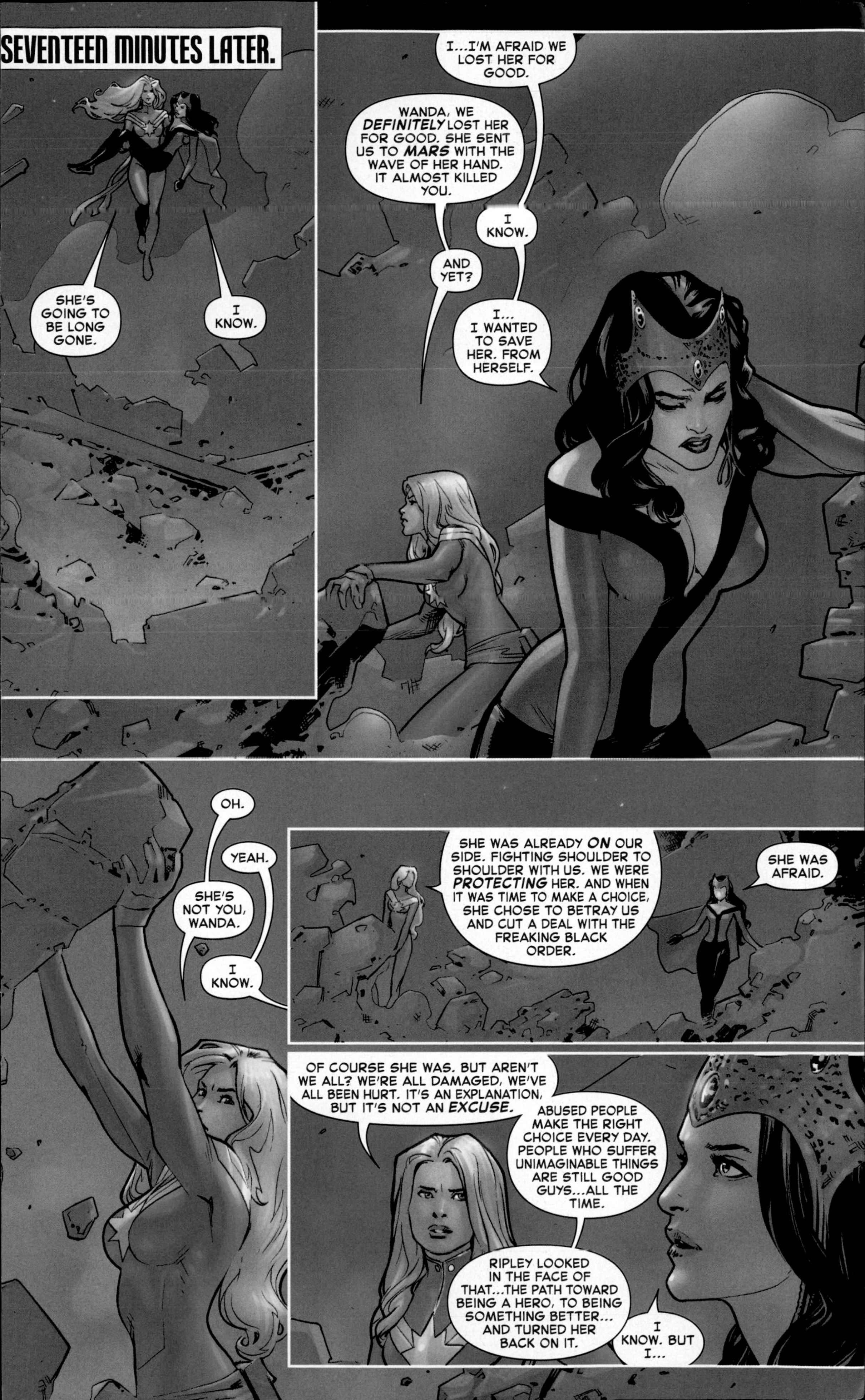

SEVENTEEN MINUTES LATER.
SHE'S GOING TO BE LONG GONE.
I KNOW.
I...I'M AFRAID WE LOST HER FOR GOOD.
WANDA, WE DEFINITELY LOST HER FOR GOOD. SHE SENT US TO MARS WITH THE WAVE OF HER HAND. IT ALMOST KILLED YOU.
I KNOW.
AND YET?
I... I WANTED TO SAVE HER. FROM HERSELF.
OH.
YEAH.
SHE'S NOT YOU, WANDA.
I KNOW.
SHE WAS ALREADY ON OUR SIDE. FIGHTING SHOULDER TO SHOULDER WITH US. WE WERE PROTECTING HER. AND WHEN IT WAS TIME TO MAKE A CHOICE, SHE CHOSE TO BETRAY US AND CUT A DEAL WITH THE FREAKING BLACK ORDER.
SHE WAS AFRAID.
OF COURSE SHE WAS. BUT AREN'T WE ALL? WE'RE ALL DAMAGED, WE'VE ALL BEEN HURT. IT'S AN EXPLANATION, BUT IT'S NOT AN EXCUSE.
ABUSED PEOPLE MAKE THE RIGHT CHOICE EVERY DAY. PEOPLE WHO SUFFER UNIMAGINABLE THINGS ARE STILL GOOD GUYS...ALL THE TIME.
RIPLEY LOOKED IN THE FACE OF THAT...THE PATH TOWARD BEING A HERO, TO BEING SOMETHING BETTER... AND TURNED HER BACK ON IT.
I KNOW. BUT I...

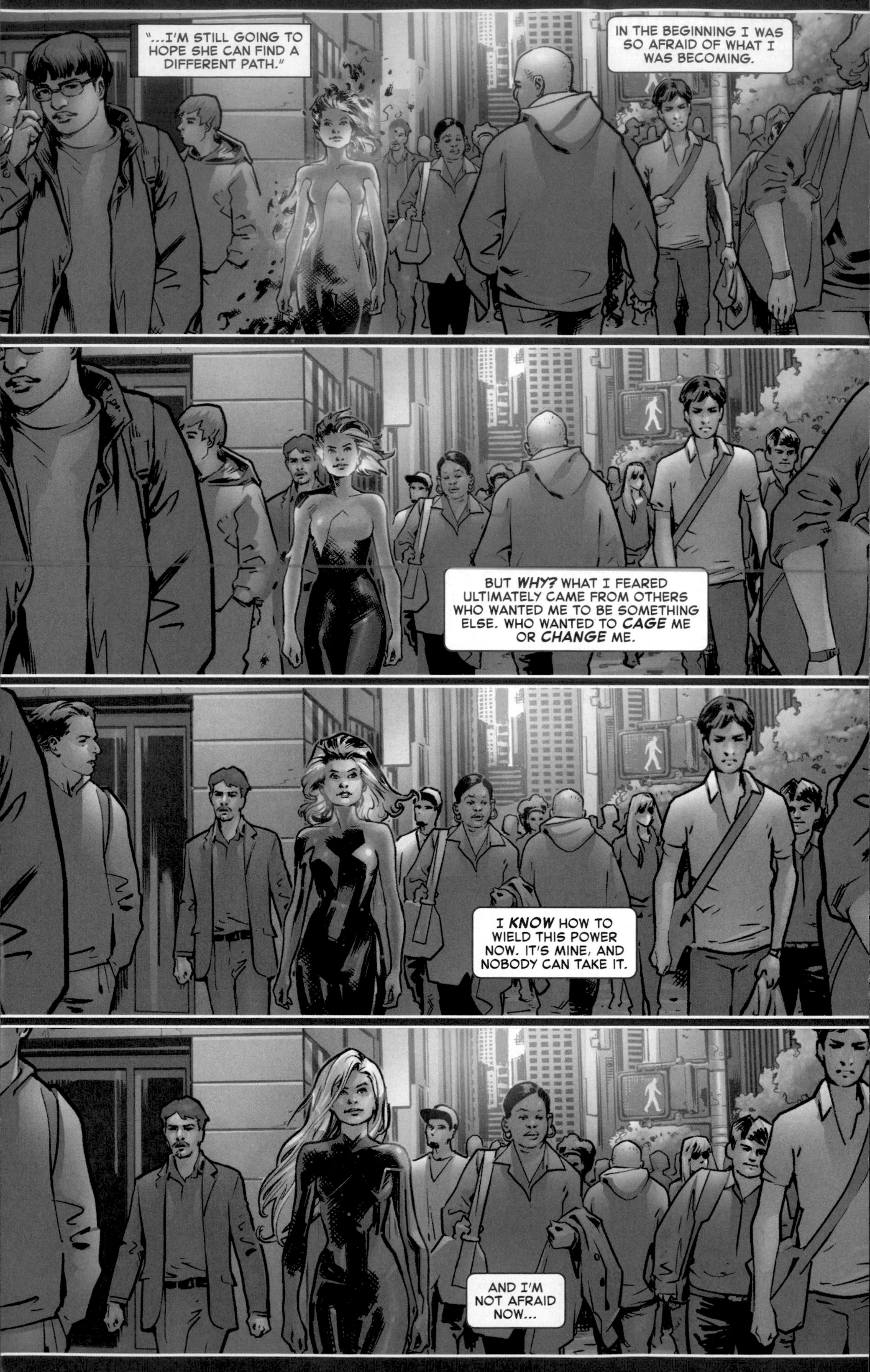
"...I'M STILL GOING TO HOPE SHE CAN FIND A DIFFERENT PATH."
IN THE BEGINNING I WAS SO AFRAID OF WHAT I WAS BECOMING.
BUT WHY? WHAT I FEARED ULTIMATELY CAME FROM OTHERS WHO WANTED ME TO BE SOMETHING ELSE. WHO WANTED TO CAGE ME OR CHANGE ME.
I KNOW HOW TO WIELD THIS POWER NOW. IT'S MINE, AND NOBODY CAN TAKE IT.
AND I'M NOT AFRAID NOW...

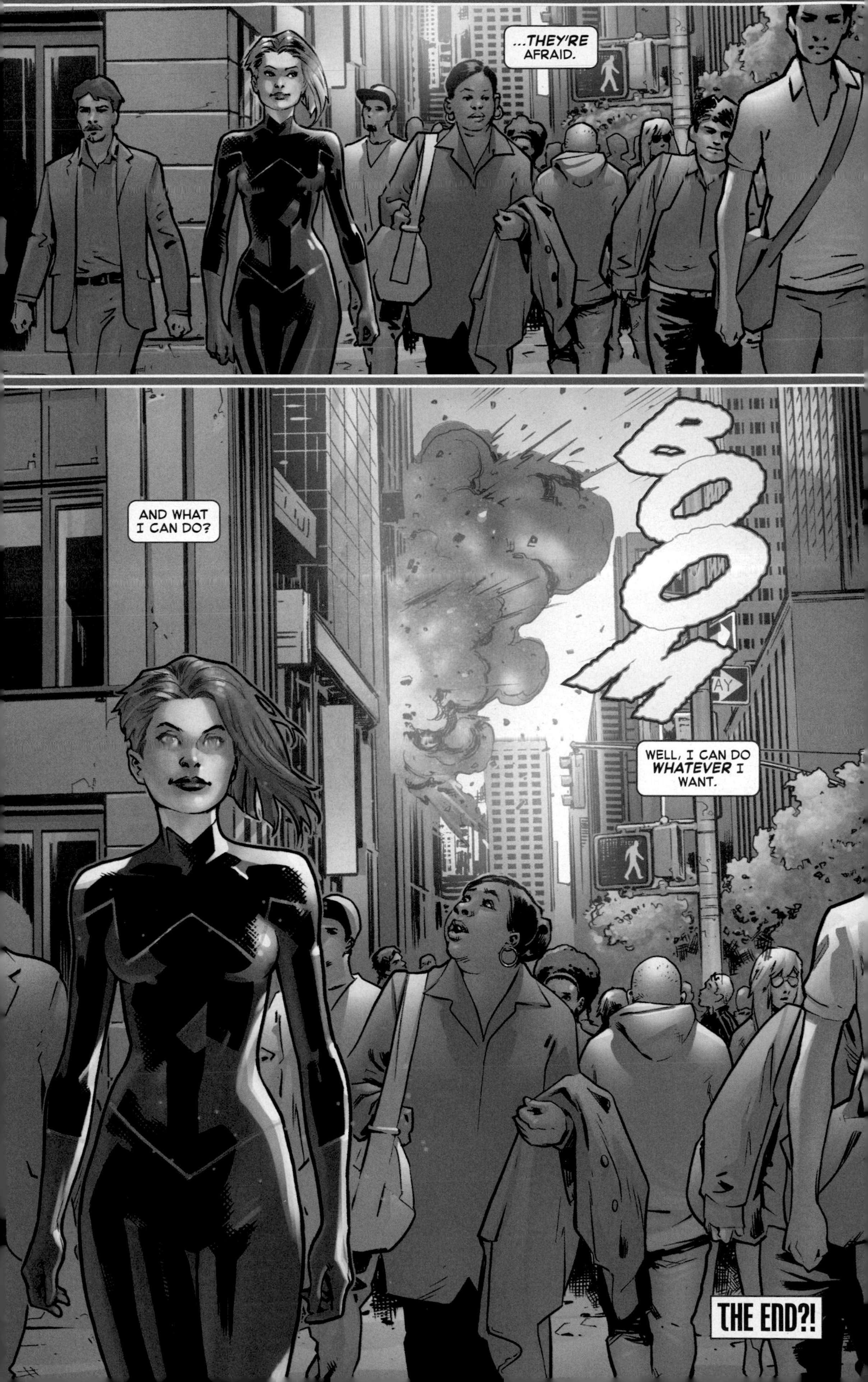
...THEY'RE AFRAID.
AND WHAT I CAN DO?
BOOM
WELL, I CAN DO WHATEVER I WANT.
THE END?!

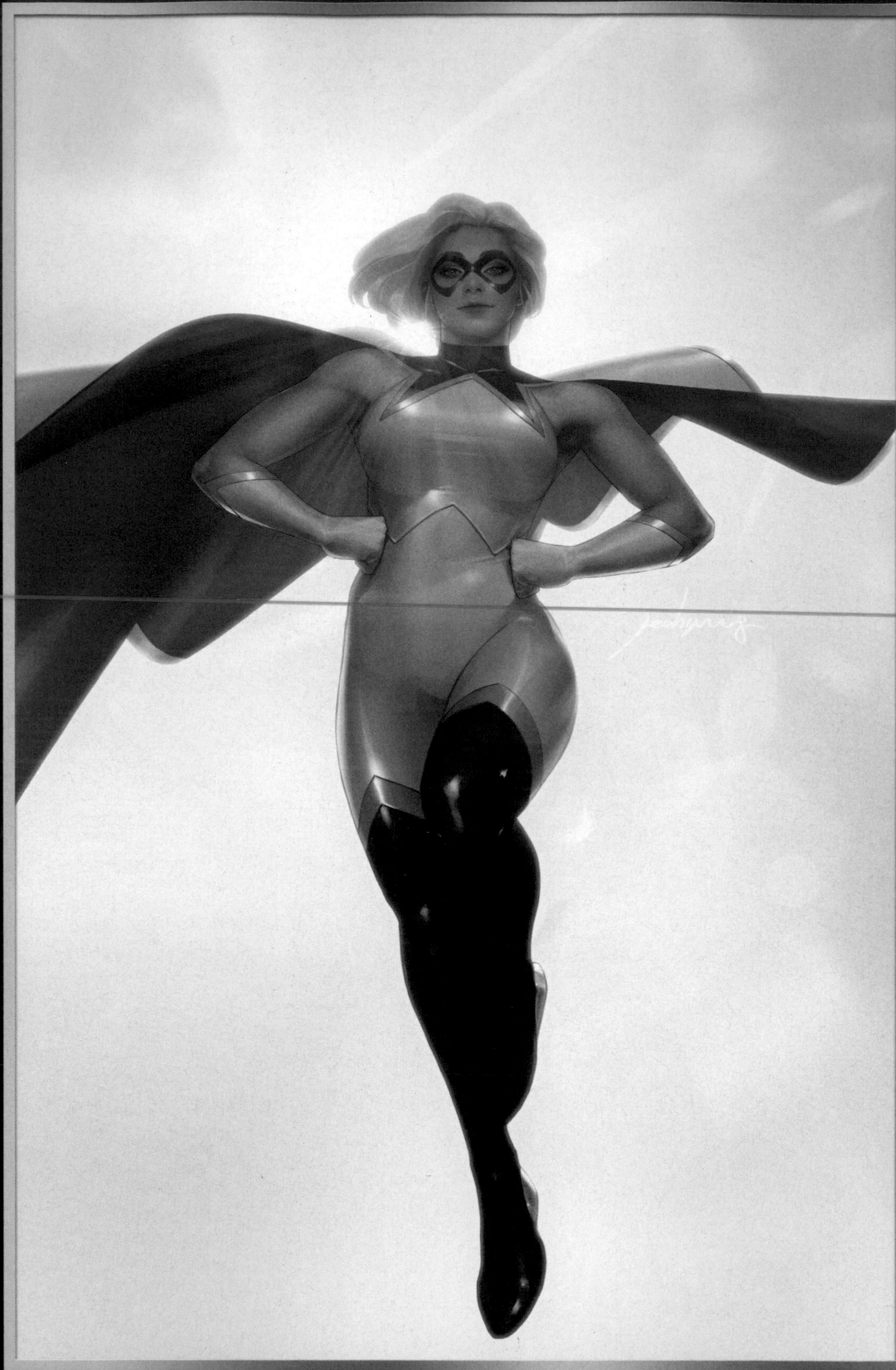

#1 VARIANT BY
JEEHYUNG LEE

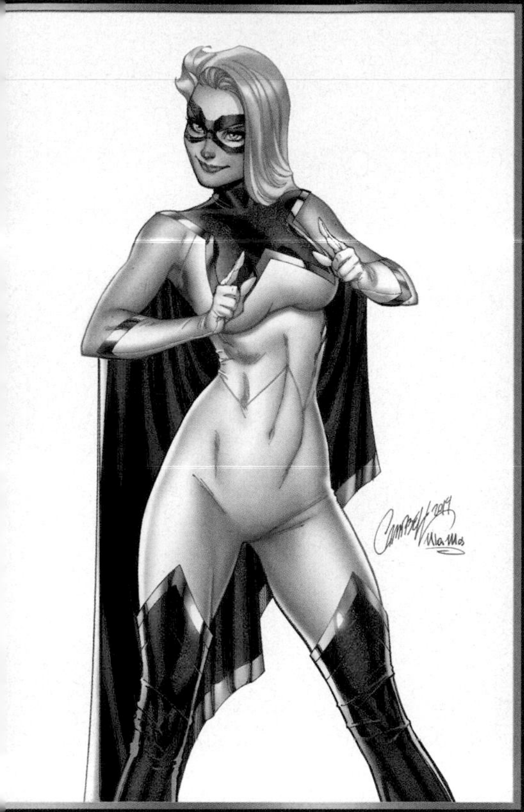

#1 VARIANT BY
J. SCOTT CAMPBELL & ULA MOSS

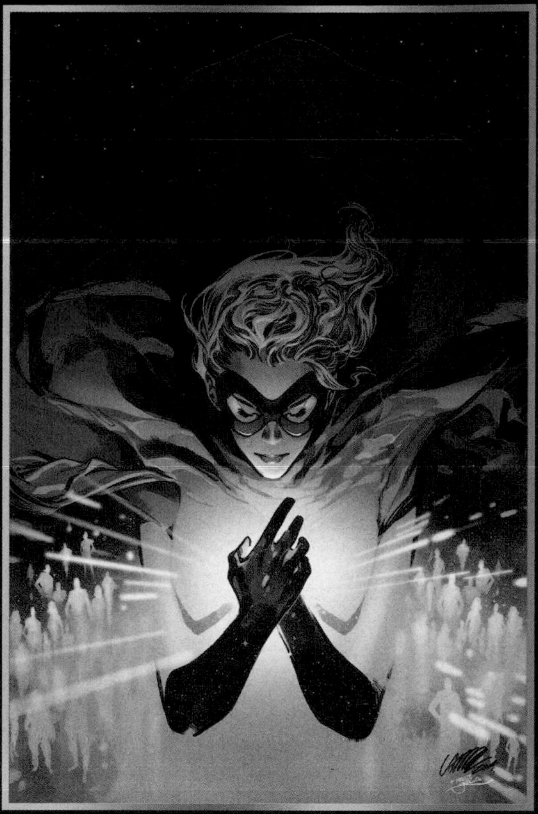

#1 VARIANT BY
PEPE LARRAZ & MARTE GARCIA

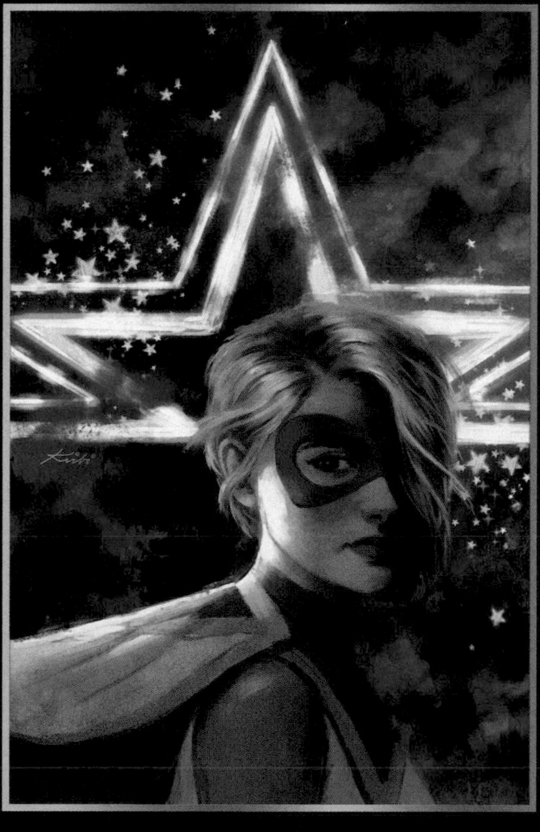

#2 VARIANT BY
KIRBI FAGAN

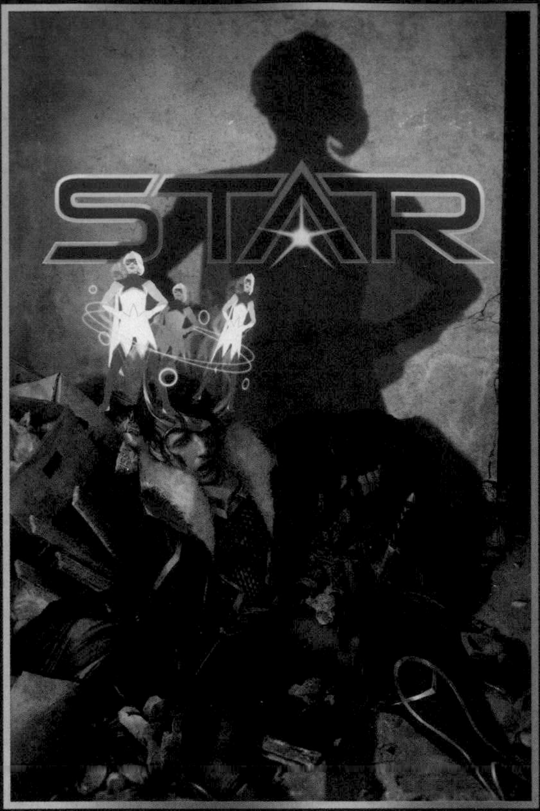
STAR

#3 VARIANT BY
RAHZZAH

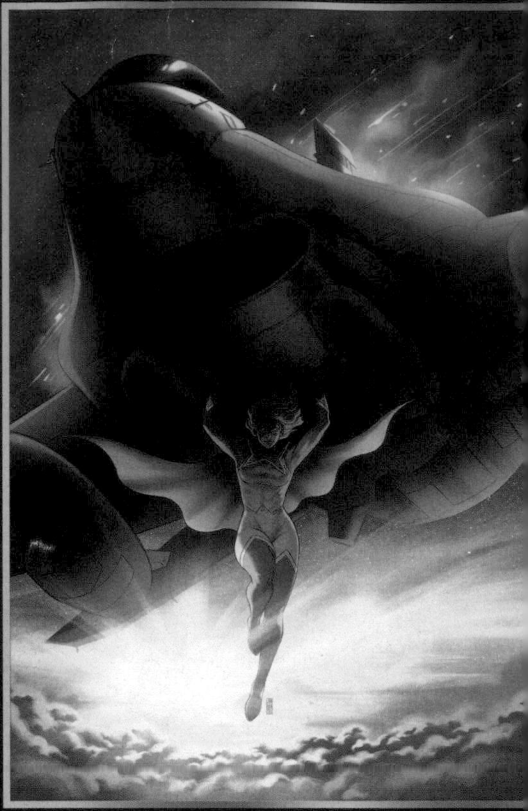

#4 VARIANT BY
JEN BARTEL

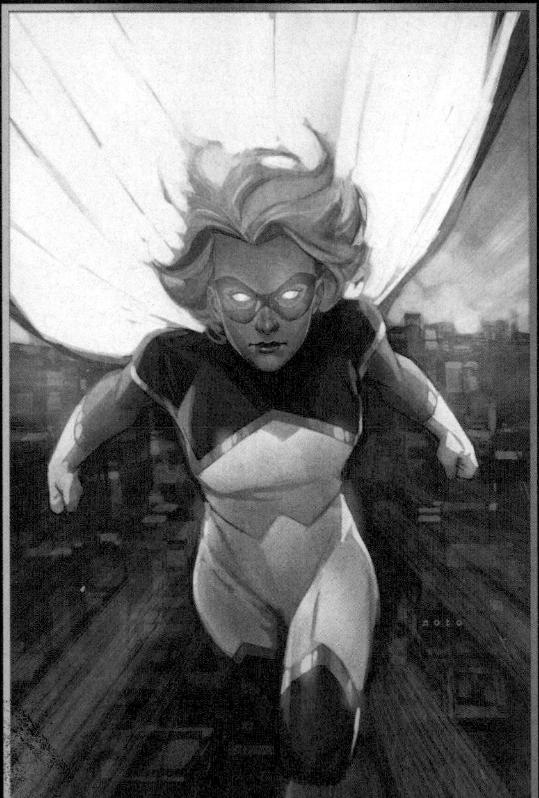

#5 VARIANT BY
PHIL NOTO

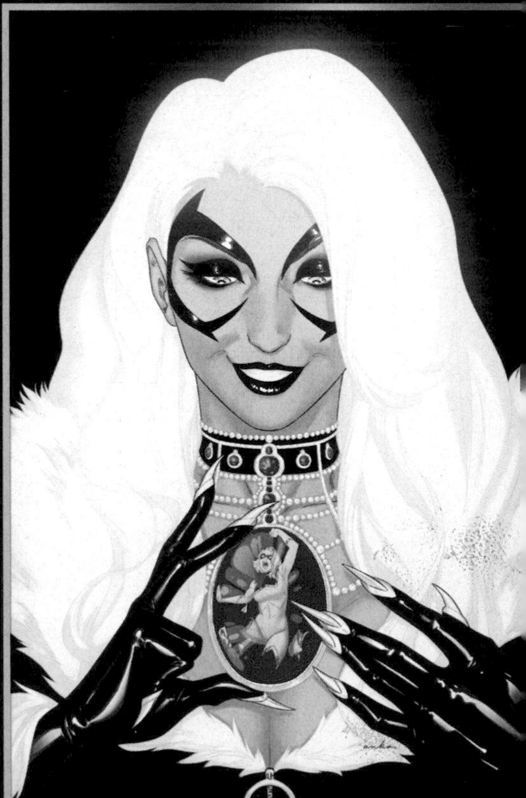

#5 VARIANT BY
KRIS ANKA